Children Growing Up

Children Growing Up

Edited by

Alan Branthwaite and Don Rogers

Open University Press

Milton Keynes : Philadelphia

Open University Press
12 Cofferidge Close
Stony Stratford
Milton Keynes MK11 1BY. England
and
242 Cherry Street
Philadelphia, PA 19106, USA

First Published 1985

British Library Cataloguing in Publication Data

Children growing up.
  1. Child psychology   2. Child development
  I. Branthwaite, Alan   II. Rogers, Don
  155.4   BF721

ISBN 0-335-15067-5

Library of Congress Cataloging in Publication Data

Children growing up.

  1. Child development.   2. Child psychology.
  I. Branthwaite, Alan.   II. Rogers, Don.
  RJ131.C544   1985   155.4   85-4838
  ISBN 0-335-15067-5

Typeset by Gilbert Composing Services, Leighton Buzzard
Printed and bound in Great Britain at the Alden Press, Oxford

For Katherine Muir
and Corinne Hutt

Contents

List of figures

Introduction

Being a child must be like being a spy. A baby has to break the code to discover the ways in which the world around works. The task is to achieve prediction and then control over a very foreign environment of people and things. To do this the baby is equipped with certain innate skills and is assisted by surrounding people. But although older people are cooperative, and usually try hard to help, we have to recognize that it is through the mental efforts of the child in observing, testing, and trying out, that mastery is achieved.

This is a book about the psychological development of the child. It concentrates predominantly on development in the younger child, partly because this is where there has been most research in recent years, but also because the most dramatic and far reaching changes in the child occur during the pre-school and early school years.

The book consists of twenty-two chapters specially written by members of the Psychology Department at the University of Keele. It has a degree of integration which would not be possible in a collection of articles, but each chapter can stand alone as a discussion of a particular topic within the general field of child development.

The book is organized into four sections, each section representing a different perspective on child development. The *social domain* deals with the child's social world, his increasing skill in social interaction, his developing understanding of others and his understanding of himself in relation to others. The *cognitive domain* deals with developments in the child's thinking, in his understanding of regularities in the world and in his skilled ability to recognize and make use of these regularities in his mastery of the world. For example, through noting regularities in the speech he hears, he is able eventually to construct sentences for himself which can be used to influence others to do things. The *personal domain* looks at the child as an individual, sharing some characteristics with other individuals and differing in other characteristics. It also explores some of the ways in which development can go awry. Finally, in the *biological domain*, various issues that were explored earlier in the book are taken up again, and considered in relation to biological factors: here, for instance, is examined the extent to which differences between children can be related to genetic factors, to hormonal factors, or to brain growth.

While these domains represent important aspects of child development, they are of course not watertight compartments, and there are very many ways in which the domains are connected. Thus, the social and cognitive domains are connected at many points – for example, the ways in which children of different ages understand the principles governing moral conduct clearly relates to social situations, and how people should behave towards one another, but also reflects cognitive issues such as the child's comprehension of the world and his appreciation of deep regularities underlying the behaviour of people; the child's discovery of language represents an astounding achievement of his intellect and thus lies within the cognitive domain, but plainly language is used in social situations to communicate with others. The four domains are also connected in discussions of differences between individuals. These are considered predominantly within the personal section, but in the social section we discuss how individuals from different social backgrounds see themselves; in the cognitive section how different cultural backgrounds affect individuals, and in particular the ways in which they remember; while in the biological section we discuss how differences between individuals can be related to genetic and other biological factors.

The sections can be read in any order. The order in which the sections appear represents our own preference, but some individuals may prefer to adopt a more traditional approach and begin with biological issues.

The politics of pronouns

There is an awkward problem in writing about child development: whether to refer to the child in general as 'he' or 'she'. Of course one can repeatedly use the phrase 'the child' but this tends to be rather awkward. By and large we have left the author of each chapter to adopt their own policy in regard to this, rather than lay down any uniform, but arbitrary standard.

Acknowledgements

We are grateful to the many people who have assisted in producing this book. In particular we would like to thank John Coleman who drew and produced the figures, and Margaret Woodward and Dorothy Masters for typing the text. The cartoons in Chapters 3 and 17 are by Glyn Prosser.

PART I

The social domain

Introduction

This section is concerned with the social world of the child. Social behaviour is in some ways like a conspiracy, whereby members of the society abide by rules subtly different for different cultures, although these rules are not stated explicitly. The child at first, of course, does not know the rules and has to discover them. In the first chapter, one aspect of the parents' role in the conspiracy is discussed: parents often treat children as though they already know the rules, as though they were already active members of society, and this in turn helps their children to become genuine members of society.

However, as might be expected, there is not one universal way of treating children, and there is not just one way in which children can become competent adults. Rather, there are many routes, and one is struck by how robust development is – children manage to grow up pretty well, despite many different rearing practices, and despite many things that go wrong. This then is taken up in the second chapter, in which the controversial issue of 'maternal deprivation' is examined – that is, what happenes when for some reason or another the child is deprived of mothering? The answer here turns out not to be a simple one, but again one is struck by the extent to which disruptions in normal social relationships can be overcome. Only if the deprivation is severe, or repeated, or several kinds of deprivation conspire together (for example, low income, overcrowded housing, unstable or disrupted relationships, poor parenting etc.) are the consequences marked. This may be one reason why research conducted a few decades ago found more evidence of effects than in recent studies. Society has taken measures to combat the effects of deprivation, so one no longer finds children in orphanages receiving physical care but unable to see out of their cots or play with others, though one may still find problems arising from a high turnover of carers so that the relationships the child makes become broken. In general there can be two kinds of deprivation: first, where there is no one to spend time playing and interacting with the child, then the child is understimulated and development of abilities for communicating, handling the environment and solving problems is retarded; secondly, disruptions to established relationships have effects on emotional development in so far as growing confidence and security is lost.

Just as there is not one universal way of treating children, so there is not one universal social world. Each family exists within larger social frameworks and reflects aspects of those frameworks: so, for example, there are differences in families from one country to another and from one social class to another. As the child grows older, he begins to appreciate the multiplexity of society, and becomes able to locate himself within the various social systems. This takes a surprisingly long time, and children make many mistakes: it is only after considerable experience that they begin to establish an accurate awareness of themselves relative to others. These issues are taken up in Chapters 3 and 4.

The child does not interact socially only with his own family, of course, and Chapter 5 says something of the ways in which children interact among themselves. This chapter shows how children actively discover by playing together some of the rules of the social conspiracy, the regulators of society. Children's understanding of the rules of society is however strongly affected by their cognitive abilities at any particular age, a theme that will take us into the material of the second section.

Methods of research in the social domain

The accuracy of knowledge we have about child development depends heavily on the methods used to collect information. This is true of any research: the findings are only as good as the methods used to obtain the evidence. If the methods are inaccurate or biased, then the conclusions will be. For these reasons, it is important to examine the methods used in research and consider their strengths and weaknesses. However, scientific research is never easy and it is extremely difficult to carry out a perfect study where the results are unbiased and conclusions can be drawn unambiguously. This is particularly true with research on children who are not as cooperative in doing what is asked as adults; whose understanding of instructions is limited; whose concentration wavers and who are easily distracted by 'irrelevancies' such as the apparatus and researcher. Nevertheless, in order to make their investigations as unambiguous as possible, researchers have progressively refined techniques and devised procedures and safeguards to make the findings as reliable as they can achieve.

From the research described in the first section of this book, we want to draw attention to the use of observational studies and comment on their advantages and disadvantages. We shall comment on other methodological issues in the introductions to other sections as they arise.

There are two broad approaches to carrying out research. One is to observe what is taking place naturally, intervening as little as possible. The other is to set up a specific experiment to compare behaviour in two or more particular circumstances that have been arranged and are well standardized or controlled. (In practice, it is not as clear as this distinction suggests and each approach often involves elements of the other.) Much of the research on social interaction described in Section I has used observations and tape recordings to examine, for example, how mothers and children interact (Chapter 1), the effects of maternal deprivation (Chapter 2), differences in languages in different social classes (Chapter 3) or the interactions between children playing (Chapter 5). Observational studies are used because the researcher is trying to discover how development proceeds in its natural setting. Often in studying interaction it is not possible to set up an experiment because that would introduce artificial elements, which would distort the normal social processes. In some case it is not ethically desirable to arrange experiments as in the case of the effects from maternal separation where one would not deprive children of their mothers for the purpose of research, although one can sometimes capitalize on 'natural' experiments where different conditions are created by naturally occurring events. However, the difference between the conditions is seldom as precise and clear cut as when they are set up by the researcher.

There are difficulties in carrying out observational studies, which can affect the validity of findings, unless there are proper safeguards:

1   There is obviously a need to make accurate observations. Events happen quickly and often when not expected so the researcher might miss a crucial aspect. When observing complex behaviour, there are many things to note and concentrate on at the same time, which may exceed the capacities of an observer. It is easy under these circumstances to 'see' what was expected or predicted would happen. Undoubtedly the accuracy of observational research has been greatly enhanced by audio and video recordings. These enable researchers to analyse critically the sequence of events several times, or have different researchers check the data. Critical events can be slowed down for more detailed analysis than could be caught by the unaided observer. These methods have been used in much of the recent research on language and social interaction. Earlier researchers did not have such facilities. Nevertheless, their investigations were often sufficiently accurate and generated considerable insights that have been checked and confirmed by later research.

2   Selectivity in sampling can be a problem in observational studies. Unless the sample on which observations are to be made is carefully defined in advance, there is a danger of making haphazard observations that are not systematic so that cases that confirm expectations stand out and are noticed while disconfirming cases are overlooked. It is essential to have a properly defined sample and to note both confirming and disconfirming instances within it.

3   Establishing cause and effect is not easy in observational studies because many other variables, which could be responsible for producing the effects found, are not controlled.

This is not to argue that all observational studies are flawed and worthless and that only data from controlled experiments can be trusted. Experiments have their problems and both approaches to research are necessary and useful; both can be carried out well or carelessly. The advantages of observational studies are that the conclusions are based in more lifelike conditions avoiding the artificialness and oversimplifications of experiments. As a general principle, by combining conclusions from research using different approaches and methods we can gain confidence in the findings. In this way we can get around the specific problems and limitations of any one method. So conclusions are often based on extrapolations from research with animals, observations of children and adults, and evidence from natural experiments and the results of experimental investigations. Knowing the strengths and weaknesses of each kind of research will help in assessing the value and limitations of the conclusions being drawn from the research described in this book.

CHAPTER ONE

Infants, mothers and intentional communication
Don Rogers

In our culture, infants spend much of their waking lives with a few principal caregivers. These are often, though by no means exclusively, their mothers. During the last fifteen years, a great deal of research has studied closely the ways in which infants and their caregivers interact with one another. It has become possible to examine very carefully the characteristics of this interaction as a result of the development of video recording techniques since patterns of interaction can be recorded, and then slowed down for study. Often, individual infants have been recorded at intervals throughout the first two years of life or more, and the resulting films carefully (and laboriously!) examined. A good deal of surprising information has been discovered, which shows that the infant is not a helpless bundle who is passively pushed about by a caregiver, but rather an active partner in an ongoing dialogue that changes as the infant grows. Several aspects of this research will be discussed in subsequent chapters, but here we will concentrate on the development of intentional behaviour, and particularly of intentional communication. While this is only one of the many interesting aspects of mother-infant interaction, it is worth close examination for several reasons. First, it illustrates the ways in which research has investigated the social world of infants and young children. Secondly, deliberate, planned behaviour is an important feature of human behaviour so it is worthwhile studying its beginnings. And thirdly, communication is one of the most important bases for social behaviour.

While many caregivers are male, and many more are not the infant's mother, the term 'the mother' will be used for the sake of convenience. Likewise, although nearly half of all infants are female, it will serve better to distinguish baby from mother, if the baby is referred to as 'he'.

The development of intention

Enormous changes occur during the first two years of a child's life. He becomes mobile, learns to walk, becomes capable of fine manual dexterity, he develops an understanding of the world around him, he begins to talk and he becomes capable of intentional, purposeful action. 'Intention' is, however, a tricky notion, and there have been great debates about whether, for example, dogs, horses and other animals can be said to behave purposefully. Perhaps it would be useful to consider what sort of evidence would lead one to think of, say, an ape as behaving intentionally. Imagine placing a bunch of bananas in front of the animal's cage so that they were out of reach. At the back of the cage is placed a rake. Surely, one would think of the animal as behaving intentionally if he found that he could not reach the bananas, turned to fetch the rake, and then drew them towards himself? In this case, the animal would be maintaining a goal in mind, while performing a subsidiary action that would enable him to attain the goal.

One can see the beginnings of behaviour of this sort in infants towards the end of their first year of life. Piaget, the great Swiss student of child development, described in 1936 the behaviour of his own children when faced with situations in which their direct access to a goal was blocked (see Ginsburg and Opper (1979) for further details).

In one of Piaget's examples, a little boy (Laurent) is described. (Ages are given in years, months and days. Thus 0; 6 (8) = 6 months and 8 days.) Page references are given to the English translation of Piaget's *The Origin of Intelligence in the Child* (1952).

> (. . .) at 0;6(0) I present Laurent with a matchbox, extending my hand laterally to make an obstacle to his prehension. Laurent tries to pass over my hand, or to the side, but he does not attempt to displace it. As each time I prevent his passage, he ends by storming at the box while waving his hand . . . Same reactions at 0;6(8), 0;6(10), 0;6(21), etc.
>
> Finally, at 0;7(13) Laurent reacts quite differently almost from the beginning of the experiment. I present a box of matches above my hand, but behind it, so that he cannot reach it without setting the obstacle aside. But Laurent after trying to take no notice of it, suddenly tries to hit my hand as though to remove or lower it; I let him do it to me and he grasps the box. I recommence to bar his passage, but using as a screen a sufficiently supple cushion to keep the impress of the child's gestures. Laurent tries to reach the box, and bothered by the obstacle, he at once strikes it, definitely lowering it until the way is clear . . .
>
> Moreover, one notes that the intermediate act serving as means (removing the obstacle) is borrowed from a familiar scheme; the scheme of striking. We recall that Laurent from 0;4(7) and above all from 0;4(19) has the habit of hitting hanging objects in order to swing them and finally from 0;5(2) of striking the objects . . . Now, this is the usual scheme of which Laurent makes use at the present time, no longer in the capacity of an end in itself. . . but as a means . . .

Piaget, 1952 pp. 217–218

The younger infant, when faced with an obstacle preventing him from reaching a goal has no way of getting to the goal (and indeed usually forgets about the goal altogether). Eventually, however, the infant can keep the goal in mind while first performing another action that will enable him to reach it. At first, as in the example above, he can only do this if the subsidiary action is something he already knows how to do, but eventually he becomes able to keep a goal in mind while performing a new action which will enable him to attain the goal. This can be seen in another of Piaget's children, Lucienne, at one year and five days. A box has been placed on the table, so that it is pivoted at the centre. A bottle has been placed on top of the box out of the child's reach.

> Lucienne at first tries to grasp the box, but she goes about it as though the handkerchief were still involved. [Pulling a handerchief was an action that Piaget had previously observed in the child.] She tries to pinch it between two fingers, in the centre, and tries this for a moment without being able to grasp it. Then, with a rapid and unhesitating movement she pushes it at a point on its right edge . . . She then notes the sliding of the box and makes it pivot without trying to lift it; as the box revolves, she succeeds in grasping the bottle.
>
> Piaget, 1952 p. 287

An important aspect of human intentional behaviour involves using other people to help us to attain goals, and this of course involves telling them what it is that we want. A number of investigators have recently begun to examine how this comes about in children–that is, how children come to realize that they can use other people as a means to attain their goals, and how they learn to communicate to them what it is that they want.

   The ability to get adults to help in attaining goals begins to manifest itself at around nine months of age, and is most clearly seen when the infant is trying to get hold of something which is out of reach. He reaches towards an object, but instead of looking only at the object, leaning towards it with arm extended to grasp as a younger infant would, he maintains the reaching movement in the direction of the object, but turns to look at the mother. Older infants vocalize at the same time, and eventually use words in conjunction with a reaching gesture towards an object; and soon the reaching movement is transformed into a pointing gesture. Thus, infants seem to come to realize that they can enlist their mothers' aid as means to attain their goals. An example in which an infant seems to be deliberately trying to communicate can be seen here:

> Jordan is a 14-month-old boy being served his lunch.
>
> Jordan: (Vocalizes repeatedly until his mother turns around.)
> Mother: (Turns around to look at him.)
> Jordan: (Points to one of the objects on the counter.)
> Mother: Do you want this? (Holds up milk container.)
> Jordan: (Shakes his head 'no'.) (Vocalizes, continues to point.)

Mother:	Do you want this? (Hold up jam jar.)
Jordan:	(Shakes head 'no'.) (Continues to point.)
Mother:	(Two more offer–rejection pairs.)
Mother:	This? (Picks up sponge.)
Jordan:	(Leans back in highchair, puts arms down, tension leaves body.)
Mother:	(Hands Jordan sponge.)

(After Golinkoff, 1983 pp. 58–59)

When infants behave like this, the impression of intentionality is compelling, partly because the infant continues his efforts to try to attain what he has in mind, and partly because he seems distinctly relieved when he finally manages to get it.

It is worth pointing out that these behaviours will only work to communicate if the person receiving them can interpret the wishes of the infant. This is possible when the infant is interacting with an older child or with an adult, who has a wide range of possible responses at their disposal, and who is willing and able to interpret the desires of the infant.

The history of intentional communication

Of course, using other people as instruments to attain goals is only one aspect of intentional communication–children also need to learn how to conduct ordinary conversations with other people, in which the aim is to chat about, perhaps, some interesting aspect of the world rather than to get them to help, but learning to ask for things is a situation in which the child's intentionality can be obvious to an observer.

The history of intentional communication is interesting. Young infants, of around three months or so, are fascinated by their mothers, and their mothers return this interest. When the infant is not actually feeding, or engaged in some other activity, mother and child spend a great deal of time engaged in face-to-face interaction.

One aspect of this involves the mother treating the baby as though he were taking part in a conversation. This can be seen clearly in an example from the work of Catherine Snow (Snow 1977). (Ann is three months old at this time);

Ann:	(smiles)
Mother:	Oh what a nice little smile! Yes, isn't that nice? There, There's a nice little smile.
Ann:	(burps)
Mother:	What a nice wind as well! Yes, that's better isn't it? Yes. Yes.
Ann:	(vocalizes)
Mother:	Yes! There's a nice noise.

Snow, 1977 p. 12

For the two little girls examined by Snow, 100 per cent of the children's burps, yawns, coughs, sneezes, smiles and laughs at three months were replied to by their mothers as though they had been deliberate, intentional comments.

At this time the baby spends most of his time interacting face-to-face with his mother, but over the next two or three months he becomes much more interested in objects around him. At around six months an infant typically becomes much more skilled at reaching and grasping objects. Often this requires assistance from his mother–she may unobtrusively hold an awkward object so that the infant can grasp it, or she may help him by passing to him an object which is out of reach. Thus, she is treating his reaching behaviour as indicative of his intent, and is helping him to accomplish his aims. At this stage, however, the infant does not look at his mother when he is reaching for an object, but concentrates simply on the object. He is not actively enlisting his mother's help, but simply receiving it.

Conversation changes as well: Snow found that mother-child conversations were different in three main respects at seven months as compared with three months. First, the mothers were much less often talking only about their children's feelings (of being tired, hungry, bored etc.), and much more often commenting on aspects of the external environment. Second, the babies were much more active partners, so that the mothers were less often having to make all the conversational going themselves. Thus, for one child at three months the mother averaged 23 conversational turns between the child's contributions (and on one occasion devoted 124 consecutive utterances to the topic of burping, before the baby did burp and the mother switched topic). For the same child at seven months the mother averaged only eight conversational turns between the child's contributions. Third, although smiles, laughs, burps and so on were still often accepted as contributions to conversation on the part of the children, mothers often commented on something that attracted the child's interest or on something that he was reaching for. Thus, reaches and looks were treated as though they were contributions to conversation. However, mothers were also a little more demanding–they often failed to respond to *any* vocalization as though it were a conversational turn, but only to 'high-quality' voclaizations: babbles.

At around six to seven months then, when the infant reaches for an object, his concentration is wholly engrossed by the object. His mother reads his wishes, and helps him to attain them, often commenting on the action or the object, and incorporating the infant's behaviour into conversation. As Harding (1983) has demonstrated, mothers are especially prone to help their children if the infant accidentally looks towards them when reaching for an object. Within two or three months, however, a large change occurs. As Bruner puts it (1978):

> . . . he begins looking towards the mother while he is in the act of reaching for an object. The gesture is changing from a . . . reach to something more like an indicator–a semi-extended arm, hand held somewhat angled upward, fingers no longer in grasp position, body no longer stretched

fully forward. His gaze shifts from object to mother and back. He can now
reach-for-real and reach-to-signal.

Bruner, 1978 p. 71

Over the next months, gesturing, pointing, vocalizing and eventually using
words become much more part of the child's constant communicative
repertoire, and are used to request objects, to enlist help from others (e.g. an
'arms-up' gesture to indicate a desire to be picked up), and to indulge in social
chat. The child plays a much more active part in conversations, and the
number of conversational turns taken by the child comes to be nearly as great
as that of the mother. The mother becomes progressively more demanding as
to what she will accept as a conversational turn by the child, and eventually
accepts largely only words–no longer are grunts, sneezes, and burps taken by
the mother as signals of intent. Thus a typical conversation between an 18-
month-old child and her mother looks like this:

Ann:	Hot
Mother:	Hot hot
Ann:	Tea
Mother:	No it's not tea, it's coffee.
Ann:	Coffee

(From Snow, 1977 p. 18)

How do infants become intentional communicators?

In brief, the history of infant communication is that mothers treat young
infants as though they were taking part in conversations. They invite
responses by questions, and treat the infant's sneezes, smiles, coughs and
gurgles as though they were deliberate, intentful conversational contributions. When the slightly older infant begins to take an interest in the world,
and reach for objects, the mother takes his reaching gestures as indicative of
intent, and helps him to attain the object. The older infant, at around nine
months, actively enlists his mother's help in gaining an object by looking
towards her after reaching for an object, and at this stage, a mother is
especially prone to help her infant if he vocalizes while reaching and looking
at her. Older infants use points, gestures and words to communicate, and
mothers progressively increase their demands on the child in terms of what the
child must contribute before they will help–at first vocalizations, then words,
and then politeness formulae such as saying 'please'.

　All of this has suggested to a number of workers (see e.g. Newson and
Newson, 1979; Harding, 1983) that infants may slowly become intentional
communicators precisely because their mothers initially treat them as though
they were behaving intentionally even when they are not. Thus, mothers react
to their babies as though they were active participants in a dialogue, they
interpret reaching gestures as requests, and as the infant becomes

progressively more capable they tighten the demands on what will count as a workable request. These processes allow the infant to gain insight into the nature of communication, and allow him to recognize that his own actions can affect the behaviour of others, so that he can use others as means to attain ends.

A spanner in the works

While this interpretation of the beginnings of intentionality seems eminently reasonable, and seems to be well in accord with a great many observations of mother-infant interaction, it has recently become apparent that there may be many other ways in which children can acquire the ability to become intentional communicators, and that mothers' attribution of intentionality to their babies may be something that occurs only in some cultures–for example in Europe and America. One of the more striking illustrations of this comes from a study by Schieffelin and Ochs, published in 1983, in which mothers and infants belonging to the Kaluli people of Papua New Guinea were examined. A number of differences were found between the behaviour of Kaluli mothers and of European mothers. In particular,

1   Kaluli mothers believe their infants 'have no understanding', and so rarely address speech to them, except for greetings.
2   Kaluli mothers do not treat actions by their infants as attempts at communication.
3   Kaluli mothers and infants do not gaze into one another's eyes, but rather the mother sits the baby facing outwards from her, towards other people.
4   Older children may address the infant, and in this case the mother will pretend to reply for the infant, using a high pitched nasal voice (though without using baby-talk words or simple sentences). However, she does not base these replies on anything the infant does.
5   Older infants (of six to 12 months) are told what to do by imperatives or rhetorical questions such as 'Is it yours?' if the infant is taking something he should not. These imperatives and questions do not seem to expect a reply.
6   When their children begin to talk, Kaluli mothers conduct 'language lessons' in which they provide a model of what the child should say, and tell him to repeat it (e.g. 'Is it yours? Say like that'), whereas European mothers very seldom do this.
7   Kaluli infants are constantly surrounded by other people, talking to one another, and frequently commenting to one another about the actions of the infant: one-to-one conversations between mother and infant are very rare.

Thus, in many respects the verbal environment of the Kaluli infant differs from that of the European infant. Unlike his European counterpart, the young Kaluli does not experience a single person talking to him alone, interpreting his behaviour, fitting her behaviour in with his, simplifying and adapting her speech, and encouraging him to be an active participant in conversation. Nevertheless, Kaluli infants learn to talk and become competent members of a community in which people can use language as a deliberate, intentional means of communication. Clearly, there is more than one way to become social.

Further reading

SCHAFFER, R. (1977) *Mothering*. London: Fontana/Open Books.
    A clear, simple introduction to the field of parent-child interaction.
KAYE, K. (1984) *The mental and social life of babies*. London: Methuen.
    Slightly more advanced. A book that casts a cool and sceptical eye on some of the more extreme over-interpretations of babies' abilities.

Discussion topics

● How do babies learn to become competent at communicating with others?
● What does it mean to say that an infant is behaving purposefully?

CHAPTER TWO

Maternal deprivation
Helen J. Graham

Much has been written on the subject of maternal deprivation during the past forty years. Most notably, John Bowlby in the 1950s began to publish the results of his research and to evaluate the short and long-term implications of the break-up of relationships between child and mother.

Observations made by Spitz (1946 a and b) of children in a variety of institutions suggested that infants in foundling homes had a far higher mortality rate and susceptibility to infection than infants raised in institutions in which their mothers were present. There also appeared to be a greater incidence of mental, social and linguistic retardation in the former. Moreover, infants separated from their mothers at a very early age were frequently characterised by lethargy, apathy and withdrawal. This syndrome was likened to a grief reaction at the loss of a relationship distinguished by the strong dependence of an individual on another, in this case that of the infant on its mother.

A number of clinical studies of the same period (Bowlby, 1946; Bender, 1947) also pointed to the frequency with which delinquency and emotional disorders were associated with institutional care and separation from the mother.

Bowlby interpreted these findings as indicating the importance of the child's attachment to the mother, and claimed that any separation from the mother in early life constitutes a bereavement for the child that gives rise to grief and distress in the short term, and consequent psychiatric or behavioural disorder. This 'maternal deprivation hypothesis' was presented in a report to the World Health Organization Expert Committee on Mental Health in 1951. This report subsequently proved to be highly influential, stimulating widespread discussion and further research into the subject. It affected, not only psychological theorizing, but also social policy and practice, and through extensive publicity given to it by the mass media, influenced public opinion and behaviour.

Subsequent research on animals appeared to lend support to Bowlby's hypothesis. Harlow (1961) noted the syndrome of anaclitic depression in infant Rhesus monkeys that had been separated from their mothers and provided with no surrogate. Typically, these unfortunate animals showed signs of acute anxiety and distress and they subsequently developed deviant social and emotional behaviours, failing to relate to other monkeys or to engage in normal sexual activities. As a result, when adult, the females proved extremely difficult to impregnate and when they eventually did produce offspring they appeared to be unable to care for them adequately, and frequently rejected or even killed them (see Chapter 18 for further discussion of this research).

Maternal love

The central thrust of Bowlby's thesis concerns the child's need for love, and its provision by the mother. He viewed mother love as not only desirable but absolutely necessary for the normal healthy development of the child and placed great emphasis on the continuity of the mother-child relationship, insisting that adequate love could not be provided by a succession of persons but must come from one primary source. He explained this in terms of what he perceived to be the child's characteristic monotrophy, or tendency to become attached primarily to one figure, and his belief that this attachment is qualitatively different from all others. On this basis he argued that any separation from the mother, particularly during the first five years of life, gives rise to a deficiency of love that causes psychopathology in later life. For Bowlby, therefore, loss of, or separation from the mother in early childhood had a simple causal status in explaining the inability to form emotional relationships in later life. Throughout the 1950s and 1960s Bowlby's views were widely interpreted as indicating the child's need for constant, around-the-clock maternal love. Moreover, the natural mother was taken as being the only possible source of this love.

Social consequences of the maternal deprivation hypothesis

The influence of the maternal deprivation hypothesis' is discernible in a number of social developments that occurred in Britain from the mid-1950s, not all of which were beneficial or desirable.

The more humanitarian developments included the relaxing of rules in children's hospital wards that formerly had been closed to parents in the belief that their visits were emotionally upsetting to the children. Institutional care of children also underwent dramatic change, conditions being generally improved and the size of children's homes being greatly reduced. In addition, the unnecessary separation of newborn babies from their mothers, which had been mandatory in many maternity hospitals, was discouraged.

Notwithstanding, Sluckin and others (1983) observe that liberalizing ideas in the field of child care can become oppressive if elevated into prescriptive dogma. This is what happened in the case of the maternal deprivation hypothesis.

The Bowlby 'doctrine' served to legitimize the re-establishment of traditional social patterns, which had become rather more flexible between 1939–45 as a result of women's employment in the war effort, whereby mothers primarily provided care for their children. Consequently, Bowlby's claim that separation from the mother during the first five years of life may adversely affect the future health of the child was propagandized to fuel the argument that the woman's place is in the home. As a result, many wartime nurseries were closed down and the establishment of creches was discouraged, making it difficult for many mothers to continue working. Those who did so were often obliged to make alternative, and frequently less satisfactory arrangements for the care of their children, which gave rise to a proliferation of untrained child-minders. Nor was the situation ameliorated when children reached school age. The application of the perjorative label 'latch-key kid' to those children whose working mothers were not at home to receive them at the end of the school day, ensured that both mothers and their children were stigmatized.

Similarly, Rutter (1981) argues that the Bowlby doctrine led some people to place an almost mystical importance on the mother and to regard love as the only important element in child-rearing. A major consequence of this view was that the role of the father in child care was minimized or almost totally ignored. Fathers were not encouraged to participate in caring for their children and little attention was paid to the child's attachment to the father, or the father's attachment to the child. Consequently, the possibility of 'paternal deprivation' was not considered. It is only recently that the father's role in child-rearing has been recognized as having potentially far-reaching consequences for child development (Parke, 1981).

A further consequence of the glorification of the mother and maternal love was the tendency to over-estimate the extent of mother-child interaction and to confound its quantity with its quality. This had important implications for both legal and social policy whereby custody of children was almost routinely awarded to the mother, irrespective of her ability to provide adequately for a child's needs, and with little or no consideration of the child's attachment to its father. Similarly, the myth that the worst of family circumstances is preferable to the best institutional care owes much to the Bowlby doctrine and has proved extremely resistant to change.

A final consequence of the over-emphasis on the mother was the growing tendency within society to blame the mother for almost every conceivable social malady, from delinquency and truancy, to mental retardation, affectionless psychopathy, and even dwarfism (Patton and Gardner, 1963), thereby placing a considerable burden of responsibility solely on the mother's shoulders.

Growing awareness of these less desirable consequences of the concept of maternal deprivation contributed to criticism of the Bowlbian viewpoint during the next decade.

Criticism of the maternal deprivation hypothesis

Despite its widespread acceptance and consequent influence, the maternal deprivation hypothesis provoked considerable controversy, and continues to do so. Critics of the concept claim that it is based on inadequate evidence, and on studies with serious methodological flaws, which failed to distinguish the multiple variables involved. Indeed, much of the criticism levelled at research in this area is justified. Moreover, some of the difficulties arise from the very term 'material deprivation', which is misleading.

It is misleading first because it confuses who the mother is with what she does–a mother may be physically present but not mothering her child, and conversely, adequate mothering may be provided by someone who is not the natural mother. It is misleading secondly because it fails to distinguish between effects that arise through loss of the mother and effects that arise through a distortion of mothering.

Alternative mothers

The studies of Harlow and Harlow (1969) indicated that young Rhesus monkeys provided with alternative mothers show minimal effects from the loss of their natural mothers. Indeed, it is commonly observed that young animals are often fostered by substitute mothers of entirely different species with no apparent ill effects. Empirical investigations (Hinde and Davies, 1972) on infant Rhesus monkeys suggest that the infant's distress following separation from the mother is not primarily the result of loss of the mother *per se*, but the effect of the consequent disruptions in mothering, and that where these disruptions are minimized so also is the distress. Similar observations have been made on human infants (Robertson and Robertson, 1967) which also suggest that where mothering is increased during separation, distress is diminished.

Research on both animal and human infants has also enabled the various components of mothering to be distinguished. Perhaps the most well-known work in this field remains that of Harlow and Harlow (1969), who in studying the effects of surrogate mothering in Rhesus monkeys focused attention on the importance of physical contact between mother and infant. They demonstrated that given a choice between a wire-frame surrogate that supplied milk on demand, or one with a 'cuddly' terry-towel covering that did not dispense milk, infant Rhesus monkeys invariably exhibited a preference for the latter. They appeared to derive comfort from clinging to it, especially when presented with any novel stimuli.

Even the observations made by Spitz in children's homes during the mid-1940s had suggested that mortality and illness in human infants were much reduced when some continuous, caring attention was provided. Moreover, it appeared to be irrespective of whether the attention was given by one or more persons. In addition, it was noted that mental retardation was more prevalent where children were confined to cots and received minimal social, perceptual and environmental stimulation. Even infants cared for by feeble-minded adults showed an improvement in their recorded IQ scores, which was attributed to the increased stimulation and attention they received. On the basis of these observations, Spitz (1945) suggested that the two factors essential to adequate child-rearing are stimulation and care. The results of both the animal and human research of the period would seem to suggest that, while developmental retardation is a probable consequence of inadequate stimulation, the syndrome of distress is probably a consequence of some disruption of care.

Considerable attention has been given to the subject of stimulation as a facet of mothering. However, researchers have emphasized different kinds of stimulation provided through mothering, including social, perceptual, linguistic and environmental stimulation. As described in Chapter 6, the infant's attention is captured by perceptually interesting objects near to the infant, and the mother's face easily captures the infant's interest. Human beings constitute the most important stimuli for infants, which is biologically useful since they provide for their survival needs. Their importance also lies in the fact that in the first few weeks of life the visual capacities of infants are relatively undeveloped and the physical environment in itself provides them with only limited stimulation. This being the case, it would follow that any physical loss of the mother-figure, or restriction of mothering during the first few weeks of life could deprive the child of much stimulation. Casler (1968) however, insisted that, while the amount of stimulation and the range of experiences to which the child is exposed are the crucial factors in child development, they are largely independent of persons, albeit generally facilitated by them. He argued, therefore, in contradistinction to Bowlby, that the human organism does not need maternal love in order to function normally.

Reassessment of the concept of maternal deprivation

During the 1960s, a growing body of opinion questioned the wisdom of the exclusive mother-child relationship, suggesting that it may do more harm than good in depriving the child of the benefits of varied stimulation and experience. In addition, an influential survey of children in England and Wales (Douglas and others, 1968) established that something in the order of one-third of all children under the age of five had been separated from their mothers for periods of a week or more without suffering ill effects.

Rutter (1981) points out in his review of the available evidence that the syndrome of distress following separation is fairly well established, and, where it occurs, is most marked in the under-fives. It is also clear that children of all ages differ greatly in their response to separation. Moreover, distress is more common in male infants–human or monkey–than in females, and less severe in all infants who remain in a familiar environment following separation.

As regards the long term effects of separation, Rutter points out that deprivation is a complex phenomenon with many aspects which operate in different ways. He suggests we can take for granted that children are retarded by admission to poor quality institutions but that separation is probably not in itself the crucial factor. What matters is the quality of care provided, the nature of relationships which ensue, and the opportunities for bonding and attachment to take place. Intellectual retardation is related to lack of meaningful experience. Delinquency and conduct disorders are a response to family discord and disturbed interpersonal relationships (whether or not there is separation). Affectionless psychopathy sometimes follows multiple separation experiences and institutional care because of the failure of early bonding to take place. Nevertheless he notes that these effects of separation can be mitigated by later positive experiences and attachments (such as in fostering and adoption).

Reviewing his position in the light of further research, Bowlby (1969) accepted that separation from the mother did not inevitably give rise to serious psychopathology, but he remained insistent that prolonged separation from the mother under the age of five is detrimental to the healthy development of the child. He also reasserted and emphasized his belief in the importance of the child's attachment to the mother-figure, and directed attention to the need for further research into the formation of this attachment in early life.

Mothering as a skill

Thus, emphasis during the 1970s shifted away from maternal deprivation as such and concentrated on the development of attachments or 'bonding' (Schaffer, 1977). This was greatly stimulated and facilitated by developments in audio-visual recording techniques that enabled precise analysis of the behaviours of mothers and infants. Significantly, this research has suggested the ways in which contact, stimulation and care are interrelated in mothering.

It appears from a number of studies (Newson and Newson, 1979) that the behaviours of infants are not random but perfectly articulated to serve their survival needs. Thus it would appear that infants emit clear signals of need, which are recognized, albeit intuitively for the most part, by the mother as attempts at communication, and to which she subsequently responds. As described in Chapter 1, mother and infant are thus engaged in a two-way communication process or dialogue. Sluckin and others (1983) have suggested that the mother's attempt to engage in this dialogue and respond to the infant's needs constitute the first signs of maternal attachment or bonding, and that being able to respond to the infant's basic needs is thus an indication that the attachment process is underway.

An important implication of these findings is that mothering, rather than being in any sense mystical, emerges as a skill–that of recognizing and responding to the infant's attempts to communicate its needs. From this perspective, mothering is monitoring and a skill that can be learned by anyone, whether they have given birth to a child nor not, or whether female or male. Recent research on some species of monkeys has shown that given the opportunity to develop this skill through access to infants, adult males can prove to make as good 'mothers' as females (Hinde, 1974).

A further implication of this research on mother-child interaction is that if the needs that an infant is attempting to communicate are not attended to (as a result of inadequate monitoring) then the infant is less likely to thrive. Furthermore, if no one is looking at the infant attempting to interact with it, its needs to communicate will not be reinforced and might therefore be extinguished over time. Additionally, the infant is likely to suffer a reduction in stimulation–social, perceptual and physical–as a consequence of this lack of attention.

It is probable therefore that it is this constellation of factors that accounts for the subsequent impoverishment of social and emotional development which concerned Bowlby, as well as much of the physical ill health and distress noted in studies of separation. Rather than being affected by different psychological mechanisms these effects would seem to be the result of a fundamental disturbance in the social interaction between the infant and its caretaker. It is therefore important to establish those factors that facilitate, hasten or retard the development of the social interaction between mother and child.

The development of bonds

Bonding has been afforded widespread publicity, much of which has placed great emphasis on the importance of the first few hours and days after birth, and also on the importance of body contact between mother and child.

Both these concerns owe much to research on animals, but one should be aware of the difficulties and dangers of generalizing from animal studies as discussed in Chapter 18. As we have noted above, Harlow's research on surrogate mothering in Rhesus monkeys pointed to the importance of physical contact in infancy. Research on sheep and goats (Collias, 1956; Hersher and others, 1963) has also shown that unless contact between the mother and her young is established very shortly after birth the mother will reject it. No clear evidence exists for a similar tendency in humans.

Nevertheless, Klaus and others (1972) have suggested that separation of the mother and child during the first three days after birth has an adverse effects on the mother because she loses intimate contact with her child at a time when she is maximally sensitive to it. They claim, on the basis of observational studies, that mothers separated from their infants in the first few hours after birth show a greater tendency towards post-natal depression and subsequent rejection of their offspring than mothers who have not experienced this separation. They also indicate that one of the striking differences noted between those mothers separated from their infants as a greater distance, rarely look them in the face and generally touch them less. Moreover, their results suggest that these differences are still apparent twelve months later and that mothers who have been separated from their infants immediately after birth are more likely to physically chastise them subsequently. Kempe and Kempe (1978) regard this as particularly significant in view of the statistics that suggest premature babies, those most usually separated from their mothers after birth, represent 30–40 per cent of battered children although they constitute only some 8 per cent of the live birth total.

Leyboyer (1977) and Odent (see Watts, 1983) have gained worldwide and almost cultic support in their advocacy of immediate contact between mother and child after birth. Sluckin and others (1983) remain cautious in their interpretation of the various data on bonding, and particularly of the emphasis placed on physical contact. They insist that no hard evidence has emerged to suggest that irreversible damage is done if the child is not placed in the mother's arms immediately after birth. They also argue that misguided ideas as to what constitutes good mothering have led in some cases to severe harassment of those mothers who have difficulty relating to their offspring in the early stages of motherhood. They suggest that the feelings of guilt, anxiety, inadequacy, depression and resentment thus engendered are not conducive to the development of maternal love and good mothering. They conclude their review of the research on bonding by advising mothers to stop worrying about the matter because the findings from available research suggest strongly that maternal attachment, and child-to-adult attachment develops slowly but surely in most cases.

Thus, while the emphasis in research has changed, controversy remains a constant factor surrounding the issue of the mother-child relationship. Nothing under the sun is new it seems, not even in Neverland:

> 'Don't have a mother' he said. Not only had he no mother, but he had not the slightest desire to have one. He thought them very overrated persons. Wendy, however, felt at once that she was in the presence of tragedy.
>
> (J.M. Barrie, *Peter Pan*)

Further reading

RUTTER, M. (1981) *Maternal Deprivation Reassessed.* Harmondsworth: Penguin.
A detailed and comprehensive review of research that presents the issues clearly.
SLUCKIN, W. HERBERT, M. and SLUCKIN, A. (1983) *Maternal Bonding.* Oxford: Blackwell.
A critical evaluation of the research on bonding, written mainly for social and health workers, general practicioners and, particularly, mothers.

Discussion topics

- Do current concerns about maternal behaviour reflect the changing position of women in society?
- What does the study of the breakdown of relations between children and mothers tell us about normal development?

CHAPTER THREE

Communication as social interaction
Glyn Prosser

Old wives, and even the not so old, have long suspected that very young babies are both responsive to communication and able to communicate. There is a strong social component to this communication. Few mothers, not to mention fathers, are able to resist those early smiles, even when under rational pressures to attribute them to the agonies of ever-present wind.

An early start

It seems the old wives were probably right: there is no reason to suppose that the infant whose age can be measured in weeks rather than months and who is apparently very 'knowing' is necessarily an exceptional child or a budding genius. He is probably quite normal, i.e. within well established norms for his group. Evidence in support of this has been coming in from developmental researchers over the past twenty years. In 1963, Peter Wolff of Boston published findings based on studies of the social play a mother can have with infants as young as six to eight weeks. Colwyn Trevarthen, working at Edinburgh in the early seventies with very young infants, argued ' . . . when a newborn is alert and coordinated, its still very rudimentary movements have, nevertheless, the pace as well as the form of activities such as looking, listening, and reaching to touch, from the start' (in Lewin, 1975, p. 64).

Recognition

Trevarthen made and analysed a number of films of young infants. He found patterns of activity that parallel the gestures that often accompany conversation between adults. Babies as young as six weeks apparently respond to people making signals, and their cooing and hand-waving as well as smiling often indicate that they actually distinguish between different people.

At the Belmont hospital near London, Genevieve Carpenter measured infants' responses to a number of situations. These situations included presentation of the mother's face alone, mother's face presented at the same time as mother's voice, and two mis-match conditions, viz. mother's face presented with a stranger's voice and stranger's face presented with mother's voice. Carpenter arranged for the infants to be seated in a comfortable well-pillowed cradle-chair facing a display of equipment that made it possible for the different stimulus faces to be presented at a distance of about 12 inches. When the small door or aperture through which the mother or a stranger could look was closed, the infant's attention was held by a display of blinking lights.

The findings of this research were that the infants differentiated between the mother and a stranger as early as two weeks of age, though whether this was on the basis of facial features or smell is unclear. They gave more attention to the mother, i.e. in terms of seconds spent fixating the face, than to the stranger, but less attention in the conditions where there was a mis-match of face with voice. The recognition of faces is described further in Chapter 6.

Interactional synchrony

William Condon, a researcher at the Boston University Medical Center, hypothesized that a newborn child moves synchronously with adult speech as early as the first day after birth. Analysing film records of the movements made by very young babies while adults were talking, he found that within the space of one second about five integrated levels of organization occurred between the child's movements and adult speech sounds. Now this is something that can be observed to happen within the behaviour of individual adults. If we watch someone talking, we shall see how the rhythm of movement not only of facial features but also of hands, arms and legs, tend to correspond to the rhythm of his or her speech. There are, of course, individual and cultural if not racial differences. Some people speak with greater animation than others. The same procedure may be observed between adults who are engaged in conversation. There is a tendency for each person to match the speech and body movements of the other. Condon (1979) refers to this as 'interactional synchrony' and, after analysing film of newborn children made within only twelve hours of their birth, he claims to have found interactional synchrony between adult speech and the babies' movements. He considers that the occurrence of such activity is evidence of participation in communication and argues, 'By the time he begins to speak he may have already laid down within himself the form and structure of the language system of his culture' (in Lewin, 1975, p. 90). Furthermore, it is by means of interactional synchrony that the child moves through the process of imitation and identification to the accomplishment of a socially based linguistic communication.

Crying

Why do babies cry and what do they communicate by their crying? Mothers, mothers-in-law and baby books suggest a check-list, very much like a fault-finding flow chart for engineers. Wolff (1969) found that newborn babies cry mainly when they are hungry. Although the babies came to associate sucking and being held with feeding, it was actually the ingestion of food that stopped them crying, and they would not be passified by sucking alone or being held. Babies also cried more when they were cold and the ambient temperature was 78°F rather than 88–90°F; because they had their clothes taken off (which was what is meant by egocentric speech (Piaget, 1926). Even when in the company be internally or externally caused. In passing we might note that rocking, at the rate of about 60 rocks per minute, seems the most effective antidote to crying (Leach, 1983).

At first the crying is simply expressive, i.e. it expresses the baby's feeling of discomfort and distress. There is no intention to communicate, though cries of hunger differ from pain cries, and some mothers learn to distinguish them. There is also an anger or grumbling cry. Soon, however, (some parents feel it could be within two or three days) the baby's crying is communicative. Not only is the baby hungry, for example, but there is the implied request, 'Feed me'. The baby learns the general lesson that crying and mother's appearance are linked; so that apart from the expression of distress and the need for feeding, there is social communication: baby seeks mother's presence and attention. Less attractively, baby can also indicate displeasure with mother's activity or lack of it by a bout of crying that is quickly identified as rage. Developmental psychologists such as Mussen, Conger and Kagan (1965) refer to this as the differentiation of emotions; although they tend to the position that learning is not the primary mechanism for this: it is a question of maturation.

Smiling

Smiling occurs very early, and appears to be associated with certain changes in brain activity or states of arousal which can be measured using EEG (electro encephalograph) equipment. It can happen without the help of any external stimulus, as early as the day of birth, but in the first week of life the infant may smile in response to mechanical noises or squeaky voices (Macfarlane, 1975). By the second and third week, the smile occurs more specifically to the human voice, especially a female voice. Smiles no longer happen spontaneously but mostly in response to some external stimulation. However the facial characteristics of the speaker have no effect. By six weeks, there are signs of real social smiling in response to the human face which is now more effective than any other stimuli in bringing about a smile. Bower (1977) has argued that the social smile occurs at 46 weeks after conception, so that it would appear at around six weeks for an infant born at the normal gestational age, and rather later for a prematurely born baby. (In fact the normal gestational time is 38 weeks, so Bower is probably referring to the time from the last period before conception.) Thus Bower argues that the appearance of social smiling depends upon maturation rather than on experience.

Trevarthen referred to the six-week-old infant's smile as a sign of recognition and, even if we may doubt whether selective smiling to familiar as opposed to unfamiliar faces occurs as early as this, it is clear that well before ten months, the age at which infants can move sufficiently well to show a preference for following their mother rather than a stranger, smiles of welcome and cries of protest at separation discriminate in favour of the mother. It is reasonable to suppose that smiling has the effect of strengthening the bonds between mother and child. More particularly, if crying can gain the mother's attention, smiling can have the effect of holding her attention. For the development of both crying and smiling as a means of communication, there would appear to be a learning component and, as a strategy for controlling the mother's behaviour, smiling gradually shows itself to be the more effective.

Language

Until language emerges, smiling, chuckling, gurgling and other attractive behaviours are the ways in which social communication is accomplished. The whole range of the young child's needs are, however, better expressed when language skills are acquired. Speech development will be discussed in Chapter 8, but some reference to the social function of speech will be appropriate here.

The process of language acquisition can be enjoyable in itself. Not only does it give the child a sense of achievement, and mastery over an increasingly interesting and complex environment, but it also brings social approval from parents and other adults. Just as both crying and smiling can attract and hold attention, so can the earliest efforts to talk. Some psychologists explain how children emerge from the baby babbling stage to produce recognizable words in terms of the attention and verbal responses that are given by adults as a kind of reward for making sounds that are close approximations. That is to say such responses are reinforced. But some writers, e.g. D.L. Olmstead (1971) have argued that the early mother-child verbal interactions are pleasurable for the simple reason that the mother's voice is already linked in the experience of the child with feelings of comfort, warmth and repletion after food. In this way, then, the process of language acquisition and, once some facility in language has been gained, that of language use, both have a strong social component. The desire for social interaction can be communicated by the use of language, and so can pleasure in the achievement of social interaction. This is linguistic social communication (Figure 3.1).

3.1   Needs are better expressed when language is acquired.

However, communication with others is not the only function of speech. Anyone who has seen a small boy in the midst of his toys talking as he selects one of them and describing the actions he is performing with it, will know what is meant by egocentric speech (Piaget, 1926). Even when in the company of other children, the child will often repeat words and phrases to himself, apparently just for the pleasure of talking. There is no intention to communicate, and when the child appears to be talking to himself in this way, he is possibly just thinking aloud. This can have useful functions in helping the child to organize and execute the task he is engaged on, an example of which can be found in Chapter 11 under the heading Study 4. However, Vygotsky (1962) held that even this kind of speech had a social function. It only appears to be egocentric because children do not realize that their private world is not shared by others.

Language and social class

As the child develops, not only does he acquire the particular language of his parents such as English, French, German or Japanese, but he learns the ways of expression that are common to their socio-economic group or class. Arguing along these lines in the early 1960s, the sociologist Basil Bernstein drew attention to what he felt were basic differences between middle-class and lower-working-class uses of language. His system has undergone a number of re-formulations since those days.

In an attempt to explain why the children of lower-working-class parents appeared to be at a disadvantage within the educational system, Bernstein suggested that whereas the middle-class use language for a wide variety of functions, the lower-working-class use language mainly to define social relationships. On this view the latter is referred to as a public language whereas the middle-class language is taken to be formal. The distinction is and, according to Bernstein, the children of lower-working-class parents are faced with the task of switching from the restricted to the elaborated code when pursuing their studies at school.

One obvious feature of restricted code is the use of 'sympathetic circularity'. The speaker indicates the need for his previous speech sequence to be confirmed or reinforced by appealing to a sense of community with his hearer. It is as though he wishes to establish that they are on common ground. So he uses such phrases as 'Wouldn't it?', 'You see?' and 'You know'. Now this looks like being a trivial matter, but the practice can be regarded as symptomatic of a basic need for speech to reflect an interchange between two social beings. It is seen as social communication, not merely the communication of information; and the speaker assumes that both speaker and hearer have something to contribute, in that they share not only a common language but a whole range of concepts and experiences. For this reason, the argument goes, lower-working-class speakers will have a greater tendency to select idiomatic phrases, which they assume will be understood; and they will organize their sentences in such a way that particular points are taken for granted. Bernstein thus sees this restricted code as a language of implicit meaning.

Evidence for Bernstein's view

Some attempts have been made to test aspects of this theoretical approach. Bernstein himself has carried out several experiments. In one of them (1962) tape recordings were made of an undirected discussion on capital punishment engaged in by five groups of five boys. Two of the groups came from middle-class famililies, the rest from working-class families. Their speech was then analysed, using methods of conventional grammar. Results of this analysis showed that the middle-class group tended to use more complex language, e.g. more subordinate clauses, passive verbs, uncommon adjectives and adverbs. They also used more egocentric sequences, e.g. 'I think', whereas socio-centred or sympathetic circularity sequences occurred more frequently in the working-class speech. The more formal nature of middle-class speech was also shown in the greater tendency to use abstract arguments.

In another study (Prosser, 1974) boys aged 13 and 14 were invited to write questions on topics such as sport, the police and the problems of teenagers. Results showed that children from middle-class families wrote questions that were longer, more complex and more abstract. They also had a tendency to ask questions that were expressed in the more formal style, e.g. 'Is it true that ...?'.

While middle-class children favoured the first person singular 'I', children from lower-working-class families had a greater tendency to use the word 'You', and to refer to their own group. This is consistent with and illustrative of the Bernstein dichotomy between egocentric and socio-centric language.

Evidence against Bernstein

Bernstein's approach has been severely criticized. In the first place, the whole concept of social class is extremely complex and controversial; and when we refer to working-class life and language, we are in danger of presenting a narrow and stereotyped view. Even Bernstein felt it necessary to emphasize that he had in mind the lower-working-class. The assumption that working-class speakers are at a disadvantage because of conceptual limitations on their linguistic expression has been tested and found wanting by Labov (1972). When he and his fellow-researchers interviewed black children from working-class homes, they sought to avoid the rather superior paternalistic attitudes sometimes adopted by white researchers and, by allowing the children to bring their friends, by introducing taboo topics and vocabularly familiar to the children, and by being prepared, when necessary, to sit on the floor with them during the interview, they changed the whole atmosphere. The hitherto inarticulate children became highly articulate and, more important, dealt with abstract concepts at a level at least as profound as that of their middle-class counterparts.

Conclusion

It is not necessary to decide between Labov and Bernstein in order to recognize that there is a powerful social component in the use of language. Some children, and adults for that matter, emphasize this social component at the expense of purely formal discussion. And the same person will use language in different ways, depending on the circumstances.

The whole question of what is the 'done thing' in behaviour or speech, (for example, in terms of 'U' versus 'Non-U') illustrates the desire of certain groups to define and delimit their own particular membership. When such people meet, they are able to express the cohesiveness or solidarity of their groups by using expressions, idioms or jargon in their own brand of 'public language'. Note that in such cases communication is social. The individual's own private feelings are effortlessly hidden, and give place to social feeling.

This exemplifies a paradox which faces us at almost every point as we investigate the development of communication skills in the young child. Gestures, cries, smiles and words all appear to derive from a primitive desire to communicate personal needs; yet as soon as they acquire some efficiency in doing this, they take on a social aspect and, in the interests of interpersonal relationships may even serve to obscure the very thoughts and feelings they were apparently designed to reveal. It may well be that this illustrates a persisting tension between the self as differentiated from others, and the self as identified with others.

Further reading

LEWIN, R. (1975) *Child Alive*. London: Temple Smith.
    A very readable account of research into different aspects of child development.
ROBINSON, W.P. (1972) *Language and social behaviour*. Harmondsworth: Penguin.
    Discusses the differences in language used by different social classes and also the functions language has in social interaction, such as defining role relationships and giving individual identity.

Discussion topics

● Describe the variety of ways in which babies communicate. Do the things that are communicated differ according to the manner of the communication?
● In what ways can language be a barrier to communication?

CHAPTER FOUR

The development of social identity and self-concept
Alan Branthwaite

Origins of self-concept

As adults, we take for granted the idea that we are separate, independent individuals with our own characteristics and inside knowledge of ourselves. But this was not always the case during development, nor is this self-awareness true for most other animals. Chimpanzees are able to recognize themselves in mirrors in the sense that they understand their image is a reflection of themselves rather than another chimpanzee. This was demonstrated in some research by G.G. Gallup (1979) who gave jungle-born chimpanzees experience with full length mirrors positioned outside their cages, and found that they learnt to use the mirrors to inspect parts of themselves they couldn't otherwise see. But this ability to recognize oneself has not been found in other animals. They treat the mirror image as if it was another, often rival, animal.

In children, the idea of self as a separate and distinct person is only gradually acquired through development. Very young children do not differentiate themselves from the environment, and they probably are not aware of a clear boundary between their own bodies and their physical surroundings. The child only gradually learns to distinguish self from the inanimate environment and other people. As Piaget (1930) described it, a distinct awareness of oneself as a separate entity is the 'result of a gradual and progressive dissociation and not a primitive intuition' (p. 128). The realization of self as an independent and separate entity arises over the first year of life out of a number of experiences. Touching oneself is important because it gives a double feeling of touching and being touched: tickling oneself is not the same as being tickled by others. The awareness of body boundary develops through touching and the exercise of coordinated voluntary movements of different parts of the body. Self recognition in mirrors also develops over the first two years. The growth of language facilitates self-awareness through the use of names and the development of

34

pronouns (I, me, mine). Out of these experiences, children develop an awareness of themselves as initiators of actions and intentions, as described in Chapter 1. Children gain experience of their own will through everyday social interchange in the potential for cooperting or not cooperating in being fed, dressed or carried about. They begin to understand more of their independence as separate entities, and gradually these 'separate entities' take on their own character as they acquire, through language, a knowledge of their own name and other personal properties.

'Who am I?'

Self-awareness involves two components: the feeling of being an independent, active initiator and controller of one's own plans and purposes; and the awareness of themselves as initiators of actions and intentions, as described in distinction was developed by Mead (1934) who conceived of the self as an 'I' (the impulsive and energizing aspect) and a 'Me' (the concept we have of ourself and other people's views of us). Once an awareness of independence and individuality has dawned, the question is 'Who am I?', that is, what is the individual's identity. During development the self-concept becomes more clearly realized and explicit. Mead believed the child actively constructed a self-concept out of social exchanges and experiences with other people. For young children the self-concept starts as a loose accretion of the labels applied to them by others and their own feelings about who and what they are. At particular times in development this question of 'Who am I?' becomes more sharply realized. Adolescence is often characterized by an intensive search to define a more explicit answer. Readers might like to try to formulate their own answers as to who, or what, they are.

Some years ago, we asked groups of students to write down 'who or what are you?' In answer, about two-thirds mentioned their sex, two thirds also mentioned their occupation (i.e. student) and one third said they were a human being. One in seven gave their nationality. Interestingly, when similar questions were put informally to groups in other countries, about half the Israelis and one quarter of Americans included their nationality. In Northern Ireland, no one gave their nationality but most gave their religion. Some struggled to express their uniqueness, and individuality, using terms such as their name, or 'me', by describing their personality, and using poetic metaphors such as: 'a speck in the cosmos', 'a shell of unique impulses'. Research into 'Who am I?' answers has found that children tend to use idiosyncratic evaluation terms to describe themselves (e.g. "I am bossy, I am untidy") whereas adults use social categories followed by personal evaluations (Kuhn, 1960).

In the main, our self-concept is influenced by three things that interact: what we want to be, the way we present ourself to others and what society and other people tell us we are. Much depends on the classification and labels given to us by parents and friends. (An interesting account of the part played by nicknames is given by Morgan, O'Neill and Harre, 1979.) When children are told they are 'a good girl' or 'a bad boy', it not only praises or admonishes but also builds up their knowledge of their place in certain social categories. A long time ago, the psychologist William James (1890) pointed out our dependence upon other people and the groups we fancied we belonged to for our appreciation of who we are, and what we are worth in terms of our society.

More recently, Bloom (1971) has drawn attention to the processes that influence our self-image in those special circumstances where society is uncertain who we are. He describes the dilemma of a man who cannot answer the question 'Who am I?' until his society has determined the social categories he belongs to. 'T' was a South African citizen whose racial classification had come into question. In 1966 two senior judges spent two days in attempting to decide who T was, which in South Africa meant his official categorization in terms of colour. T was appealing against a decision of the Population Registration Board, which had issued him his first identity card when he was 22 years old and which indicated he had been classed as a coloured person. Previously T had grown up thinking of himself as white, mixing with white people and having white friends. Until the court settled who T was he could not know to what job or profession he could reasonably aspire, who would be his friends or neighbours. If he was confirmed in the status of 'coloured' he would have been restricted in his social world and have to relearn who he was.

While the method of legal classifications in South Africa dramatizes the process by which we form our identities, essentially the same social mechanisms operate everywhere informally to label and categorize us as belonging to particular groups. It is out of this matrix of group memberships that we develop our concept of who we are.

Group memberships and self-concept

Sex identity is one of the earliest aspects of self-concept to develop in children. Perhaps this should not be surprising because the sexual identity of a child is of major importance to parents and relatives long before the child realizes the significance of blue and pink clothing. Between the ages of three to five years, children indicate preferences for playing with members of their own sex. This is one of the first prejudices to develop (Rubin, 1980). In answering the question 'What are you?' children between six and eleven years answered overwhelmingly in terms of their sex (Jahoda, 1963). The way in which gender identity develops is considered more fully in a later chapter, so we will not expand further on it here.

Of particular interest to social psychologists has been the use by children of racial group membership to define their self-concept, and what consequences this awareness might have for adult pesonality.

At first young children don't understand racial labels when asked about them. In one study (Hartley, Rosenbaum and Schwartz, 1948) when asked 'Are you Jewish?', the child replied 'No, I'm only four. I'll get Jewish'. When asked 'Are you American?' another child answered 'no, my father is American, I'm a girl'.

A clear awareness of racial identity dawns between three and five years old according to research carried out in America, though the timing is influenced by the surrounding social climate and emphasis placed on racial differences by adults. In the 1930s and 1940s the Clarks presented three to seven-year-old children with dolls that were identical except that some were brown with dark hair and the others white with blonde hair. The children were asked to pick out the doll they liked best, the one that looked bad, the one that looked like a white child, the one that looked like a Negro, and the one that looked most like themselves (Clark and Clark, 1947). It was found that the brown doll was most often rejected and disliked often because it was black or 'ugly'. The majority of black children liked the white doll best and this was the one they would prefer to play with. Even the three year old children were not only aware of which group they belonged to but also the undesirability of being black. Some of the children became very emotional when it came to indicating which doll looked like them. The proportion of children who identified themselves with the black doll varied according to the child's own skin colour. More of the darker children picked out the brown doll as being like them than did the lighter skinned children who more often identified themselves with the while doll. One five-year-old explaining his identification with the brown doll said, 'I burned my face and made it spoil'. (The Clarks, it should be noted, were black. The influence of the investigator's skin colour is discussed in Milner, 1983.)

From many studies in America, it was clear that by the age of four, children were aware of themselves and others in terms of racial identity and the values associated with different groups in society.

Similar investigations were carried out in this country during the late 1960s and early 1970s, with similar results. Milner (1983) asked British children of West Indian, Asian and English descent, between five and eight-years-old, to pick out the doll that looked like them and that they would prefer to be. The dolls were specially produced for the research to achieve a life-like appearance with the correct facial features, skin colour, eye colour and hair type of each racial group. The children were given two dolls to choose between one of which represented the child's own racial group. The other doll represented a white person for the West Indian and Asian children, or the dominant immigrant group for the white children.

The results indicated that 100 per cent of English children identified themselves as looking like the white doll, while only 76 per cent of Asian and 52 per cent of West Indian children identified themselves with their correct racial group. 24 per cent of Asian and 48 per cent of West Indian children misidentified themselves by indicating that the white doll looked more like them. In terms of which doll they would prefer to be like, the results show that 100 per cent of English children would prefer to be like the white doll while 82 per cent of West Indians and 65 per cent of Asians would also prefer to be like the white doll. The study showed that black children in Britain, just like their American counterparts, recognize racial differences and have a strong tendency to devalue their own group.

There were no general age trends in the findings, apart from some decline in the numbers of older black children identifying with the white doll. Milner interprets the mis-identifications by black children not as showing lack of awareness about racial identify but *rejection* of that identity on the part of children from negatively valued groups. The relative inaccuracy of the coloured children's self-identification reflects not ignorance of self-concept but an unwillingness to accept the social identity implied by the coloured dolls. Milner describes the implications of his findings in these terms:

> One of the central problems for the black child is that of establishing for himself a viable identity. He is socialized into a world in which the social valency of his skin colour is highly negative . . . In other words he may have difficulty in creating a stable, positive sense of himself. As self-esteem is an important part of adjustment and mental health, the black child appears particularly vulnerable.

(Milner, 1975 p. 140)

Similar studies have been carried out with children of Pakistani descent in Glasgow but using a different technique. Jahoda and others (1972) used an 'identikit' apparatus in which there were three shades for skin colour (dark, light and intermediate), three eye colours, three hair colours and two shapes each for the face, nose and mouth. This gives over 200 possible faces by superimposing different features. In particular the use of three shades for skin colours meets a criticism made of other studies that light-skinned Negroes may have been more accurate in choosing the white doll rather than the black doll when there was no intermediate available (Greenwald and Oppenheim, 1968).

Jahoda allowed the Pakistani and Scottish children two attempts to construct a face that looked as much like themselves as possible. These attempts were classified as correct or incorrect, taking into account the colour of the child's skin. There is no strong evidence of greater misidentification on the part of the immigrant children in this research. Among the six-year-olds, 33 per cent of Pakistani children made one or both faces incorrect compared with 20 per cent of white Scottish children. Among ten-year-olds, 21 per cent of Pakistani children made one or both faces incorrect, compared to 14 per cent of Scottish children. Jahoda also asked the children to say 'what are you?' and, interestingly 61 per cent of Pakistani children used ethnic identification compared to 14 per cent of Scottish children. So ethnic membership would appear to be more salient for the Pakistani children as part of their self-image.

Finally, ethnic preferences were obtained with the identikit by asking each child to build up a face they would like to have. 59 per cent of six-year-olds showed a preference for their own pigmentation, but there was a difference among ten year-olds. While 66 per cent of Scottish children preferred their own pigmentation, 63 per cent of Pakistanis preferred another (lighter) pigmentation. Blue eyes also featured prominently in their construction of preferred faces. Two researchers were used in this study, one white and one Asian. Preferences were biased towards the colour of the interviewer for all children, but, overall, the Pakistani children still showed a preference for lighter features.

The evaluation of social groups

It is the evaluation of particular social groups in society that poses problems for the emerging identity of children from minority groups. There is no doubt that children become aware of these evaluations at an early age; long before they have absorbed any facts about particular groups and nationalities, they know whether they are for or against them. For example, there was found to be more agreement among six to seven-year-olds about which countries they liked and disliked than about their relative sizes (Tajfel and Jahoda, 1966). Here, as so often, attitudes lead, and predetermine, knowledge.

Most children by the age of six have learned to positively evaluate their own group. Children in five European countries judged photographs of men they liked better as being from their own country (Tajfel and others 1972). The exceptions to this were children from nationalities with low standing even though there may not be marked physical differences. Scottish children and oriental Israeli children did not positively value their own group, preferring the English and European Israelis respectively. Even at the age of six, these children had absorbed the subtle distinctions made in society as to which groups are preferable and more positively evaluated.

Changing social evaluations

We have seen how a child's developing sense of identity and realization of personal qualities draws on the group memberships and social classifications that are ascribed to the child. We have also discovered that this process can pose acute problems for the children of minority racial groups who learn that their group, and therefore their personal identity, is negatively valued by the wider society. However, there are indications that social change in the standing of black people in society is beginning to affect the attitudes and identities of black children.

Vaughan noticed these social changes taking place among Maoris in New Zealand. Four studies had been conducted between 1961 and 1971 with Maori children, showing them dolls and photographs and asking them which they were like and which they would prefer to be. Vaughan (1978) observed that if he ordered his studies in terms of when the data were collected and whether they were conducted in a traditional rural region or more progressive urban locations, then the results fell into a pattern. It was found that Maori children showed increasing preferences for their own group and greater identification with their group as a function or urbanism and time. This trend was apparent in the five to eight-year-olds but stronger in the nine to twelve-year-olds. So, less Maori children identified themselves with the white doll and would have preferred to be white in the more recent and urban studies. Vaughan speculated that this trend reflected the effects of social change, in that in towns, Maoris have recently become less subordinate to whites. This change is occurring more slowly in the more traditional rural areas. Furthermore, there is more awareness in towns, from the media, of black and brown power movements. Vaughan's analysis is also interesting in demonstrating that the white New Zealand children were also undergoing change in that their preferences and identifications were less and less exclusively in favour of being white. However, Vaughan's analysis should be treated with some caution because of the way the four studies were ordered, which involved a degree of arbitrariness and the possibility for bias.

There is, nevertheless, corroborating evidence from other recent studies that black children are identifying more positively with their own group. A study reported in 1980 of Asian, West Indian and white children living in Britain found that the black children were no more likely to say that they looked like a white child than white children were to identify with a black child (Davey and Mullin, 1980). Only 8 per cent of West Indian, 16 per cent of Asian and 18 per cent of white children, aged from seven to ten years, misidentified themselves. These proportions are much lower than those found in the late 1960s for coloured children by Milner and Jahoda, indicating a decline in the frequency of misidentification. This would seem to be true despite differences in methods and stimuli used to test identification in each study, which makes comparisons difficult. Interestingly, white girls were the group who most frequently misidentified themselves (28 per cent compared to 9 per cent for the boys) and this seemed to be based more on detailed similarities of the hair style and dress of the children shown in the three photographs that they were asked to choose from, although in fact the Asian, West Indian and white children in the photographs wore identical clothing.

When the children were asked which of the children shown in the photographs they would wish to be like, the results were that about half the coloured children would prefer to be white whereas only 12 per cent of white children preferred to be like the coloured children. This level of outgroup preference among coloured children is somewhat less than the percentage found by Milner and Jahoda but it is still very substantial. There was no pattern of differences in the results between children in the north and south of England, or between Asian and West Indian or the proportions of coloured and white children in their schools. Also there was no trend with age over the range used in the research from seven to ten-year-olds. This serves to confirm that the influence of ethnic group membership in children's identity is established at a much earlier period of their lives.

Davey and Mullin interpret their results as showing that coloured children have developed an identification and pride in their own race and culture but an awareness of the more favourable status of the white majority. Despite the passage of time and the apparent improvement in the sense of personal worth among minority children, this situation is no more healthy (for society) than that found in the earlier research. Although there is an improvement in individual's self-concept, the unfairness and injustice of their social position is clearer.

Conclusion

In concluding, we should try to put this discussion of the influence of racial categorization on the development of individual identity into context. We have used this particular group membership to illustrate the ways in which identity is formed in children. Ethnic categorization is only one of the many groups to which children belong and out of which they form their self-concept. It is probably not the most important group membership on which young children base their identity. Age and sex are probably most important at the youngest ages and then their school and the gangs they belong to will also feature in children's self-concepts. Supporting particular football clubs and belonging to current fashion cults are ways of distinguishing identity at older ages. Advertising also plays a role in elaborating the identities which are on offer to young consumers.

However, in this rich array of group memberships, ethnic group is of more significance for the children of minority groups. It is also potentially critical to the development of a harmonious and well-adjusted society. Ethnic identity relates the individual to society and influences both the feelings they have about themselves, and the way they see society working, as in, for example, the injustices of unemployment or their perceptions of harassment by police (Brown, 1984).

Further reading

LEWIS, M. and BROOKS-GUNN, J. (1979) *Self-cognition and the acquisition of self.* New York: Plenum.
  This book describes research and theory on the self-concept and its development through childhood.
MILNER, D. (1983) *Children and Race: ten years on.* London: Ward Lock Educational.
  This is an up-dated account of the way race and prejudice affects children in Britain. It is a practical book which looks closely at the implications of such research for education and society.

Discussion topics

- Should the misidentification of black children found in research be interpreted as a lack of awareness of their ethnic identity or a rejection of their identity?
- How do children of minority groups learn that their group is thought of as inferior in society?.

CHAPTER FIVE

Moral development
Alan Branthwaite and Angus Gellatly

The concept of moral development is an elusive one for psychologists to come to grips with. It is also a concept with implications extending far beyond the bounds of psychology itself. In this chapter we will be dealing with three major aspects of the topic, namely: moral feelings, judgements, and behaviour.

Each of these aspects is bound up with other features of development: moral feelings with the development of personality, moral judgements with cognitive development, and moral behaviour with such social phenomena as conformity. In discussing moral development, therefore, we will need to draw together a number of developmental strands that tend, as a rule, to be studied in isolation from one another. But before attempting to do so it is worth pointing out that studies of moral development are of more than purely academic interest, they have broader implications. For instance, many legal decisions rest upon implicit assumptions about the moral qualities of human beings and how they come to be as they are. Prevailing assumptions determine the answers given to questions such as: What should be the age of legal responsibility? What limits should be set on the control that parents are granted to exercise over their children? What are sufficient grounds for a plea of diminished responsibility? Studies of moral development can play a part in causing changes and refinements in underlying assumptions. They also bear upon larger social issues concerned in the transmission of moral values from one generation to the next.

Moral feelings

Contemporary thought about the development of moral feelings, or conscience, has been dominated by the thinking of Freud. The theory that Freud developed is too complex to be described in the space available, so in this section we will confine ourselves to giving a summary of some of his conclusions regarding moral development and an assessment of their current standing.

Prior to the late nineteenth century, conscience was generally viewed as the inborn voice of God. It was a faculty that, if exercised with sufficient diligence, enabled an individual to discriminate right from wrong, good acts from bad acts. Freud challenged this view in two ways. He argued that conscience is not instilled by God but derived from society, and that moral imperatives – standards of right and wrong – are culturally relative, not absolute. He explained the acquisition of conscience as part of psychic development, that is the development of the mind and of personality.

According to Freud, newborn infants are solely concerned with their own appetites and desires, they have no morality and act only to achieve self-gratification. As experience teaches them that other people and the nature of the world itself can frustrate their wishes, their behaviour comes to be governed by a degree of expediency. They learn to take account of other people but only from a sense of self-interest, not of moral compunction. They are intent on what they can get away with yet there is also a need for love and self-esteem. These can be obtained only by complying with, and eventually adopting, the standards of the culture, and of the parents in particular. To a large extent the children must relinquish their own wishes in favour of those of their parents. Identification with the parents means that their values are internalized as the voice of conscience, roughly what Freud termed the superego, and in this way the values of the culture are transmitted. A result of internalization is that children become capable of feelings such as guilt and shame in respect of their own behaviour and thoughts, judging themselves as they believe their parents would judge them. The intensity and strength of such feelings indexes the strength of conscience, which differs between individuals. Freud argued that the more of the child's desires that were relinquished, the stronger the resulting conscience would be. This was because frustration of personal satisfactions, instead of being expressed outwardly as anger, is turned inwards as self-criticism. The more the frustration, the greater the self-criticism or voice of conscience.

Because Freud's theory concerns inner processes and feelings it is not easily tested experimentally. However, three predictions deduced from the theory have been intensively investigated (Brown, 1965). The first prediction is that a stronger conscience develops when parents discipline a child with 'love withdrawal' rather than with physical punishment. The second prediction states that the individual who has a strong conscience and generally behaves with moral restraint will, rather unfairly, also be the person to feel most guilty at moral failings, precisely because of having a critical conscience. The third prediction, which can be understood only by working through Freud's theory itself, is that males will on average develop a stronger conscience than females. A large body of research, conducted mainly in the 1950s and 1960s, tested these predictions by correlating indices of conscience, such as resistance to temptation and ratings of honesty by parents and teachers, with type of discipline experienced, frequency of reported feelings of guilt, and sex difference. The third prediction was overwhelmingly falsified, with girls if anything found to have stronger conscience than boys. The other two predictions, however, found a broad measure of support. Love withdrawal was found to be an effective means of fostering the development of conscience, provided that there existed a warm parent–child relationship. And stronger conscience was found to be associated with greater guilt feelings, even over trivial transgressions.

There has, therefore, been some support for the Freudian theory, but the two successful predictions can also be accommodated within other theoretical accounts. More recently, increasing emphasis has been placed on the importance in moral development of the peer group and of adults other than the parents, e.g. teachers (Hoffman, 1979). In addition to identification with the parents, straightforward imitation of adult models, which plays only a small part in Freudian theory, has been stressed. There is also evidence that children as young as two-years-old can display rudimentary signs of guilt (Hoffman, 1979), much earlier than the theory allows.

Although Freud attempted to explain how the child learns to identify and label moral feelings, this theory inevitably remains incomplete as an account of moral development. This is because it does not explain the growth of moral judgement. A child may be capable of appropriate emotional responses such as guilt or disapproval but the appearance of these is dependent upon a conception of moral accountability. The emotional response can only be subsequent to some kind of judgement of responsibility. Generally speaking, you do not feel guilt unless you judge yourself, rationally or not, to be responsible for some particular happening. In the next section we turn to an examination of this aspect of development.

Moral judgement–changing awareness about rules of conduct

Morality can be thought of as a system of rules in society about appropriate conduct and what is right and wrong. All societies have a great many rules, which children are taught and expected to follow: closing doors after them, not speaking while others are talking. Many of these rules are to do with polite conduct that shows appropriated respect for other people and their rights. Not all of these rules are matters of morality, although many are–such as not telling lies, not stealing, not cheating at games.

The development of morality in children can be studied from the point of view of the way in which children acquire social rules and how they understand these rules. One such study was carried out by Jean Piaget (1932). Although conducted many years ago, this remains an important study which set the scene for later research. We will describe it in some detail taking into account refinements and qualifications found by later researchers (e.g. Graham, 1972; Wright, 1971).

Most social and moral rules for children come from parents, or other adults, so they are backed by parental authority. Moreover these adult rules are usually set so that children have little opportunity for influencing them or participating in their formulation. Piaget wanted to study how children treat rules when they are free from adult control and sanctions. He did this by studying rules of children's games, in particular the game of marbles. Here the rules are operated by the children themselves. (A distinction might be drawn between traditional children's games, which have evolved among children themselves, and games devised by adults for children, such as Monopoly, where the rules are formally written down for the children to use. Our interest is in the former type).

It may seem surprising to study lofty matters such as the acquisition of morality by analysing the way children play marbles. However, these games present somethings of a microcosm of society with their own complex rules, folklore and social order. It is a world that is in the control of children themselves. Playing marbles seems to stop after roughly the age of 14 and these early adolescents are the acknowledged leaders and experts. The rules of marbles in its mature form are highly complex involving special words that allow players to make certain moves, while other players can prevent this by using other key words in advance.

Piaget studied two aspects in children's playing of marbles. First, developments in their use of the rules and secondly, changes in consciousness and awareness about the rules. Piaget distinguished four stages in the use or application of rules and three stages in the corresponding consciousness of rules. However, it is important to emphasize that the process of development is a continuous one where one type of awareness merges into the next and features of both may coexist for an intermediate time. This kind of development makes it difficult to fix characteristic age limits for stages. In any case, the ages at which stages occur are very variable according to experience, ability and other factors (Graham, 1972). What is more fundamental is the notion of an orderly progression through the stages. The ages indicated should be treated cautiously and are only given to provide a notional idea of the kind of children being referred to.

Stages in the use of rules

(i) *Motor and individual play (under 2 years)*

The young child, given some marbles, plays a haphazard way, handling them at the dictate of her desires and motor habits. The child tries sucking, biting and dropping the marbles but there seems little or no continuity or direction in the behaviour, i.e. no purpose to it. However, through these activities the child discovers something of the nature and properties of objects, such as: they are hard, tasteless, slippy and they roll. The child is believed to be doing two things in this exploration:

(a) *assimilating* the novel object to existing understanding of the world. So she is testing the nature of marbles in terms of existing preoccupations and ways of structuring objects (predominantly whether they can be eaten).

(b) *accommodating* existing ideas about the world to take account of new features and discoveries. In this way existing ideas are extended and developed to take account of broader, more complex realizations.

During the later parts of this first stage, ritualized patterns of behaviour appear where certain actions are strung together and repeated as a sequence over and over. Piaget describes the example of his daughter who was stroking her hair while in the bath and then let go of it and splashed the water. Immediately she repeated the movements in turn, stroking her hair then splashing the water. Over the next few days this activity became ritualized so that she didn't strike the water without first outlining the movement of stroking her hair. The two actions together amused her and they were performed over and over again. Piaget believed that it was these rites that anticipated the rules of future games, but that for the ritual to become a rule there must be some conscious obligation. We will see more about this later when we come to examining stages in the consciousness of rules.

(ii) *Egocentric stage (beginnings 2–5 years old)*

This stage begins when the child takes notice of the way other (often older) children are playing, and the sequences of behaviour they use, and tries to imitate their game. In this way, the child receives from others the example of rules and copies what she believes others are doing. However, during this stage the child plays essentially for herself, in parallel with other children but without interacting in a proper game. The play is essentially individual though it is a copy of what others appear to be doing. Although the child believes she is playing like the others, she plays in an individualistic manner using her own ideas and interpretation of what the game is about, which is why it is called egocentric.

On interesting feature of this stage relates to winning. When Piaget inquired who had won the game it transpired that children believed everyone had won. Winning corresponded to having had a good time and there was no attempt to compete.

(iii) *Cooperation stage (beginning at about 7–8 years)*

Often it is unclear what precise determinants cause development from one stage to the next. Piaget notes that around this age there is a desire for mutual understanding. Children at the beginning of this stage seek to compare and evaluate themselves against others. We might speculate about the influence of schools in encouraging this process but they are probably not the prime cause. Attention now becomes focused on winning in terms of doing better than others. Children who play together begin to concern themselves with the rules to establish a common basis for competing and a decisive winner. The game of marbles is now a social interchange involving a mutual evaluation of competing powers which leads, through the observation of common rules, to an acceptable conclusion. The rules provide social controls.

However, detailed observation of children who play together regularly reveals that, despite their intentions, knowledge of the rules is vague and inconsistent.

(iv) Codification of the rules (beginning about 11–12 years old)

The third stage merges into this final stage as children become more familiar with the rules and tighten up procedure. Ultimately every detail is fixed in the procedure and rules are devised to anticipate all manner of circumstances. At this stage the code of rules is widely known and agreed upon. The dominating interest is in discussing the rules themselves more than playing the game.

Stages in the consciousness of rules

Conscious awareness and the ability to articulate and comment on what one is doing lag behind action. Actions have to be practised for some time and internalized before thinking catches up with these physical skills. Consequently, the three stages in the consciousness of rules overlap the stages in the use of rules.

(i) No consciousness of rules

During the motor and individual stage in the use of rules there are rituals and regularities in the child's actions but no awareness of external rules governing actions. The rules relating to marbles are seen as interesting examples of what to do but carry no obligation to perform them. There is no consciousness of coercive rules which carry obligations. Awareness of rules, in their social and moral sense, only appears when the child accepts a command emanating from someone she respects. This appears later during the egocentric stage.

(ii) Heteronomy in the consciousness of rules (begins at 5-7 years)

During the 'egocentric stage' when children begin to imitate the play of others, no matter how poorly or idiosyncratically, they treat the rules of the game as sacred and untouchable. Children believe there is a proper way of doing things. Piaget asked whether their way of playing could be changed and whether the rules had always been the same. Any suggested alteration strikes children as a horrible transgression. They have a deep respect for rules as permanent and emanating from other people (adults, or even God) hence the term heteronomous. Although in practice the children play as they choose and vary the rules, this is more through lack of understanding and knowledge. Each child firmly believes she is following the proper rules set by others.

(iii) *Autonomy and reciprocity (beginning around 9–10 years old)*

During the 'stage of cooperation', as children concern themselves with unifying the game and operating mutual control, there is a growing realization that the rules have no intrinsic value in themselves. This arises out of working with the rules, discussing them, and putting them into practice, so the children begin to exercise their control over rules (rather than vice versa). Autonomy leads to seeing the rules as invented and capable of alteration by the people using them, provided that all agree. Laws are worthy of respect in so far as they enlist the consent and cooperation of people involved. A democratic attitude exists among the players of marbles in that it is no longer seen as a crime to express an opinion about the rules. The agreement of the majority is what is important.

Changes in children's judgements about moral conduct

What does the study of marbles tell us about children's moral development? Children's judgements about what is right and wrong follow a similar progression to their consciousness about rules in games. In terms of key areas of moral conduct which affect children, such as lying, stealing, clumsiness, and telling on others, young children consider adult laws as sacrosanct and any violation as naughty and reprehensible. There are three features of this stage:

(a) obedience to a rule or adult command is good, regardless of what may be required. So acts that do not conform are bad. These rules are external and imposed by others (heteronomous).
(b) the letter rather than the spirit of the law should be observed.
(c) actions are evaluated not in terms of their motive and intention but in terms of their objective appearance and consequence.

At this stage then, lies are defined as 'naughty words' and equated with swearing. They are understood as things that must not be said or punishment will follow. The reason for lies being forbidden is not understood and the intention to deceive is not appreciated. A little later lies are understood as 'things that aren't true', but mistakes and deliberate attempts to deceive are lumped together and the judgement is still external and objective. So saying a 'dog was as big as a cow' is especially naughty because it is impossible and can't be believed. On the other hand, giving an adult false directions deliberately is not naughty if the adult could not know it was wrong. To the extent that adults are taken in by the lie, it is not a lie. For young children, in making moral judgements, what matters is breaking the rules. Their judgements tend to be *objective* in that they evaluate the amount of damage cause by clumsiness, the degree to which a lie departs from the truth, or the amount that is stolen.

With age, children move from using heteronomy to autonomy and reciprocity in evaluating social rules for moral conduct. After the age of about 7–10, children make moral judgements on the basis of motives and intentions behind breaking the rule, such as the aim to deceive and mislead in lying, or whether breaking an ornament was accidental or deliberate. Judgements are based not on the breaking of some rule but whether there is misuse of trust that would disrupt social relationships. These children appreciate rules not as categorical commands from authority figures, but as growing out of social relationships and providing a mutual basis for avoiding conflict and unfairness.

Factors underlying the development of judgement

There are two factors underlying the changes described from heteronomy to reciprocity in the appreciation of rules. The first is related to changes in children's thinking and the second to changes in relationships.

(i) *Changes in thinking*

The heteronomous view of rules, both in games and moral affairs, as fixed by external authorities and demanding obedience is related to a particular type of thinking found in young children, which is known as egocentricity. The characteristics of egocentric thinking are a limited ability to take the point of view of others and, indeed, an unawareness that others have a different point of view so that one's own perspective is not universal (see Chapter 9). Correspondingly, the child does not differentiate what goes on in her head from what is external reality; fantasies and imagination are not distinguished from real events. There is no awareness that there may be alternatives to personal beliefs and knowledge, nor that such ideas are not shared by everyone. Such a manner of thinking encourages the view of rules as absolute dictates, which are incapable of being modified or having any alternative. As Wright (1971) puts it, 'since he now sees things that way, that is the way they must be; his inability to differentiate what is thought from what is external reality means that the rules he has accepted are part of the external reality to which he must adjust' (p.158).

As they grow older, children become increasingly capable of thinking that recognizes the points of view of others and the differences between thinking and external reality. Rules can now be seen as alterable to accommodate different perspectives.

(ii) *Changes in relationships*

The sophistication of moral judgement also depends on the kind of social relationship existing between people. Piaget distinguished two types of social relationship:

On one hand, there exists a relationship of constraint and unilateral respect where one person holds power over another in a top dog to underdog fashion. This relationship goes with a heteronomous view of rules because they are external and imposed from outside by others with the threat of punishments and sanctions for disobedience. This is the social relationship often imposed on children by adults. Even if not deliberately imposed, this is the way it is often conceived by children because of their inferior standing and their awe for parents. But relationships of constraint are also common to adults in terms of our standing towards the law, employers, etc. Sometimes we have no direct participation in the formulation of rules or in varying their application. This encourages a heteronomous view and explains why we so often seek to fulfil the letter rather than the spirit, or to disobey except when we are in danger of being caught out. So laws such as speed limits do not enjoy wide conformity, probably because they function in a relationship of constraint and appear arbitrary and inflexible.

On the other hand, relationships of cooperation and mutual respect between people on an equal footing encourage reciprocity in their attitude to rules. The intrinsic value of rules is then more appreciated as being in the interests of regulating social relationships. In so far as the rules stem from cooperation and democratic consensus there is wider adherence to their spirit.

It was through the need for cooperation in regulating their game of marbles that the 11–13 year olds came to appreciate the social values of rules. Because the game of marbles is dropped by 14 or 15, they were the seniors in the game so they enjoyed a sense of autonomy, which comes from being paramount and which gave rise to morally sophisticated judgements.

Research into Piaget's theory

A great deal of research has tested various aspects of Piaget's theory, and is reviewed by Graham (1972). These later findings confirm the transition from judging morality by outcomes and consequences to judging intentions, although the age at which this happens has usually been lower than Piaget suggested. There has also been support (e.g. Stuart, 1967) for the belief that these changes are influenced by the child's ability to 'decentre' and appreciate more than one perspective (the move from egocentricity to reciprocity).

However, there has been less clear support for Piaget's idea that moral judgements are influenced by the type of social relationships involved. Often this is because attempts to test this idea have not been very well thought out. Piaget emphasized that maturity of judgement developed more readily in peer relations where there was equality. This is not quite the same as expecting that children who have more experience of peer groups (in a Kibbutz for example) will be better able to judge actions by their intention in a range of abstract problems. The essential point may be that relationships involving authority and constraint inhibit the expression of existing moral autonomy, and of ideas about reciprocity and mitigating intentions. Ruffy (1981) has shown that children judge actions between children in a more mature way than actions towards adults. Ruffy's research also demonstrated that discussions and interactions between children fostered decentring and the achievement of higher level moral responses, which tends to support the importance of cooperative social interaction in the development of moral judgement.

Moral behaviour

Although in this chapter we have paid particular attention to the study of moral judgement, and to a lesser extent moral feelings, it remains to say something about actual behaviour. The fact is that our actions are by no means always consistent with our judgements and feelings of right and wrong. Not only may we sometimes yield to our less worthy impulses, but our behaviour is often controlled by the external factors or unacknowledged motives. One way in which this has been demonstrated is in studies of conformity (see, Aronson, 1984) of which probably the most influential were Milgram's experiments on obedience. In these experiments, subjects were asked to act as the teacher in a learning experiment with a second subject as the learner. Uknown to the teacher-subject, the learner-subject was actually a confederate of the experimenter. The teacher and the learner were put in separate rooms connected by intercom and the teacher had to test the learner's memory for word-pairs and to administer increasingly powerful electric shocks following each mistake. The sham 'Shock Generator' had an instrument panel with switches calibrated from 15 volts up to 450 volts, the latter being labelled as 'dangerous'. When the teacher administered 'shocks' to the learner he heard groans of pain over the intercom that increased with the severity of the shock. Typically the teacher protests and tries to withdraw from the experiment, but Milgram found that with prodding from the experimenter as many as 62 per cent of the teachers continue giving shocks, as they believe, up to the maximum of 450 volts.

Miligram's results are disturbing. They also contrast strongly with the predictions made by both laymen and psychiatrists when told of the experimental set-up and asked how subjects would behave. Apparently, when pressed to obey by an authority figure such as a scientist, people will often fail to live up to their own moral standards.

The power of such conformist tendencies has also been confirmed in a number of studies by Darley and Latane (see Aronson, 1984). They showed that a lone subject was much more likely to offer assistance to someone apparently in need of help than were subjects in pairs or groups. The presence of other individuals seemed to inhibit any one of them from making the first move. Conversely, it was found that car drivers were far more likely to stop and assist a motorist with a puncture if they had shortly before witnessed a similar act of helpfulness than if they had not. Conformity, or imitation, can lead people into or away from altruistic acts.

The fact is that behaviour does not only reflect our internal values, it may also be caused by features of the social environment, or result simply from habit. Actions are not always preceded by conscious deliberation. Frequently the reverse is the case. We follow through a course of action and only subsequently seek to rationalise the behaviour into consistency with our moral knowledge, hoping to evade condemnation by our own consciences and by others (I was not responsible, I was dutifully following orders). To this extent, the development of moral behaviour can be equated with the development of any habitual practices, or with habitual compliance with particular conventions or sources of authority.

Concluding remarks

The dramatist, Tom Stoppard, puts the following words into the mouth of one of his characters:

> A small child who cries 'That's not fair' when punished for something done by his brother or sister is apparently appealing to an idea of justice which is, for want of a better word, natural . . . it is well to be reminded that you can persuade a man to believe almost anything provided he is clever enough but it is much more difficult to persuade someone less clever. There is a sense of right and wrong which precedes utterance.

(Stoppard, 1978, p.90)

Stoppard is suggesting the existence of a natural moral sense which perhaps need not be acquired at all, or is developed at an early age. By contrast, Freud appears to have viewed the infant as a moral alien and ethical ignoramus. For Freud, morality is slowly and grudgingly acquired in acquiescence to superiors. Freud's explanation has some similarities to Piaget's stage of heteronomy but it may only deal with the beginnings of the process. His account may partly reflect his era and the social relationships between parents and children at the time he wrote. On the other hand, Piaget's views may not be all that antithetical to Stoppard's if we investigate further. Young children seem able to make ready (natural) inferences (see Chapter 9) but they frequently fail to make the inferences that seem obvious to an adult. We can say that their sense of inference has to be socialized, or educated. Perhaps children also display a natural moral sense in the way that they tend towards the need for a moral order as something valuable in its own right, a necessary property of 'society'. Children seem spontaneously to seek some form of moral order, although the particular form it takes may be a matter of learning the kind of moral reasoning prevalent in a society, and of bringing their developing cognitive skills to bear on specific problems. For instance, although Piaget found that seven and eight-year-olds usually ignored intentions and judged actions solely in terms of their consequences, it has been shown that even four-year-olds *can* take intentions into account in some circumstances. A result very similar to that found with inference making. In other words, we might concur with Stoppard in granting the child a natural moral sense that is proof against sophistry while still hesitating to set her up as an arbiter of complex moral problems.

Further reading

BROWN, R. (1965) *Social Psychology*. New York: Macmillan.
  A comprehensive and easily readable summary in two chapters of the main approaches to explaining moral development.
WRIGHT, D. (1971) *The psychology of moral behaviour*. Harmondsworth: Penguin. A more comprehensive description of empirical research into various aspects of moral behaviour.

Discussion topics

- How could you test which stage of moral development a child has reached?
- Why do children sometimes act in a way that they know to be wrong?

PART II

The cognitive domain

Introduction

This section is devoted to the ways in which children's thinking and understanding change and develop through their use of experience. The chapters in this section demonstrate some key principles of child development and you will find many instances and illustrations of these principles in the chapters. We have listed them here so that you can be alert to them:

1 Abilities evolve out of experience and are tuned to the child's needs to handle particular environments. This is an active process on the child's part to discover the properties of things, make events predictable and control what happens.
2 Children's understanding of the world around them differs from that of adults. Development involves the correct identification of different kinds of problem and the ability to apply an appropriate strategy for solving that problem.
3 Development proceeds by progressive differentiation of experience; and the evolution of more complex skills proceeds by adapting and integrating simpler, well rehearsed abilities.

1. The abilities that children have at birth are primitive but they serve the immediate needs of the child. Children are born with some capabilities that are 'pre-wired' and inborn and more will be said about these in Section IV.
These basic abilities are quickly developed and adapted to cope with widening horizons in what the child can perceive and the action that can be effected. The child is progressively able to handle experiences at wider and wider distances from himself in space and also time, and at levels that are freed from immediate sensory experience by representing events in memory and as symbols. This process is described throughout the chapters in this section of the book. Chapters 6 and 7 illustrate how, in visual perception, the process begins with the ability to organize sensory experience, discriminate and identify objects and then recognize symbols for objects.

Of great importance in development is language acquisition which enables objects to be represented by symbols such as spoken and written words. This capacity allows something like a quantum leap in the child's ability to organize experience and handle the environment. We saw some of the benefits of language as an instrument for controlling others to fulfill needs and purposes, in Chapter 1. The way in which facility with language develops illustrates the active role children play in exploring the features of the world around them and incorporating the results into their capabilities, as described in Chapter 8. The detection of rules and the organization of language gives clear evidence of the developing child's active search for pattern and predicability in their experiences.

Notice that all the growing abilities of the child function to meet the needs and purposes of the child – development rarely happens for its own sake, but serves the needs of the child to operate on the environment in more and more ambitious ways.

2   Children's ways of thinking about the world are different from those of adults. This is clearly illustrated in Chapter 9 which describes the errors children make because of their limited appreciation of the complexities of the world and their lack of experience. Much of development involves matching the skills and ways of thinking of the child to the problems encountered in the environment and the accepted ways of operating in a particular culture.

Chapter 10 argues strongly that the particular skills and facilities a child acquires reflect the demands of the culture in which he develops. A point made in many of the chapters (notably 7, 9 and 10) is that what chiefly differentiates children and adults is the amount of experience they have had in manipulating the world. It's not so much that children cannot think in the way adults do as that they have not the familiarity with a sufficient range of experiences to rehearse potential solutions and identify the most successful. Adults make childish mistakes when dealing with new and unfamiliar materials and problems. Opportunities are required to explore in order to recognize and identify the critical features of problems. This point is expressed in the discussions of decentering in Chapter 9, the description of categorization as an aid to memory in Chapter 10, and the ways of improving memory described in Chapter 11. Sophistication in thinking relies not so much on maturational processes, as the opportunity to experience problems in a variety of contexts, to work out appropriate solutions and to identify the applicability of such solutions to different kinds of problems, i.e. to discern the limits where such strategies are helpful or need revising and rethinking.

3.   Cognitive skills progress by practising new techniques and abilities until they become automated and habitual. This is clearly shown in the way children do the same thing over and over again, for example in the use of words and language. More complex and sophisticated skills evolve by adapting and integrating established skills into new repertoires of behaviour. Chapter 9 demonstrates that many of the logical deductions we make automatically as adults and which we use automatically to solve the problems

we encounter, are based on the groundwork of skills we mastered as children. Similarly, the ability to express ideas in language (Chapter 8) and drawing (Chapter 12) requires the integration of separate skills which were each painstakingly acquired and rehearsed but when mastered can be used to develop more complex expressions.

Methods of research in the cognitive domain

From the point of view of the methods used to gather information, the various chapters in this section illustrate the ingenuity of researchers to devise investigations that will demonstrate the skills and abilities of children. The first chapter in this section (Chapter 6) gives a good account of the problems faced by researchers in eliciting information about the capabilities of children, especially when they are unable to talk so that they cannot describe their experiences or answer questions. The studies described in that chapter and succeeding chapters (especially 7, 9 and 10) illustrate the power of experiments to test precisely alternative explanations for a phenomenon. By setting up carefully thought out problems for the children to respond to, these experiments test which of several alternative (and mutually exclusive) processes were being used to make a decision or come to a solution. By controlling the alternatives a clear answer can be found. In reading about the research, note the clever way in which some researchers have devised their experiments so that the child's responses discriminate which of several possible processes was used.

The precision of experiments contrasts with the procedures in studies which make observations and recordings of ongoing, naturally occurring events as found for example in Chapters 8 and 12. These studies can only make guesses and inferences to the mechanisms and processes underlying the results obtained. Nevertheless, the ingenuity and insight of researchers can be remarkable in noticing particular events and occurrences that rule out some explanations and strengthen the case for other interpretations. One example is in the kinds of mistakes made by children in their language as described in Chapter 8.

Finally, a particularly challenging problem for research is in comparing development in different cultures and societies. This is useful to attempt if one is to establish the generality of laws about development and to measure the influence of different social, and physical environments. The difficulty is that a given research task may not mean the same thing in different cultures so that performance may be affected by interest in the task, motivation and the inherent reasonableness of what children (and adults) are being asked to do. This is a problem that has affected studies of differences in intelligence between races, which we will learn more about in Chapter 19. Too often such studies have assumed that differences in results reflected differences in ability of people in different cultures. A much more enlightened and reasonable approach is shown in cross cultural research described in Chapter 10. Here the differences in results were taken to indicate more about the cultural practices, and their influence on development, than the individual's abilities. Experiments can be devised to test particular aspects of a culture which are responsible for the differences in performance and development.

CHAPTER SIX

Infant perception
John Sloboda

Red-green colour-blindness (*Deuteranopia*) affects about one in 200 people. It entails an inability to distinguish between red and green hues. One standard screening test for colour-blindness involves asking people to identify numbers which are printed in red on green backgrounds or vice versa. Although most people perform this task with ease, deuteranopes find it extremely difficult.

Deuteranopia is an inherited condition whose precise causes need not concern us here. What I wish to focus attention on in this section is the *method* by which we may assess perceptual abilities and deficits such as this, particularly in the very young.

Imagine that you are a medical psychologist who has been approached by a colour-blind parent who wishes to discover whether her three-week-old baby has inherited her colour-blindness. Assume that there is no way of finding this out by making internal physical or biochemical observations on the baby. You have only external behaviour to go on. How would you proceed? Before reading any further take a few minutes to write down some of the problems you think that you might encounter, and some of the observations you might make.

The problems you have been grappling with are not trivial ones. They have tested the ingenuity of many experienced psychologists. If you came up with only one or two of the ideas to follow then you did well. I shall group the problems under three main headings; they concern *communication*, *control*, and *motivation*.

Communication

When we probe the perceptual world of adults we typically use our shared language to mediate our investigation. We present our subjects with verbal instructions and expect them to report their experience verbally. In the colour-blindness test described above the experimenter might say, for example, 'please look at this picture and tell me what number you see'. Then the subject replies '2' or 'I don't see any number' as the case may be. Such verbal mediation seems almost inevitable when we consider the *private* nature of perceptual experience. One person cannot see into another person's mind in the direct way in which she can experience her own mental life. Speech may seem like the only way that private perceptual experiences can be communicated to the outside world.

Young babies can neither talk nor understand speech. This fact has led some people to conclude that whatever experiences the baby has, they are unknowable to anyone else. The lack of language certainly places severe limits on the extent of our knowledge, but it is, perhaps, pessimistic to believe that we can know nothing. What we *can* do, as those who study animal behaviour have particularly shown us, is infer things about perceptual capacities from the type of behaviour we observe. The general form of the inference is- 'if the animal is able to do X then it *must* be capable of perceiving Y'.

On technique employing this sort of inference, which is extensively used in animal research, is known as *discrimination training*. Although the name is technical, such training is, in essence, used by anyone who has ever owned a pet. The technique involves rewarding the animal for performing an activity in one context (A) and punishing it in another context (B). If the animal learns to perform the activity *only* in context A, then this *proves* that it is capable of telling A and B apart. House-training is a commonplace example of applied discrimination training. Most domestic pets are soon able to restrict eliminative behaviour to the precise locations required by their owner. This proves that they can perceive a difference between acceptable and unacceptable locations. In this real-life example there are many potentially perceptible differences between acceptable and unacceptable locations. Therefore, we do not know *which* of the many available cues of sight, sound, and smell a house-trained animal actually uses. Psychologists can tighten up the situation by attempting to train an animal to behave differently in two contexts which differ in only *one* perceptual respect (such as, for instance, colour). Successful training is uncontrovertible proof that the animal can perceive differences in that one quality.

In a typical discrimination learning experiment the animal is placed in a cage facing two doors who surfaces can be marked by a variety of different visual displays. Thus, the animal might see a red door and a green door. The position of the colours is switched in an unpredictable way from trial to trial so that no association with a particular position can be built up. Each time the animal chooses to go to the red door it is rewarded, typically by a small food pellet, but when it goes to the green door it receives no reward (or may receive some aversive stimulation such as electric shock). At first the animal will choose a door at random, sometimes getting reward and sometimes not. If, however, it is capable of distinguishing the two colours it may eventually come to consistently choose the colour associated with reward.

Before asking how this technique might be applicable to babies, it is worth commenting on a major shortcoming of this and other such techniques. Whilst it is true that successful discrimination proves the existence of the relevant perceptual capacities, it is *not* true that failure to succeed proves the *absence* of such capacities. There are a number of other important reasons why failure might occur. One is that the animal may be unable to *relate* the particular perceptual quality to the presence and absence of reward. For instance, rats can learn to associate different *tastes* with subsequent feelings of gastric wellbeing or upset. This is why they are able to learn to avoid rat poison. They are, however, unable to learn to avoid *sounds* that are followed by gastric upset. It seems as if they are 'prewired' by their genetic constitution to be able to learn only certain types of associations. This is partly adaptive. It is highly unlikely that, in the natural environment, something that an animal simply *hears* (but does not eat) is likely to upset its digestion. However, if the situation is changed somewhat, so that the sounds lead to *external* rewards or punishments (such as electric shock) rats will now learn to avoid the sounds.

A second reason why an animal may fail on a discrimination task is that the response required of it is not under voluntary control. Early attempts to teach chimpanzees a simple language were blighted by a failure to take this into consideration. The investigators tried to teach chimps to *speak*. It turns out, however, that chimpanzee vocalizations are not under full voluntary control, but are instinctively controlled signals of motivational state. When later researchers used a modified manual sign language, they achieved much greater success. Chimpanzees have good voluntary control over their hands. We shall return to the issue of control in the next section.

A third and final reason why an animal may fail on a discrimination task is that it may not be adequately motivated. For food to be an appropriate motivator, the animal must be hungry. A well-fed animal is more likely to curl up in a corner of the cage and go to sleep then repeatedly run towards coloured doorways. In the standard experimental situation the animal is hungry, and receives only a small food pellet on each trial, so that it is motivated to keep working for more. We will discuss the problem of infant motivation in a later section.

So, in summary, lack of verbal communication is not an inpenetrable barrier to the discovery of perceptual capacities. Procedures such as discrimination training allow many organisms to communicate their perceptions to us *indirectly*. Their actions betray their capabilities.

Control

If we take a superficial look at the movements of a newborn baby, it is very tempting for us to conclude that they are not controlled in any significant way. Limbs and trunk seem to flail about aimlessly without any coordination to one another or to any external event. Even when it seems to us that the baby is trying to express intention or fulfil some purpose we usually feel that the behaviour is not capable of reliably transmitting that intention. The baby seems to be in the same kind of relation to all its movements as an older person is when attempting some novel skill such as riding a bicycle. Movements have unintended effects that result in clumsy and sometimes disastrous outcomes. No matter what reward we might offer a beginner for successfully negotiating a bicycle along some pathway, there is little chance that success will be achieved.

Fortunately, in the case of babies, the impression of complete incompetence is partly illusory. Although a young baby has nothing like the full repertoire of coordinated movements which are necessary for locomotion or grasping, she does have early and unmistakable control over some movements, particularly those of head, eye, and mouth. For instance, most newborn babies are capable of maintaining moving objects in view by tracking movements of head and eye. Young babies also seem to be capable of turning their heads towards the location of an unseen sound (Wertheimer, 1961). These inborn skills ensure that babies are able to sample the visual environment in an adaptive way, for instance, by allowing them to maintain visual contact with their mother as she moves around.

Nonetheless, there is still a more general problem of control to solve. Newborn babies are not always in the alert and calm state that allows their limited competence to be tapped. When drowsy or distressed a baby is not responsive to experimental contingencies. To put it bluntly, one cannot do perceptual research with a howling bundle of rage. If, as one may well suppose, babies undergo sudden and unpredictable swings of moods, they may well be impossible subjects for any kind of training experiment that requires attention over a period of time. Fortunately, it is now known that much of a newborn baby's mood changes are regular and predictable. They seem to go through a regular cycle of biologically determined *states* which always occur in the same order (Wolff, 1959). These are: sleep, fretful wakefulness, feeding, alert wakefulness, drowsiness, and then back to sleep. An average newborn baby completes this cycle about once every two to three hours. If the experimenter can 'catch' a baby just after feeding then he can hope to have a reasonably attentive subject for anything up to 15 minutes. Posture can affect alertness too, and a baby that is propped up to sitting position is less likely to become drowsy than one who is lying down. Finally, most instances of infant distress have very definite causes. Babies do not, on the whole, cry for nothing. They cry when hungry, uncomfortable, too hot or too cold, or unwell. Attention to all these matters can ensure a reasonably sanguine and cooperative baby.

Motivation

We have already seen how a reward such as a food pellet can motivate an animal to persist at a discrimination learning task. Food (i.e. milk) is not, however, an appropriate reward for a baby. When a baby is hungry it howls, and is not in the right state to observe or learn anything. It goes on howling until it has had enough to satisfy hunger. One would not to able to interrupt a baby after a single mouthful and expect it to work for the next one. We need a motivator that can operate on a well-fed (and thus reasonably content) baby. One such motivator is mild novelty or surprise. From a very early age babies are attracted to any sort of change or motion. One simple action which delights most babies is the 'peek-a-boo' in which an adult pops up from behind a barrier and then disappears again. This action can be repeated again and again, well beyond the tolerance of most adults, and the baby goes on being delighted. Suppose we set up a situation such that the baby can obtain another 'peek-a-boo' by making some movement. Now we are ready to try a discrimination training experiment. This is precisely the technique that has been pioneered and extensively used by the British psychologist Thomas Bower (1966).

The 'peek-a-boo' technique

Although Bower has not used this technique to test colour vision, it would serve well for our purposes. We would proceed in this way. The baby would be harnessed into a chair with a specially constructed head rest. Inside the head rest is a switch which closes whenever the baby moves its head in a certain direction, say towards the left. In front of the baby is a screen onto which can be projected various visual displays. The baby and the screen are on separate tables. An experimenter is concealed in the gap between the two tables, ready to pop up at appropriate times. To train the head-turning response we would begin by always presenting a single colour, say red, on the screen. The baby moves its head this way and that in exploration. When, by chance, the head-switch is closed, the experimenter immediately pops up and gives a 'peek-a-boo'. Soon the baby realizes that a left head turn always produces a peek-a-boo and deliberately repeats the action. At this point, the discrimination training can begin. Sometimes we show a red display and sometimes a green display. Head turning gets a reward *only* when the red display is present, never when the green display is present. If the baby is discriminating between red and green we should observe a gradual drop in frequency of head-turns to the green display. She is learning that rewards never come when the green light is on.

The prediction for a colour-blind baby would be, of course, that such discrimination training would fail. Suppose, then, that the baby you have been asked to test fails to learn the discrimination between red and green. Are you entitled to tell the parent that colour-blindness has indeed been inherited?

Unfortunately, it is not as easy as that. Before concluding that colour-blindness is present, you have to establish two other crucial facts:

1. That normal babies of the same age *are* capable of discriminating colours.
2. That the baby you are testing is capable of normal visual discrimination in respects *other* than colour.

The first condition is required to guarantee that the baby you are testing is abnormal. It might be the case that *all* normal three-week-old infants are unable to discriminate colour. In fact, the available evidence tells us that babies of this age *can* discriminate colour. Notwithstanding this, you would be prudent to test normal babies on *your* apparatus to check that it really did work.

The second condition is required to guarantee that the failure is one of *colour perception* and not of some other component of the task. For instance, the baby might have a profound visual handicap which would render it incapable of *any* visual perception. Or there might be some general handicap in ability to attend or learn, and so on. To eliminate all such possibilities we need to show that the baby can perform quite normally on other visual discrimination tasks (such as, say, size or brightness) and only fails on the colour blindness test.

Habituation and surprise

We have spent the first part of this chapter examining the major difficulties that beset researchers attempting to study infant perception, and have introduced one powerful investigative technique that overcomes many of the difficulties. It is, however, good scientific practice not to put all one's eggs in one basket. Psychologists have developed a *range* of methods that can be used to study infant perception. If several different approaches yield the same sort of answers, then one's confidence in the findings is greatly increased.

A different technique, which has yielded much useful information about infant perception, makes use of the fact that even very young infants possess a rudimentary memory. When presented with the same stimulus over and over again, a baby 'habituates' to it. This involves a general loss of interest in or attention to the habituated stimulus. When something perceptibly new happens, however, a baby will 'dishabituate', responding to the novelty by facial expressions of surprise, changes in heart rate, and increased attention to the new object.

Any consistent behavioural change to novelty proves that the baby is discriminating between the old and the new. By carefully controlling the nature and degree of differences, we can probe the infant's discriminatory powers (e.g. Lewis and Goldberg, 1969).

Developmental changes in discrimination

In the case of colour discrimination we see few radical developmental changes during childhood. The basic discriminatory power is present almost from birth. In many other abilities, however, this is not so. One of the most striking and socially significant changes occur in the area of face perception. Below the age of two months we have no evidence that babies can tell one face from another, provided that the two faces are matched for size, brightness, and other global features. This finding contributes to the conclusion that young babies have profound deficiencies in the perception of visual form on shape. Many other findings also support this conclusion. For instance, young babies cannot discriminate different orientations, and cannot tell straight from curved. The research on face perception, which was pioneered by the American psychologist Robert Fantz (1961), has shown that young babies make little distinction between a conventional schematic face and one in which all the features had been jumbled up (see Figure 6.1).

6.1 Schematic and jumbled-up faces.

It is now believed that very young babies see the world, not in terms of shape and form, but in terms of disconnected points of 'salience' spread over the visual field. If we examine the eye movements of a newborn infant as it scans a visual scene, we find that gaze tends to be 'captured' by such things as edges between light and dark areas, vertices and where several lines join one another, areas of particular brightness, and areas of high contrast. Movement of an element within the field is also a cause of capture. The baby can certainly locate and track salient events, but it is not capable of recognizing or integrating separate events.

Around the age of three months, this pattern begins to change. Eye movements become more controlled, and tend to sweep right around distinct objects, focusing on points that may not be particularly salient in terms of the properties listed in the previous paragraph. Discrimination begins to take place along such dimensions as orientation and curvature, and complex forms such as faces now begin to be recognized. One of the important social consequences of this is that the smiling response, which begins by occuring in many situations, becomes specific to human faces, and eventually, to familiar faces. Distress reactions to strangers typically begin to be observed around five or six months of age.

How do we explain this change? One rather convincing explanation rests on brain development. It is known that brain growth is not complete at birth (see Chapter 20). In particular, the cortex appears to be markedly inmature, and shows patterns of electrical activity different from that of older babies. At around three months, the cortex begins to function normally. We now have a great deal of evidence that there are specific areas of the cortex that are essential to the perception of form. If these areas are not functioning properly at birth then we would expect deficiencies in form perception.

Our knowledge about cortical function rests primarily on work with animals, particularly on a technique pioneered by American psychologists David Hubel and Torsten Wiesel (1962). This technique, known as single-cell recording, involves removing a small portion of skull and inserting a very fine moveable electrode into the brain. This electrode can enter a single cell and record details of electrical activity within that cell.

In the visual area of the cortex, most cells are activated by visual stimulation. But each cell is selective in its sensitivity. One type of cell responds best to a line or an edge at a particular angle. A given cell may become very active in the presence of a vertical line, but respond hardly at all to a horizontal line. The net effect of many such selective processes is to provide a very detailed point-by-point analysis of the visual field in terms of features such as angles, edges and connections. This supplies the information which allows significant forms and objects to be located and identified.

We know that this cortical activity is necessary for form and object perception for several reasons. One reason is that damage to visual cortex disrupts form perception. The British neuropsychologist Lawrence Weiskrantz (1972) has carried out investigations on monkeys whose visual cortex has been surgically removed. These monkeys are profoundly handicapped in form perception, being unable, for instance, to discriminate a vertical from a horizontal bar. Nonetheless, they do retain some residual visual capacity, being able, for example, to locate and track bright or high contrast objects. Their visual capacities seem very similar to that of the newborn human baby.

A second source of evidence comes from some ingenious work carried out on cats by another British neuropsychologist, Colin Blakemore (1973). He reared kittens from birth in visually restricted environments. Some kittens were able to see only vertical lines (Fig. 6.2). Others saw only horizontal lines. After several weeks they were let free in normal environments. Blakemore discovered that those kittens reared in a 'vertical' environment were effectively blind to horizontal lines (and vice versa). They exhibited this blindness by colliding with obstacles orientated in the horizontal plane, whilst avoiding vertically oriented obstacles. Subsequent single-cell recording from their visual cortex showed that most cells were tuned to respond only to *vertical* lines. It seems as though the lack of horizontal stimulation caused disruption in the normal development of horizontally tuned cells, leading to horizontal 'blindness'.

6.2   Kitten reared in environment of vertical stripes.

Work such as this has convinced psychologists that the young brain is particularly sensitive to environmental stimulation, and requires a wide range of normal stimulation to develop normally. Such stimulation is provided in abundance in cultures where mothers carry their babies around with them all the time. One may question to what extent the 'civilised' practise of confining babies to cots and cribs is in their best interest.

From sensation to cognition

Gross brain development can account for a set of striking perceptual changes in early infancy. But such brain power marks the beginning, rather than the end, of another developmental story. This is the story of how a baby comes to *interpret* its sensations as providing knowledge of an external physical and social world. When you or I look at a visual scene, we effortlessly see it *as* a collection of familiar three-dimensional objects existing and interacting in space. The scene 'makes sense'. But much of this sense is dependent on our prior knowledge. For this reason, perceptual processes are inextricably entwined with processes of interpretation, memory and attention. In the next chapter we shall examine this interaction more closely as we ask how children come to make sense of sensory experience.

Further reading

COHEN, L. B. and SALAPATEK, P. (1975). *Infant Perception: from Sensation to Cognition*. New York: Academic Press.
A fairly complete source of detailed information on all aspects of infant perception.

HAITH, M. H. (1980). *Rules that babies look by: the organisation of visual activity*. Hillsdale, NJ: Erlbaum.
An up-to-date monograph on visual preferences and scanning patterns of infants.

McGURK, H. (1974). Visual perception in young infants. In B. Foss (ed.) *New Perspectives in Child Development*. Harmondsworth: Penguin.
A good introductory chapter written with undergraduates in mind.

Discussion topics

- What particular difficulties arise when one tries to discover the capacities of very young babies? How can they be overcome?
- How does perceptual discrimination develop in the first few months of life?

CHAPTER SEVEN

Perception and Knowledge
John Sloboda

As I struggle to compose this sentence I am looking in front of me. On my desk I see various familiar objects, such as my telephone and my coffee mug. As I look upwards my gaze falls on a window. Through the window I see some distant trees. I know, without effort, that my telephone is a small object near enought to be picked up if I stretch out my arm. I also know that the tree outside my window is several times taller than a man and stands about 100 metres away.

That I know these things is without doubt. *How* I know them is not so clear. The size of the visual images cannot directly inform me of the true size of the objects. The image of my telephone is considerably larger than the image of the tree, yet I see the telephone as small as the tree as large.

Philosophers and psychologists have been attempting to explain the 'how' of perceptual knowledge for centuries. One line of explanation rests on past experience of common objects like trees and telephones. One comes to discover that telephones are small enough to be picked up whereas trees are not, and that when one is near enough a tree to touch it, then it appears far larger than a telephone. One also comes to discover that objects appear to shrink as one recedes from them, and so one learns to make appropriate compensations. I *know* trees are big. The tree I see out of my window appears small, therefore it must be far away.

This type of explanation (associated with a school of thought called 'empiricism') is undoubtedly the right one for certain aspects of perception. For instance, it helps us to understand how we may misinterpret the size and position of unfamiliar or ambiguous visual objects. Perhaps some of you will have shared an experience that I once had. I was looking out of a window and saw what looked like a large bomb descending through the sky about half a mile away. It was only when it failed to disappear behind some nearby buildings that I suddenly saw that it was a speck of dirt falling from the roof just outside my window. My initial misinterpretation of size and distance were based on a wrong hypothesis about the *nature* of the object.

Critics of empricism argue, however, that there are some cues to properties such as distance that are independent of knowledge about the nature of particular objects. One of these cues is provided by the slightly different information provided by the two eyes (sometimes called 'binocular disparity'). When an object is very close to an observer it will appear to be markedly different to the two eyes. As it moves away, the two images will become more similar. This fact allows distance to be estimated from the degree of binocular disparity. Does one need to learn this kind of knowledge?

A strict empiricist will argue that one needs to learn through discovery that physical closeness (and 'touchability') is invariably associated with high binocular disparity. It is, however, possible that such knowledge is genetically built in to our perceptual system. In recent years, psychologists have been providing evidence which allows us to begin to resolve such disputes.

The visual cliff

One of the most important experimental contributions to our understanding of the development of visual depth perception is that of American psychologists Richard Walk and Eleanor Gibson (1961). They developed an apparatus called the *visual cliff* (see Figure 7.1). It is a simple apparatus, consisting of a glass-topped table with a central raised platform onto which babies (or animals) may be placed. On one side of the platform is an apparent drop to the floor several feet below the glass. On the other side, an opaque patterned covering is fixed to the underside of the glass.

Walk and Gibson placed their subjects on the central platform and simply waited to see which way they would move. In the case of human babies an

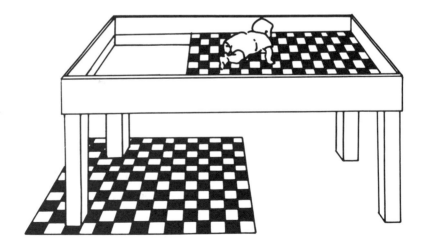

7.1 Visual cliff apparatus.

inducement to move was sometimes provided in the form of the mother beckoning to the child from one or other side of the apparatus. The general result was very clear. Six-month old babies (and a variety of other young mammals) refused to step off the platform onto the apparent drop (even though they might *feel* its solidity with a limb), but would only move onto the apparently raised side. Since visual depth was the only difference between the two sides, this shows that babies were, in some sense, accurately assessing depth and the consequences of approaching a cliff.

Walk and Gibson were also able to test the *nature* of the cues that were most important for successful discrimination. By blindfolding one eye they showed that detection of binocular disparity was *not* necessary. Avoidance of the drop still occurred. What turned out to be crucial was the existence of 'motion parallax'. When an observer moves about in a visual environment there appears to be relative motion between near and distant objects. The most striking case of this is to be observed from the window of a rapidly moving vehicle such as a train. Nearby objects appear to flash by whilst distant hills remain apparently stationary. The phenomenon occurs, however, in any visual environment, as can be easily experienced by moving one's head from side to side. On the visual cliff, motion parallax takes the form of the two surfaces apparently sliding apart as one approaches the cliff.

One shortcoming of the visual cliff technique is that it only yields results for babies who are old enough to crawl. We cannot be certain whether six months is enough time for babies to have *learned* depth perception (by, for instance, falling off platforms), or whether they might have the appropriate knowledge from birth. To resolve this question we turn back to the work of Bower (introduced in Chapter 6), who examined six-week old babies in a 'peek-a-boo' discrimination learning experiment.

Depth perception in early infancy

Bower (1966) trained babies to respond to the presence of a 30cm cube placed one metre from the eyes. When the response was established, three new stimuli were interspersed with the original. One (*A*) was a 30cm cube placed three metres away (same real size, different distance, different aparent size). Another (*B*) was a 90cm cube placed one metre away (different real size, same distance, different apparent size). A third *C*) was a 90cm cube placed three metres away (different real size, different distance, same apparent size). Figure 7.2 represents these conditions diagrammatically.

Bower was concerned to discover whether the learned response would generalize to any of these new stimuli, and if so, which. The stimulus obtaining most response would, Bower argued, be the one that appeared most similar to the original. The nature of the stimuli selected allowed one to discover whether perceptual similarity was in terms of apparent size (baby chooses *C* most often), distance (baby chooses *B* most often) or real size (baby

CONDITIONED STIMULUS	TEST STIMULI		
	A	B	C

		A	B	C
TRUE SIZE				
TRUE DISTANCE	1	3	1	3
RETINAL SIZE				
RETINAL DISTANCE CUES		DIFFERENT	DIFFERENT	SAME

7.2   Illustration of cubes used in Bower's research.

chooses *A* most often). The empiricist argument suggests that baby should choose *C* most often, since apparent size is immediately apprehensible. Bower obtained exactly the opposite result. Babies responded to *A* (same *real* size) more than the other stimuli. The correct compensation to apparent size in virtue of perceived distance was already being applied at six weeks of age. These babies already seem to know that the same object looks smaller when it is further away.

Could such knowledge have been learned from nothing in six weeks? It seems hardly likely. Rather, it seems as though some aspects of knowledge about the world are built in at birth. We should not be overly surprised at this. After all, many newborn mammals perform appropriately on the visual cliff. The mechanisms for gauging size and distance are so useful to survival that it makes sense for evolution to have selected for them to be preserved in the genetic constitution.

Just as in the visual cliff, Bower showed that distance estimation depends primarily upon motion parallax. His babies still showed the same pattern of choice when one eye was blindfolded. Even when unable to crawl, a baby makes enough side-to-side head movements to experience motion parallax. The visual cliff performance and the ability to respond to real size seem to be manifestations of the same underlying perceptual capacity.

The status of empiricism

Where do these data leave the empiricist account of perceptual development? They show, at the very least, that some aspects of knowledge about the perceptual properties of physical objects are present as early in life as it is possible to test for them (see also the discussion of object concept in Chapter 9). If learning is responsible for these phenomena then it must be a very rapid learning, quite unlike the lengthy trial-and-error process that seems to underlie much learning. Such rapid learning is only possible if the organism has special inbuilt predispositions to acquire just such knowledge. For instance, it is possible that the newborn infant 'expects' some correlation between apparent size and distance, requiring experience simply to calibrate changes in one property against changes in the other.

When talking of infants' knowledge, we are, of course, referring to 'implicit' knowledge which displays itself in appropriate behaviour. It does not follow that such knowledge is in any sense conscious or 'explicit' such that an infant can reason with the knowledge or manipulate it internally. Such explicit knowledge is only acquired gradually, usually in association with language development. It is possible to argue about whether implicit knowledge is 'real' knowledge, on philosophical and conceptual grounds. My use of the term is not meant to presuppose that such conceptual problems are solved. Discussion of them, however, falls outside the scope of the present book.

The demonstration that a particular aspect of behaviour or knowledge appears to be unlearned (or 'innate') does not, of course, amount to a general refutation of empricism. Psychologists have shown that neither the innateness nor the learnedness of any particular phenomenon may be assumed. It is a matter for empirical discovery. We now turn to some aspects of perception where learning appears to be extremely important.

Recognition

When we recognize or identify something, we are, in effect, deciding that a sensory input is sufficiently similar to something experienced earlier to deem it to come from the same object (e.g. my car) or class of objects (e.g. *a* car). Psychologists by no means understand all that is involved in skilled recognition. One problem is posed by the incredible speed with which most people can recognize familiar (or not so familiar) material. Another problem is that few perceptual patterns are identical in *every* respect to previous ones from the same object. The angle of view or the distance may be different. The lighting conditions may be different. The object may have changed in itself. It is, for instance, quite remarkable that we are able to recognize people we have not seen for decades, despite all the normal changes which ageing brings about.

One suggestion concerning how we recognize objects rests on the notion of *distinctive features*. According to this notion, associated particularly with the work of Eleanor Gibson (1969), we recognize objects or classes of objects by noticing features that act to distinguish them from other objects. Recognition is not, therefore, a matter of matching a present visual scene to a previously remembered one, as one might try to superimpose two photographs. It is more like going through a checklist of vital features, and discovering which remembered object shares the most features with the present situation. We increase our perceptual skill, in both childhood and adult life, by *learning* new features which make our discriminations more efficient and fine-grained.

A much quoted example of this is provided by the experience of many Westerners that 'all Chinamen look alike'. This experience arises, arguably, because we try to characterize a Chinese person by a set of features which, although they help to tell people apart in our culture, are common to most Chinese (e.g. sallow skin, slanting eyes, high cheekbones). To become more efficient at recognizing individuals we must learn a *new* set of features that are actually discriminating ones.

A classic experimental study on this topic was carried out by Anne Pick (1965), an associate of Eleanor Gibson. She trained children to discriminate a standard shape from other similar shapes that differed from it along predetermined dimensions. Examples of materials used in the training task are given in Figure 7.3(a). When the children were able to select the standard from among the other shapes without difficulty, she split the group into two, and gave each group a different 'transfer' task. In the first condition (Figure 7.3b) the standard was the same as in the training task, but the 'distractor' shapes differed from it along new dimensions. In the second condition (Figure 7.3c) there was a new standard, but the distractors differed from it along the same dimensions of difference as in the training task.

Pick argued that if children learned the first shape by, as it were, building up a mental 'photograph' of it, then they should continue to do well in the first transfer condition, where the shape remains exactly the same. If, however, children learned the shape by noticing its distinctive features (e.g. straight rather than curved, large rather than small, etc.) then they should do best in the second transfer condition where, although the shape was new, the distinctive features were the same. Her results strongly supported the second hypothesis. Children transferred most easily to the second condition (new shape but same distinctive features).

Learning to read

A clear application of the principle of distinctive features comes in the psychology of learning to read. A common difficulty experienced by children concerns left-right orientation. They are prone to confuse letter pairs such as b/d and p/q (misreading 'bark' as 'dark' for example). They also make order reversals (misreading 'was' as 'saw' for example). These errors are best explained by supposing that, up to the point of beginning to read, left-right orientation is not a useful distinctive feature for most perceptual tasks. It makes little difference to recognition of a cat or a cup whether it is facing left or right. The important thing is the configuration of elements that gives their

a. Training task

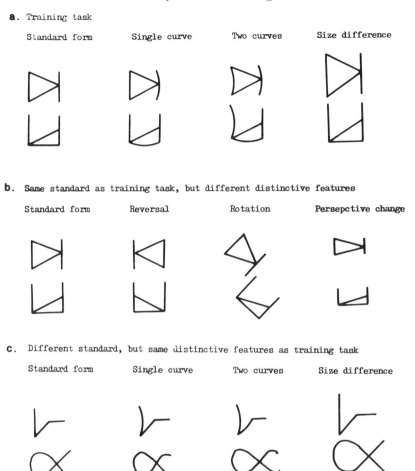

7.3 Materials used in the discrimination task.

distinctive shapes. In reading, probably for the first time, the very identity of an object (a letter) depends upon which way it is facing. This new feature has to be learned before children can become effective readers.

Reading is one of a class of *symbolic* activities, where what is perceived stands for, or represents, some aspects of reality not actually present. For instance, although one can ride a bicycle, one cannot ride a picture of one, or the word 'bicycle'. The capacity to deal with symbols seems to be a crucial property of humans, and is certainly one which starts early in life. As well as their precocity with language (see Chapter 8), children often spontaneously develop their own idiosyncratic notation systems for number or language, before they are taught 'official' notation. Most young children will proudly proclaim a mess of self-produced squiggles to be 'a picture of mummy' (see

Chapter 12). Nonetheless, a full understanding of the essential arbitrariness of many symbol systems only grows slowly. Many pre-school children, for instance, imagine that words for big objects must be longer than words for small objects.

It is hard for experienced readers to imagine just how daunting a page of print must appear to the novice. One way of appreciating this is to undertake to learn an unfamiliar alphabet (such as Cyrillic or Chinese). Another, less arduous, way has been used as the basis of a series of investigations by the Canadian psychologist Paul Kolers (1972). In these investigations he asks readers of English to attempt to read goemetrically transformed text (for example, upside-down or mirror-reversed). Examples of such transformations are given in Figure 4. People are typically very bad at reading such texts– they are slow and make many errors. If you try to read texts of this sort, you will find yourself having to piece words together letter by letter, with much effort. The task is perceptually and intellectually tiring. Kolers found that, because of this, his adult subjects started to do what a lot of beginning readers do; that is, guess words from the preceding contexts. Such guesses tend to be grammatically and semantically appropriate, and it seems to involve less mental effort to guess in this way than to decipher each and every word.

How does reading change from an effortful and error-prone process into the effortless and accurate process that most of us enjoy? 'With much practice' is one general answer. But what, precisely, does practice do for us? One possibility is it enables us to make better guesses about what is coming next from the context. According to this explanation, it is not so much *perceptual* skill that improves as our knowledge of language and the world. Even if the skilled guess or prediction is part of the answer, it cannot be the whole one. Adult reading is usually very accurate, but language is just too rich and varied for prediciton to be always accurate. Consider the sentence 'Jane decided to go out, so she put on her   '. We could plausibly insert many words in the gap (e.g. coat, hat, shoes). Some inspection of the text is necessary for the right word to be chosen. Furthermore, one cannot predict one word unless one has already accurately read some other words. At very frequent points the reader *must* use detailed information from the page.

A second explanation for reading improvement is that frequent exposure to combinations of letters allows one to recognize them, not as four or five separate objects, but as a single meaningful pattern. On this view reading skill depends upon the processes of letter recognition and integration becoming automated to such a degree that there is no experience of intellectual effort between seeing a group of letters and the immediate recognition, or failure to recognize, that it is a word in one's language. There now exists much evidence that skilled readers can identify *words* as quickly as they can identify single letters. They have build up a large storehouse of knowledge about letter patterns such that the appropriate knowledge is automatically 'triggered' by the presence of a pattern in the perceptual input.

*Expectations can also mislead us; the unexpected is always hard to
perceive clearly. Sometimes we fail to recognize an object because we

*Emerson once said that every man is as lazy as he dares to be. It was the
kind of mistake a New England Puritan might be expected to make. It is

*These are but a few of the reasons for believing that a person cannot
be conscious of all his mental processes. Many other reasons can be

*Several years ago a professor who teaches psychology at a large
university had to ask his assistant, a young man of great intelligence

*On his first day in topsy-turvy land he was thoroughly disoriented.
His feet were above his head; he had to reach for things when he

*A very young child sees of dangers as if it an object was merely a
visual image that enters and leaves the field of view begrictiously,

*Psychology became an experimental science during the closing decades of
the sixteenth century, at a time when European thought was curtained by

*Imagine two different pictures. One shows a bright red circle on a pale
yellow background, the other a bright green circle on a gray background.

7.4 Geometrically transformed text. (This figure appeared originally in *Experiments in Reading* by P.A. Kolers, *Scientific American,* July 1972, and is reproduced by permission of W.H. Freeman and Company Publishers.)

'Development' versus 'learning'

Pattern knowledge is not only of use in reading, it is vital in almost every area of perceptual skill. It is now agreed by most psychologists that many changes in perceptual and intellectual behaviour are not so much a result of growing older as of experience with the relevant material. Of course, gaining experience *entails* growing older, but it is possible that a given child may have more experience in a particular area than a given adult. In such a case, the child may be more advanced or 'developed' than the adult.

If this view is correct, then in much of what is commonly called 'developmental' psychology, there is no real need to make a distinction between children and adults. It just so happens that most people undertake particular kinds of learning in childhood. We need to look at processes of learning and skill acquisition in themselves.

An example of this approach is provided by the work of two American psychologists William G. Chase, and Micheline T.H. Chi (1980) on chess perception. One of the tasks they used was a version of 'Kim's Game' in which subjects were shown a chess board with about 20 pieces arranged on it. They were allowed to examine the board for five seconds. They then had to reconstruct as much of what they had seen as possible, from memory, on another board. The arrangement of pieces was taken from the middle of an actual chess game. They found that the greatest predictor of success at this task was, not age, but chess expertise. Children who played chess well remembered many more pieces than adults who could not play chess well. The children who played chess well were not born that way. They achieved expertise through many hours of practice. It is reasonable to suppose that their good memory for chess positions was, thus, dependent on those hours of practice.

How do chess experts manage to do so well? Part of the answer is provided by looking at what happens when one asks people to reconstruct boards on which chess pieces have been placed at *random*. In this situation experts, of whatever age, are not better than novices. Performance is uniformly poor. This shows that good memory performance is dependent on the existence of some familiar structure in the material to be perceived. In the case of chess, it seems that experts perceive boards, not as a set of independent pieces, but as strategic configurations or patterns, each containing several pieces. Some of these patterns have names (e.g. knight fork, concealed check), others do not. Repeated experience of these patterns in chess games has allowed chess experts to build up a 'library' of many thousand such patterns in memory, so that 20 pieces may be automatically and effortlessly seen as four or five easily remembered groups.

Further reading

DODWELL, P. C. (1970) *Perceptual Learning and Adaptation.* Harmondsworth: Penguin.
    A collection of reprinted studies, many of them classics in this field.
CROWDER, R. G. (1982) *The Psychology of Reading: an introduction.* New York: Oxford University Press.
    An up-to-date and well-informed student text.
GIBSON, E. J. (1969) *Principles of Perceptual Learning and Development.* New

York: Appleton Century Crofts.
A comprehensive text which outlines the evidence and marshals the arguments to support the 'distinctive features' theory.

Discussion topics

- Is the human infant born with an understanding of three dimensional space?
- How does the notion of 'distinctive features' help us to understand perceptual development?

CHAPTER EIGHT

Language Development
Don Rogers

What is language?

When people communicate, they convey information by both verbal and by non-verbal means. The non-verbal aspects of communication are especially good at indicating our current emotional state; revealing our attitudes (for example, whether we like or dislike someone); showing our degree of interest, understanding or appreciation of what someone else is saying; and maintaining a smoothly flowing conversation. Using non-verbal means we can also indicate to a limited extent our wants and desires – by for example pointing and gesturing; and we can to some degree get others to do what we want – for example, a child might indicate that she wishes someone to pick her up by raising her arms. However, it is clear that the precision with which we can control the behaviour of others and indicate our desires is greatly augmented by language, as is the scale of time and space over which we can operate. Thus, by means of language we can indicate that we want some precise thing which is in another room; we can instruct people to perform some precise action, at some future time, in a distant location ('Meet me by the left-luggage lockers at Euston station at 10.30 next Tuesday morning'). Moreover we can do a number of other things that are not at all possible without language. Thus, for example, we can inform people of facts that they do not know; we can plan future actions; we can tell jokes and make up stories. Language is, then, a flexible means of communication which enables us to move away from the constraints of the immediate present and make use of the experience and expertise of others.

An important characteristic of language is that it is *creative*. We can easily produce a new sentence that we have not heard before– and a listener can easily understand it, provided that (a) speaker and listener understand the words of the sentence in the same way, and (b) the speaker's sentence conforms to the rules of grammar of the language, and the listener shares a knowledge of those rules.

In many cases, listener and speaker also rely on a shared knowledge of the world to understand one another. For example, in the following conversation:

A. Will you buy some potatoes?
B. It's half past seven.

Speaker B's remark is perfectly comprehensible as an answer if both know that the potato shop is closed at 7.30.

Languages then work by virtue of shared knowledge– knowledge of words, of grammar, and of the world– and within a framework of shared knowledge speakers can create new sentences and be understood.

While languages obviously differ from one another, they all share important characteristics, which enable speakers to understand one another and create new meanings. Each language has (1) a relatively small number of individual sounds, which can be combined to produce (2) a much larger set of words; and (3) these can be combined in rule-governed ways to produce an indefinitely large number of understandable sentences. In addition of course, sentences can be put together to produce narratives and conversations.

Often the ways in which sentences are understood in context is not wholly predictable simply on the basis of the words and syntax. For example, when people tell someone else what to do, it is frequently considered impolite to frame this as a direct imperative (e.g. 'Close the door!'), and so they prefer an indirect request e.g. 'Would you mind closing the door?' 'Don't you find it cold with the door open?' etc. Notice that it would usually be considered odd to answer these indirect requests by answering 'Yes' or 'No', although they have the syntactic form associated with questions for which such answers would be appropriate.

The beginnings of speech

From the discussion so far, it is clear that in order to speak the child needs to acquire a knowledge of the sound system of his language; a knowledge of the words of his language and of their meanings; a knowledge of the syntactic rules of his language; a knowledge of the social and functional significance of utterances in context; and a sufficient knowledge of the world to be able to interpret utterances when their framework is not made fully explicit.

In order to accomplish this, two broad problems are faced by the child. First of all he needs to work out the meaning of speech addressed to him, and its relation to the world; and secondly he needs to work out ways of constructing his own utterances, so that others can understand. In making an initial breakthrough to linguistic communication, children are greatly assisted by certain characteristics of their mother's speech, and by the situation in which such speech occurs.

The primary situation in which an infant during the second year of life hears speech is when he is with his parents and often his mother. This may involve the mother and infant reading a book together, playing with toys together, the mother feeding the infant, and so on. While doing these, the mother may draw the child's attention to something ('Oh look, there's a rabbit'); comment on something ('See, he's digging a hole'); instruct the child to do something ('Let's find your rabbit') and so on. In these situations, mother and child are both interested in the same activity, and the mother's gestures and pointing indicate what she it talking about. Very frequently, in fact, she follows the child's lead, and comments on something that has interested him. Consequently, it is fairly easy for the child to work out the relationship between her speech and some object or event in the world.

Conversely, since the mother is able to see what the child is looking at, and has shared a great many of his experiences, she can understand what the child is trying to say. For example, I recorded the following exchange between an 18-month-old child and her mother:

> Child: (pointing at a picture of a cat) Nana.
> Mother: Yes, it's just like Nana's cat, isn't it?

Clearly, without access to the child's experience, the child's comment would seem like a bizarre misunderstanding, but since the mother knows her child well, communication is able to take place.

Other aspects of the mother's speech are also helpful to the child both in understanding what his mother is saying, and in working out some of the characteristics of the language he is hearing (see Snow and Ferguson (1977) for further details):

First, mothers' speech tends to be in the 'here and now'– mothers talk to young children predominantly about immediately present events, actions and objects, so that their speech relates to the ongoing physical situation.

Secondly, mothers use short and simple sentences when talking to young children, and rather longer and more complex ones when talking to older children.

Thirdly, mothers tend to repeat themselves a great deal, but with variation. This arises from two different sources. Often, mothers are concerned to be understood, so that as Snow (1972) found, mothers are much more likely to repeat when talking to two-year olds than when talking to ten-year-olds. For example:

> Pick up the red one. Find the red one. Not the green one. I want the red one.
> Can you find the red one?

Repetition also occurs through the frequent use by a mother of similar sentence frames– for example:

> Where's . . . Here's . . . Let's play with . . . Look at . . . That's a . . .
> Here comes . . .

Fourthly, mother's speech to young children tends to be slow, with pauses between sentences, with an exaggerated intonation contour, fairly high pitch, and with well formed and complete sentences.

Fifthly, the words that mothers use when talking to young children tend to be ones that are likely to be relatively easy for the child to understand, and useful in a number of contexts. Thus, Rosch (1977) has pointed out that many objects in the world can be grouped in different ways, for example a particular object could be called a 'musical instrument', a 'guitar' or a 'Hawaiian steel guitar'. Notice that the category 'musical instrument' contains a great many different-looking objects with only a rather abstract property in common; on the other hand, 'Hawaiian steel guitars' are very much like 'Spanish guitars', 'classical guitars', 'twelve-stringed guitars' and so on–these categories are similar in most ways but differ in only minor respects such as the number and type of strings. The category 'guitar', however, contains members which are all perceptually very similar to one another, and fairly dissimilar to other categories. One might expect then, that mothers would use the term such as 'guitar', rather than the other alternatives when talking to their children–and one would be right.

Sixthly, children are not merely the passive recipients of maternal speech–rather they are active participants in an ongoing dialogue, and much of the time their mothers are replying to initiatives by the child. These replies can take a number of forms, but very often they involve extending and commenting on something that is currently engaging the child's interest.

In these ways then, the situations in which children hear speech can enable them to understand how the utterances they hear relate to the world around them. Children hear careful, simple, slow and interesting utterances, which are fairly easy to understand in relation to the physical context, which contain a good deal of repetition and which match the focus of their current interest and attention. That this is important can be seen by the fact that children do not seem to learn language if speech is not directed at them in particular. Clark and Clark (1977, p. 330) cite two relevant studies: in one, it was shown that a hearing child of deaf parents did not learn very much at all of spoken language, although he was exposed extensively to television; in the other it was shown that young Dutch children who watched German television every day did not learn to speak German (though recall the discussion of Kaluli mothers in Chapter 1).

Words and early grammar

Children produce their first recognizable words at around 12 months, and expand their vocabulary, rather slowly at first, from then on. It may be that, to begin with, children do not realize that the words they are using have meaning. McShane (e.g. McShane and Whittaker, 1983) has suggested that children may at first simply take part in a ritual game whereby their mothers say 'See the ball' when showing the child a picture, and the child gleefully utters a sound 'ba!'–without realizing its significance. Eventually, the child achieves the insight that everything has a name, and that a name applies to the same category of objects in any situation: at this point there is an explosion in the child's vocabulary. This insight is graphically described in the autobiography of Helen Keller, a child who was both blind and deaf, but who was taught to communicate through finger-spelling by her teacher, Anne Sullivan.

> The morning after my teacher came she led me into her room and gave me a doll . . . When I had played with it a little while, Miss Sullivan slowly spelled into my hand the word 'd-o-l-l'. I was at once interested in this finger play and tried to imitate it . . . I did not know that I was spelling a word or even that words existed; I was simply making my fingers go in monkey-like imitation. In the days that followed I learned to spell in this uncomprehending way a great many words, among them *pin, hat, cup* and a few verbs like *sit, stand* and *walk*. But my teacher had been with me several weeks before I understood that everything had a name . . .

> We walked down the path to the well-house, . . . Someone was drawing water and my teacher placed my hand under the spout. As the cool stream gushed over one hand she spelled into the other the word *water*, first slowly, then rapidly. I stood still, my whole attention fixed upon the motions of her fingers. Suddenly I felt a misty consciousness as of something forgotten–a thrill of returning thought; and somehow the mystery of language was revealed to me. I knew then that 'w-a-t-e-r' meant the wonderful cool something that was flowing over my hand . . . I left the well-house eager to learn. Everything had a name, and each name gave birth to a new though.

> (Keller, 1958, p. 25-26)

However, even when children realize that words have meanings, they may have some difficulty in appreciating quite what the meaning of a word is, and quite often seem to use words inappropriately. This may happen in several ways:

1   The child may base her guess about the meaning of the word on the wrong aspects of the situation in which it is used. Bowerman (1976) for example, cites the case of a child who used the word 'hi' when something was resting on her hands (e.g. small toys held on her fingers), and when she inserted her hands into something which covered them. Bowerman suggests that the child's guess was based on having seen a finger puppet that nodded and said 'hi'.
2   The child may 'underextend' the word–for example, treating 'doggie' as applying only to the family pet, or (in an older child) calling furry mammals 'animal' but refusing to use the word 'animal' to refer to a praying mantis (Anglin, 1977).
3   The child may 'overextend' the meaning of a word–for example, treating 'doggie' as applying to all four-legged animals.

Most attention has been paid to overextensions, especially in the work of Eve Clark (see e.g. Clark, 1973). She suggests that children only slowly acquire a full knowledge of the meaning of a word, and initially overextend meanings on the basis of one property of the original referent. For example, she cites the case of one child who learned the word 'tick tock' and initially applied it to a watch; this was then extended to clocks, then to all clocks and watches, then to a gas meter, then to a firehose wound on a spool, and finally to a bathscale with a round dial. In Clark's view, as children acquire more words, and more knowledge about the conditions under which adults use words, so they progressively narrow down the range of reference for a word. Thus, a child who applies 'doggie' to all four-legged animals, may acquire the word 'moo' to apply to cows, then 'gee-gee' for horses, and so on. At the same time, he will see more instances in which 'doggie' is used by adults, and realize that properties other than four-leggedness apply—fur, barking, biting and so on.

Other factors may well affect children's overextensions, however. One reason why children may overextend is that they may deliberately pretend. If, for example, a child sticks his foot in a box and says 'boot', it is probably not the case that he is confused about the meaning of 'boot', but rather that he is pretending that the box is a boot (Winner, 1979). Furthermore, if a child does not know many words, and wants to talk about a horse he may use the nearest available word to do so and thus call it a 'doggie'. That this may frequently be the case is supported by an experiment cited by Clark (1979) in which it was shown that children who overextended words in their own speech would often not do so in a comprehension task—for example, a child who in speech overextended 'apple' to balls, cherries, tomatoes etc. would point only to apples if asked to 'Point to the apples'.

An interesting aspect of children's use of words is their readiness to invent new uses for words—uses which they have not heard—and indeed to invent new words (e.g. a 'fix-man' for a mechanic, 'lessoner' for teacher, etc.) Eve Clark (1982) has examined this aspect with respect to children's readiness to use nouns as verbs. For example:

Age (years and months)	Innovation
2; 11	(Not wanting mother to sweep room) 'Don't broom my mess'
2; 3	(Talking about getting dressed) 'Mummy trousers me'
2; 8	(After roaring with 'claws' outstretched at a towel) 'I monstered that towel'
2; 3	(When the stove timer went off) 'The buzzer is buzzering'
2; 4	(To mother preparing to brush hair) 'Don't hair me'

Presumably, innovations of this sort (which are a rather general process in English–compare 'He plastered the ceiling'; 'She captained the boat'; 'They weekended in the mountains', etc.) arise because the child does not know a suitable verb, and so makes use of an appropriate noun. Clark points out that it does not arise simply because the child *confuses* verbs and nouns–it is very rare for children to use a verb as a noun, but common for a noun to be used as a verb.

Children are faced with many problems in working out the meanings of words and in using them correctly. Some words seem to be more difficult to work out than others. For example, 'tall' seems to be harder for children to use correctly than the more general 'big', presumably because it applies to only some cases of bigness; and particularly difficult are words such as 'bring', which indicate that the hearer should not just carry something, but carry it towards the speaker, whoever he may be. (See Clark, 1978, 1979, and Carey, 1982, for further discussion.)

When children first begin to produce recognizable speech, and for six months to a year after that, they produce speech one word at a time. These words do not always correspond to a single word in the adult language–for example, a child might request drinks by saying 'cupatea'–but they act as a single unit in the sense that 'cupatea' would not be broken down into 'cup' or 'tea', and would not be recombined as 'cupamilk', 'cupajuice', etc.

Towards the end of the second year, children usually begin to put together the words they have been using singly into longer sequences–mostly at first into sequences of two words–and soon rapidly add new words to their stock.

In order to interpret what the child seems to mean by early word combinations, the child's speech needs to be related to the context in which it occurs. This is clearly shown in a famous example from the work of Lois Bloom (1970), in which a 21-month-old child said 'Mummy sock' on two different occasions. On one occasion she said it when the mother was picking up one of her own socks, so that here the child seemed to be talking about the owner of the sock, i.e. '(That is) Mummy('s) sock'. On the other occasion the child said 'Mummy sock' when the mother was putting one of the child's socks on the child. Presumably here the child was trying to say something like 'Mummy (is doing something to my) sock'.

By trying to interpret what children say in context, it has been possible to show that they often seem to be expressing a small group of meanings. Often the two-word sentence seems to relate to two aspects of an action situation–sometimes the action and the doer (e.g. 'Mummy push'); sometimes the action and the thing receiving the action (e.g. 'Eat dinner'); sometimes the action and the place where it happens ('Play garden'). On other occasions children name things –e.g. 'This truck' (= 'This (is a) truck'); talk about recurrence ('More milk', 'Other egg'); and talk about non-existence ('Allgone egg'). These meanings occur over and over again in the speech of children, even ones learning widely different languages (Brown, 1973). However, it is difficult to work out the best way of capturing precisely what children seem to intend, and there is a good deal of disagreement about the best way to do it–and some people have even suggested that these descriptions are really describing how adults intepret what children mean, rather than what children intend (Howe, 1976).

It is interesting to note that deaf children who are not exposed to sign language sometimes invent signs and put them togehter in combinations very like the two-word combinations on hearing children. Feldman, Goldin-Meadow and Gleitman (1978) studied several children in this situation, and found that they invented gestures. Most of these referred to actions (e.g. flapping arms for *fly*, hands making pedalling motions for *riding a bicycle*, etc.) and some to attributes like *big* (arms extended) or *floppy-eared* (hands behind ears and flapping forwards and backwards). They also pointed to objects in the environment, for example to people, animals, toys, food and so on: much the same categories that hearing children refer to by words. The deaf children (aged between 18 and 54 months) mostly produced points or gestures one at a time, but on about one-quarter of occasions these were combined smoothly into longer sequences. For example, when a deaf boy wanted his sister to give him a toy motorcycle, he pointed to his sister and then to himself; when he wanted another child to give him a mask he made a 'give' gesture (open palm, facing upward, arm extended towards listener) and pointed to himself; when he wanted his mother to give him a book, he pointed to the book, made the give gesture, pointed to himself and then pointed to the book again. Thus, the gestures and points that were used indicated the actions, objects and principal actors in action sequences and, in just the same way as the speech of the hearing child, could be used to comment on a situation or to request an action on the part of another.

Some trends in later development

As children grow older, their utterances grow longer. This trend can be seen in Figure 8.1 (after Brown, 1973), which also shows the extent to which children of the same age can differ. Thus, just after their second birthday, the average length of Eve's utterances was more than twice that of Adam's, and he did not reach Eve's two-year-old level until he was three years six months.

This increase in length arises for two reasons: first, children include more grammatical elements in their speech, so that for example they indicate location by prepositions ('in', 'on', and later 'under'); indicate plurality by putting /s/ on nouns ('Two shoes'); indicate possession by putting /'s/ on nouns ('Mummy's sock); and begin to use definite and indefinite articles ('the' and 'a'). As Brown has demonstrated, the order in which these, and other, grammatical elements are acquired is fairly consistent between different children, and interestingly enough is not particularly related to their frequency in parental speech: *the* and *a*, for example, are said much more often by parents then are *in* and *on*, but children produce them later. Brown

Don Rogers

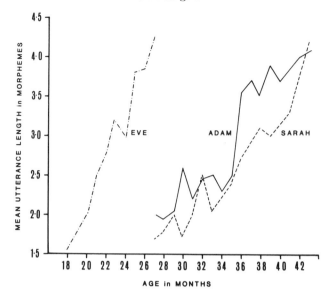

8.1   Average length of utterance for 3 children.

suggests that the order in which these elements emerge in children's speech reflects the relative conceptual difficulty of the elements, rather than how often they are heard.

Second, children become able to include more ideas in a single sentence. There seems to be some preference at first for tacking clauses together by 'and', rather than putting one clause inside another. This is clearly seen in a child studied by Slobin and Welsh (1973). The child, whom they call Echo, happened to enjoy imitating what was said to her, and at the age of two years and four months showed that she could understand a sentence in which a main clause was interrupted by a relative clause, but preferred to repeat it as two successive clauses. Thus, on hearing 'The man who I saw yesterday got wet', Echo said 'I saw the man and he got wet'.

As well as children's utterances getting longer as they get older, they also become more complex. There seem to be two senses in which this is true; first, constructions that are grammatically more complex appear later, and second constructions that are conceptually more complex appear later.

In order to show that grammatical complexity can be independent of conceptual complexity, it is necessary to find cases in which children clearly express the underlying notion of a construction before they have mastered the means to express it fully. Instances of this abound: for example, children can ask questions long before they master the full adult means of doing so. Children at first ask questions simply by raising pitch at the end of utterances, ('Mummy eggnog?', 'See hole?' etc.). It is some time before they master the means of inverting subject and auxiliary to ask questions ('Does lions walk?', 'Oh, did I caught it')

In some cases, however, a construction can be grammatically fairly simple, but represent a notion that is hard to understand, and in this case it too will appear late in development. Moskowitz (1978) suggests that the future tense is like this – in English its form is much more regular and much simpler than the past, but instead of representing something that concretely has happened, it represents something that might happen, and which has to be imagined. And the future, she says, is acquired later than the past.

Language learning as an active process

Children are not passive recipients of language, which they then slavishly imitate. Rather, language learning is a remarkable achievement of the child's intelligence in which the child reveals himself as an active constructor of his own speech. Even when children do imitate, they do so by recasting the sense of what is said into forms that appear in their spontaneous speech (as can be seen in the examples given from Echo, above). Nor indeed are many of the things they say likely to be imitations – adults typically do not say 'Allgone sticky', 'Byebye hot', 'More page' and so on.

Instead of imitating, children seem to produce speech in accordance with their own rules. Two examples of this are past tenses and negatives.

In English, there is a regular form for past tenses, which applies to most verbs. Thus, I hope – I hoped; he jumps – he jumped, etc. However, a number of the most common verbs have irregular forms for the past tense: for example, I bring – I brought; he comes – he came. Children typically go through four stages in their acquisition of past tense forms. In the first stage no past tenses are used. In the second stage a few *irregular* past tenses may be produced, e.g. 'went', 'broke', 'came' etc. In the third stage the *regular* past is used both for regular and irregular verbs, so children say 'I goed', 'I buyed', 'I breaked', 'I comed' and occasionally 'I wented'. This stage can persist into the early school years. Finally, in the fourth stage children achieve adult usage, and sort out the appropriate irregular forms, reserving the regular form for regular verbs. Notice that in stage 3, the child is producing forms that he has never heard, but which are consistent with the rule he has derived from other verbs – the child has observed a systematic property of the language, and is actively applying this to the speech he produces, even though this means ignoring counter-examples that he hears, and which sometimes he has himself produced at stage 2.

With respect to negatives, the evidence that children are constructing rule systems for themselves and producing speech in accordance with these rules seems even stronger since in several ways children's negatives are remarkably unlike those of adults. As Klima and Bellugi (1966) have described, children's early negatives are ones like 'No singing song'; 'No want stand head'; 'No Fraser drink all tea', in which children appear to construct negatives by placing *no* (or *not*) before a normal positive statement. Gradually, other negative words (*don't* and *can't* at first are added, and the child begins to use more complicated rules, in which the negative can stand between the subject and the verb: 'I can't catch you', 'I don't sit on Cromer coffee'. However, a lot of details concerning within-sentence agreement still need to be sorted out so that children say things like 'I didn't did it'; 'You don't want some supper'; 'You didn't caught me' and so on.

Initially, then, children seem to construct negative sentences in accordance with a very broad rule: *put 'No' at the beginning,* which applies to anything they want to negate; they then move on to more complex and detailed rules which apply in more restricted circumstances, but which still operate as though a negative term can be inserted into a positive sentence without altering the rest of it.

Children, then, seem to produce speech in accordance with 'rules' which they have worked out for themselves. As Moskowitz points out, if a child's utterances are, from his own point of view, grammatically correct, then he will be relatively impervious to correction. A famous example suggests that this is the case (McNeill, 1966). A two-year-old, who is presumably producing negatives according to a rule, which states that a negative sentence must have an explicit negative word to indicate it, has the following conversation with his mother:

Child: Nobody don't like me.
Mother: No, say 'nobody likes me'.
Child: Nobody don't like me. (Seven repetitions of this dialogue, and finally:)
Mother: Now listen carefully, *'Nobody likes me'*.
Child: Oh! Nobody don't *likes* me.

McNeill, 1966 p.69

It might seem surprising that the mother would implicitly confirm her son's anxieties rather than reassuring him, but this example (and many others) do suggest both that children construct ways of speaking for themselves, and that to correct their ways of speaking would be ineffective as well as hindering communication.

Further reading

AITCHISON, J. (1983) *The articulate mammal.* London: Hutchinson. Second edition.
    Provides a sensible account of child language and introduces a number of issues in the study of language development.
DE VILLIERS, P. A. and DE VILLIERS, J. G. (1979) *Early Language.* London: Fontana/Open Books.
    An attractive book which is easy to read.

MOSKOWITZ, B. A. (1978) The acquisition of language, *Scientific American,* 239, No. 5, 82–96.
A short article which covers a surprising amount of material in an interesting way.

Discussion topics

* How do parents help children learn to talk?
* In what sense is learning to talk an 'active' process on the part of the child?

CHAPTER NINE

Development of thought
Angus Gellatly

Introduction

Consider a nine-month-old infant examining a coloured ball in which she is interested. Now you take the ball and, in full view of the infant, hide it under a cloth at position A. Obviously delighted by this game, she reaches out and retrieves the ball from its hiding place. Several times more you place the ball under cloth A, and each time the infant successfully discovers it. She appears to be a competent retriever of hidden objects. However, if you next place the ball under a second cloth, at B, a curious thing happens. It is very likely that the infant will search under cloth A but pay no attention to the spherical bulge in cloth B. She is not, after all, so adept at locating hidden objects, and we can ask the reason for her failure on such an apparently trivial problem. Why does she make the mistake? How do her thinking and understanding differ from what they will become as she grows older? These are questions about cognition and its development.

Cognitive development is the development of thought and understanding about oneself, about other people, and about the world. It is a fascinating subject for the good reason that, as the above example illustrates and most parents will readily confirm, the ways in which infants and children act and speak, and presumably think, are themselves fascinating. At times children seem so like little adults, at other times so alien. The similarities and differences are revealing not only of the child's mind, but also of the adult mind and its furniture. Indeed, Jean Piaget, the Swiss investigator whose work dominates the field, took up the study of cognitive development because he believed it provides the only proper approach to philosophical questions of the adult mind. Only by studying the growth of mind, Piaget reasoned, is it possible to appreciate its mature state.

Early in his career, Piaget was forcibly struck by the apparently bizarre difficulties that can be caused by problems such as the one with the ball and the cloths. He studied children at all ages, and he invented a series of tests graded with respect to the age at which children typically succeed on them. On the basis of his studies with these tests, Piaget (1952) devised a theory of cognitive development according to which the infant is as mentally distinct from an adult as a fertilized seed is structurally distinct from a fully grown plant. In other words, Piaget regarded the child's mind as qualitatively different from that of an adult, and he proposed that to reach intellectual maturity she had to pass through a series of stages, some of the features of which are described in this chapter. (See Donaldson, 1978 for a summary of the stages.)

Despite the enormous influence of Piaget's thinking over the last thirty years a number of psychologists have begun to question his conclusions. The common focus of their criticism has been his engagement with tests on which children fail. They claim that his emphasis on failure, and on inferred cognitive deficiencies, led him to underestimate the abilities of children and the continuity of cognitive functioning across different age groups. For these psychologists, the child differs from the adult not in the structure of her mind but only in the *quantity* of her experience and understanding.

In this chapter we will examine several of the ingenious tasks that Piaget originated and which he believed to be diagnostic of the cognitive abilities and deficiencies of children at various stages of their development. In each case, his findings and claims will be contrasted with the discoveries of those who have endeavoured to extend and to criticize his work. The chapter can provide only an introduction to the study of cognitive development; there is not the space to attempt a full exposition of Piaget's theory, nor to give a complete evaluation of its various strengths and weaknesses.

Object permanence

The simplicity and ingenuity of the experiment with the ball and two cloths is typical of Piaget's originality as an investigator of children's behaviour. Only a truly creative imagination could have sensed that such seemingly perverse failure might, if properly construed, allow an insight into the world of the infant. Moreover, the experiment is highly reliable; the result described is readily obtained with infants of the appropriate age. Nonetheless, a correct construal of an infant's failure at object retrieval is not to be easily arrived at. Piaget's radical proposal was that failure was due to the infant lacking an adequate idea of object permanence. In the beginning, he suggested, the infant's world is nothing but the experience of constantly shifting sensations. Visual scenes follow one another like a random sequence of meaningless snapshots. There is no sense of the self as an individual, nor of an external world of persisting people and objects. All of these are cognitive constructions, concepts that the infant will come to invent in order to make sense of her experience. For Piaget, each child begins by unselfconsciously groping in a formless world and goes on to develop (implicit) theories to explain the consistencies she encounters, like a scientist. Just as chemists came to postulate persisting elements that underlie the world of changing appearances (e.g. in a chemical reaction) so the child will eventually come to conceive of permanent objects that can look different from different angles, or that can disappear behind or beneath one another without annihilation. Initially, however, she does not have this concept. Its earliest form is one in which objects are defined solely in terms of her own actions. The nine-month-old believes her action of lifting cloth *A* causes the ball to be created, or re-created, there. When it disappears at *B*, she repeats her previously successful action of lifting *A* in order to create it once more. The intention is to bring a ball into existence, not to search for a still existing ball.

It is hard to know how to test so far-reaching a claim, but some psychologists prefer to interpret the ball-and-cloths results in terms of inappropriate strategies of search and retrieval rather than of an undeveloped object concept. In one experiment, a baby saw someone else retrieving a hidden object from under cloth *A,* yet she searched there herself after the ball subesquently disappeared at *B.* Since she was not simply repeating an action of her own, she must have possessed some notion of objects as independent of her actions. Her error could as well represent a confusion about how to search for missing objects as about objects themselves. This argument is supported by the results of studies by Harris and by Butterworth (Harris, 1979). They repeated the usual experiment but used perspex containers instead of cloths. The ball 'hidden' in container *B* remained visible, yet infants still attempted to retrieve it from container *A.* Since the ball had not disappeared its continued existence should not have been in question, and once again the error might be interpreted as the failure to adopt an adequate retrieval strategy. Harris (1979) gives an analogy to explain this more clearly: when a magician makes his assistant disappear, we do not doubt her continued existence. But we may be unsure of her whereabouts or how best to retrieve her. Harris proposes that the baby, inexperienced at dealing with the world, faces a similar problem with objects that have been moved away.

The issue of how babies conceive of objects and what search skills they have remains unresolved for the present. Discussion of it has served to provide an introduction to the differences between Piaget's theory that children lack logical abilities, and competing explanations of their behaviour which emphasize undeveloped cognitive skills. In the following sections, these differences will be elaborated upon with the help of further examples.

Egocentricity

A central theme of Piaget's theory is the egocentricity of the child. By egocentricity is meant an inability to take another point of view than one's own, and the younger the child the worse afflicted by it she is supposed to be. The newborn infant is worst off of all. Having no conception of herself or others as individuals, she has no possibility of 'decentring' from her own immediate impressions. Even by the age of three or four, when she has already constructed a world of objects and people, she is still thought to be incapable of appreciating any viewpoint other than her own present one.

There is an intuitive appeal in the idea of the young child as naturally egocentric. Anyone who has ever asked a four-year-old to recount the story of a film she has seen will be aware of how few concessions are made to the uninformed listener; events are under-reported, characters may be identified only by pronouns, and there is no sense of a developing storyline. Less anecdotally, Piaget devised what is known as the mountain test in order to demonstrate that the child cannot decentre. The task involves a three-dimensional model of three mountains, distinguished by features such as snow on one, a house at the summit of another, a cross atop the third. The child sits at one side of the model and a doll is placed at some other position round it. The child has to decide what view the doll sees. Since a verbal description would call for complex language skills, the child may be shown a number of pictures taken from different angles and asked to choose the one representing what the doll sees of the model. Children up to about eight or nine find this very difficult to do, and they have a strong tendency to settle for the picture corresponding to what they themselves see. For Piaget, this is evidence that they cannot decentre.

Donaldson (1978) argues that although children frequently display egocentricity, the same can also be said of adults. What is important is whether children are invariably egocentric. She describes an experiment that makes use of two intersecting walls in the form of a cross (Figure 9.1). Policemen dolls

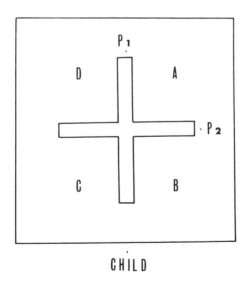

CHILD

9.1 Diagram of the apparatus described by Donaldson.

are placed at positions *P1* and *P2,* where between them they can observe areas *A, B* and *D,* but not *C.*

Individual children are then asked to position a boy doll so that he will be hidden from both policemen. Even a three or four-year-old correctly places him at *C.* The child thereby demonstrates that although she sees the boy doll at *C* she appreciates that the policemen cannot; she can take account of more than one viewpoint at a time. Donaldson argues that children succeed on the policeman task because they understand what is going on; hiding from someone is an activity they have engaged in themselves, it makes human sense. By contrast, the purpose of the mountain task is arbitrary and obscure to the child. Donaldson suggests that a child will decentre in an unthinking way during the course of an everyday activity, but may be unable to call upon the ability when an unfamiliar and explicit problem is to be solved. What the young child lacks is not the ability to decentre, but the capacity to engage in decentring outside the context of a well understood and purposeful activity.

A similar conclusion has been reached by Gelman (1979). She discusses a study in which four-year-olds were asked to talk to two-year-olds, other four-year-olds, and adults about their toys. It was found that the length, complexity, and content of their utterances varied appropriately with the age of the listener, indicating that they took account of the level of understanding to be expected, and therefore that they were able to decentre in these circumstances. Such taking account of the listener must surely be essential to language acquisition, yet it is not always evident in children's speech, as illustrated by the example of the child recounting the plot of a film. In this case, poor performance may not reflect egocentricity but a lack of story-telling skills (see Chapter 10). Having had little experience at telling, as opposed to listening to, stories, the young child will not know how to make use of narrative structure and conventions, or how to handle the introduction of characters. What appears on the surface to be egocentricity may be no more than a result of being unpractised with the subsidiary cognitive skills that the task requires.

Conservation

Probably the best known and most controversial of the many Piagetian tests are those concerned with 'conservation' of quantities such as volume, length, number, and weight. In the prototypical conservation of volume test, a child is shown two identical beakers, each filled with liquid to the same level, and is asked which, if either, contains more to drink (see Figure 9.2). Equality of the two volumes is usually agreed. Then, in full view of the child, the experimenter pours the contents of one beaker into a differently shaped container and again asks which has the greater amount of liquid. Now the child will say there are different amounts, usually indicating the container with the higher level as having the greater.

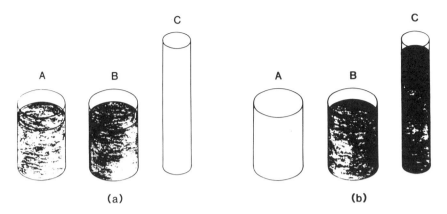

9.2 Conservation of volume: in (a) the child typically agrees that *A* and *B* contain the same volume of liquid. In (b) the child typically responds that *C* contains a greater volume than *B*.

Piaget's explanation of this failure is in two parts: first, he claims that a five-year-old cannot coordinate all three spatial dimensions, but instead becomes fixated on one, usually the height of liquid in this example; secondly, the child is said to lack 'reversibility', she cannot carry out in her head the reverse operation of returning the liquid into its original beaker to arrive back at the original level. It is only at a later stage of development that such mental powers are thought to be acquired, and that conservation becomes possible.

Although 'non-conserving' responses prove remarkably stable, Piaget's theoretical explanation has been open to question for some time. For instance, if the child is shown the liquid being transferred but can only see it disappearing behind a screen which hides the new container, she will repeat her initial judgement that the two quantities are the same. In other words, she will give 'conserving' responses when not misled by the sight of liquid at different levels (Bruner, Olver, and Greenfield, 1966).

Other evidence of conservation in young children has also been discussed by Donaldson (1978; 1982) in relation to conservation of number. In one form of this test, a child is shown two rows of eight counters lined up in one-to-one correspondence (see Figure 9.3). The experimenter asks which row has most counters, or whether they have the same number. The child says they are the same. The experimenter then spreads out one of the rows, and repeats the question. Now the child is likely to reply that the spread out, and therefore longer, row has more counters. Donaldson argues that failure on this standard test is not due to the inability of the child to conserve but to other factors, such as undue deference to the experimenter and a tendency to attend to the whole social meaning of the experiment rather to its purely linguistic and logical aspects. The 'important' adult brings about a change in the array, and draws attention to it in a manner that indicates it must be an 'important' change.

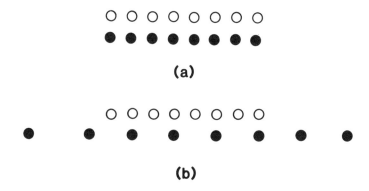

(a)

(b)

9.3 Conservation of number: in (a) the child typically argues that there are equal numbers of light and dark counters. In (b) the child typically responds that there are more dark counters.

The child is liable to accept this evaluation of importance, and, faced with the perceptual feature of length that distinguishes the two rows, to give a non-conserving response. If the experiment is differently presented, so that the alteration of the array is made to seem accidental, or otherwise unimportant to the task, Donaldson and others find large increases in the number of children who conserve. Similar results are also observed in Gelman's 'magic task' (Gelman, 1979). Apparently magical changes in the number or spacing of items in an array are made while the array is out of sight. Subsequently, young children spontaneously comment on changes in number and remark on the addition or subtraction that must have taken place invisibly. For spacing changes, however, they say the number of items is the same, thereby showing an ability to conserve number.

The very young *are* able to conserve – one might say that they have the *assumption* of conservation – but they are readily led into error. Both Donaldson and Gelman argue that their real difficulty is a failure to disembed, or decontextualize, the logical task from its social and linguistic setting. The child must have not only the abilities necessary to reach a correct solution, she must also be able to identify, and to attend solely to, those features of the task that the experimenter defines as logically relevant. It is the development of these social, or cultural, skills rather than of logical ability itself that Piaget's tests inform us about.

Transitivity

The making of inferences from given information is fundamental to successful cognition. If 'Adam is taller than Bill' and 'Bill is taller than Charlie', we should all be able to say who is the taller of Adam and Charlie.

This is known as a transitive inference. Piaget found that children below the age of eight who were given the problem verbally could not reliably make the correct inference, and he concluded that they had not developed an understanding of transitivity. To support his conclusion, he showed that the same children did not succeed on a measurement task that called for a transitive inference. The children were asked to compare the heights of two brick towers, one on a table, the other standing on the floor. A measuring stick was available that could have been used as the middle term in a transitive series analogous to 'Adam is taller than Bill' etc. The child would have found the first tower (*A*) was taller than the stick (*B*) which was taller than the second tower (*C*). But young children did not take advantage of the stick and tended instead to depend upon unreliable judgements by eye of the relative heights of the towers.

Bryant and Trabasso (1971) suggested that failure on the verbal problem might be due to a child's poor memory for the premises A>B and B>C, rather than failure to comprehend transitivity itself. They gave children a task in which there were five differently coloured sticks of decreasing length. The children were thoroughly rehearsed until they could recall all the premises, e.g. red is longer than green, green is longer than blue, blue is longer than yellow, yellow is longer than brown. Under these conditions even four-year-olds could often give the correct answer to the question: Which is longer, green or yellow? Transitive inference, it seemed, was not beyond them. However, further studies have established that success under these conditions does not result from making an inference as such, but from working with a mental image. That is, during rehearsal of the premises a child will come to order the terms, *A*, *B*, *C* into a single image. When asked to compare *A* with *C*, she can read off the answer from the image just as she would from a picture of the three items in order. Piagetians, therefore, have argued that transitivity proper has not been demonstrated. While, on the other hand, it can equally be argued that ordering the terms into a single image is itself indicative of an 'implicit' understanding of transitivity.

It can be seen that whether or not a child has transitivity has proved to be a less than straightforward matter. Piagetians have sought to maintain a distinction between the 'implicit' transitivity that can suffice for a young child to solve the verbal problem and 'operative' transitivity upon which the voluntary use of measurement is dependent. However, Bryant recently showed that children who make by-eye comparisons on the towers problem will sometimes resort to measurement on a task that allows no perceptual basis for comparisons. Asked to compare the depths of two holes drilled in pieces of wood, some children did use a measuring stick. Furthermore, Bryant (1982) reported experiments in which six-year-olds were *required* to solve the towers problem with a measuring stick. Under certain specific conditions of learning, the children then made spontaneous use of measurement to solve subsequent tower problems. Even 'operative' transitivity need not be confined to those over eight. In appropriate circumstances younger children can be induced to solve more difficult tests of transitivity, although it should be emphasized how fragile their grasp of the relevant skills is and how easily it is disrupted by apparently minor changes in the experimental task.

Cognitive Development

On the basis of what we have seen of how cognitive development has been and continues to be studied, three general conclusions can be drawn, the second requiring lengthiest discussion. First, the influence of Piaget remains all pervasive. His research set the stage for all subsequent investigators, their research is conducted against the backdrop of his work and his theory.

Secondly, there can be no doubt that Piaget did underestimate the abilities of young children in a variety of ways. Failure on his seemingly simple tests is not diagnostic of logical deficiencies, or certainly not of the kind that he originally proposed. Children can fail the tests for all manner of reasons other than a lack of certain logical abstractions such as object permanence, conservation, or transitivity. Indeed it may be impossible to say whether a person has or does not have these abstractions. Success may elude the child because she does not differentiate logically relevant from irrelevant features of the task, because she relies overmuch on perceptual information, because she is unpractised with certain subsidiary cognitive skills the task requires, or because she is unable to access and put to conscious use those fragile skills she does possess. Transfer of skills to new settings is a major problem. Most probably this is because children are unconscious of their abilities and skills, which come into play only automatically in certain familiar contexts. In this respect they are not unlike a novice learning to drive a car with manual transmission. She has been making movements of her ankles her whole life, but now she must separate them out from all the other leg movements of walking, running etc., bring them under exquisitely fine control, and learn to access them as dictated by traffic conditions, the sound of the engine, visual indicators of speed, and so on. The child must go through a similar refinement of her fundamental abilities as she learns to apply them in a skilful manner to an ever widening range of cognitive problems.

Yet, while it must be agreed that children do possess abilities that Piaget would have denied them, that is not the whole picture. For part of Piaget's undertaking was his attempt to describe the world of the child. Those psychologists whose work has been contrasted with his have not entered into this attempt, they have been content to demonstrate abilities previously thought to be lacking. It may be that there is no means of fully rendering the child's world into adult language. But surely an infant searching at *A* for the ball visible at *B,* or a child garbling an account of a film, must inhabit a rather different sort of world to an adult. New technological, scientific, or artistic expertise both reflects and conditions the adult conception of the world. In an analogous fashion, the developing cognitive expertise of a child must equally involve altered conceptions. Improved search strategies and story-telling skills must entail an enhanced understanding of objects and of communication. The form of the child's understanding will be determined by the kinds of expertise she acquires and by the socially constructed reality into which she is inducted (Berger and Luckman, 1966). So far only Piaget has attempted to describe the way in which this takes place.

Thirdly, and lastly, the study of cognitive development helps us to increase our awareness of the skills that subserve adult cognitive performance. The surprising failures of children lead us to a recognition of those cognitive skills and habits of our own that are so ubiquitous as to be normally invisible. Piaget was absolutely correct when he asserted that a full understanding of the adult mind can only be built upon a knowledge of the mind's development.

Further reading

DONALDSON, M. (1978) *Children's Minds*. London: Fontana.
  A highly readable introduction to the problems of understanding cognitive development.
GELMAN. R. (1979) Preschool thought. *American Psychologist,* 34, 900-5.
  A succinct review of research demonstrating the often unsuspected skills young children.

Discussion topics

• What are the problems in understanding the mind of a child?
• What is cognitive development the development of?

CHAPTER TEN

Memory development: the cultural background
Ian M. L. Hunter

When you go shopping for a long list of items, it helps if your list is organized rather than haphazard. A commonly helpful organization is by categories–fruit, electrical goods, books, confectionary, clothes, etc. In this chapter, I shall focus on one type of memory task in which remembering by categories looms large. The task involves the free recall of a set of clusterable items. I shall use this task as a window through which to view some aspects of memory development in children and the influences that cultural background has on that development.

The chapter has three sections. Section One describes the task, the developmental trend that shows when the task is given to schoolchildren, and the striking absence of this trend when the task is given to children in a traditional culture. Section Two considers the relation between cultural practices and mental development, notes that members of a culture develop the skills that the culture encourages, and looks at one large difference between traditional and technological culture with regard to the practices that elicit learning and remembering. Section Three returns to the free recall task and considers what happens when modified, more culturally compatible versions of the task are given to traditional adults and older children.

Section One

The free recall task

Here is an example. You are told that you will hear all these words: Yellow – lion – doctor – zebra – teacher – giraffe – postman – tiger – lawyer – pink. You now try to remember as many of the words as you can.

Notice two things about the task. First, it asks for free recall. You are free to recall the words in any order you choose. You are not, for example, constrained to recall the words in the order in which they were presented. Secondly, the words are clusterable. They can be grouped into categories, e.g., four words relate to colour, four to animals, four to people. However, these categories are not pointed out to you and, in the list, words in the same category are not presented next to each other but separated by words from other categories.

When you recall the words, you are likely to cluster them – recall the colours together, the animals together, the people together. The extent of such clustering can be expressed as a numerical index of clustering. Further, there will be a close relation between the extent of clustering and the amount you recall. This relation is not a statistical artifact because the index of clustering takes account of the total number of words recalled. The relation reflects the empirical fact that, almost automatically, you organize the list into categories, use this organization to guide your recall, and recall more words as a consequence of this organization.

School children

This type of task has often been given to school children of different ages. The items have been words (spoken or written), pictures, objects. The details of the task have been varied in many ways. Many of these investigations are reviewed in Kail and Hagen (1977) and more simply and accessibly in Kail (1979).

The main finding is that there is a clear, age-related increase in the extent of clustering and in the number of items recalled. Older children, more so than younger ones, cluster their recall and, thereby, recall more. With commonly familiar items which can be grouped into commonly familiar categories, clustered recall is usual in children of ten years and older, rare in younger children, and usually absent in children of seven years and younger. Basically, older children are more spontaneously sensitive to the organization in the list (items fall into categories), and more spontaneously inclined to use this organization to guide and monitor recall (to recall by categories).

Finer details have been made clearer by various experiments. It has been discovered that children who do not cluster their recall, nevertheless, may be well able to categorize the items. If given the items on cards and asked to arrange the cards into groups, these children produce the categories. Or if asked to point out the animals, colours, and so on, they do so. Thus, absence of clustering in recall does not necessarily mean that the categories are undetectable. It means, more often, that the children do not, of their own accord, identify the categories within the list.

Another finding is that, even when the categories have come to their notice, younger children do not use the categories to guide recall. If these children are prompted to recall by categories (e.g., asked to say what were the animals, then asked to say what were the colours, and so on), they recall by categories and there is an increase in the number of items recalled. In other words, younger children often have items 'in memory' but do not organize their recall procedures so as to bring all of them out. When their recall is organized for them by the experimenter, this external scaffolding enables the children to recall more than they recall when left to their own devices. A dramatic demonstration of this effect of external scaffolding is given by Kobasigawa (1974) whose experiment is described and discussed by Hunter (1976).

In summary, school children of seven years and younger do not cluster their recall because, in large part, they have not yet discovered and begun to master the habit of using categories as a memory-aiding device. After the age of seven, school children make progress in using this device. By the age of ten years, most school children use it as a matter of routine when faced with familiar items which are clusterable into familiar categories.

This developmental progression is a securely established finding. So much so, that we might be tempted to view it as inevitable in all normal children. However, such a view would ignore that there are cultural contexts in which normal children do not show this progression. Let us turn to these children.

Kpelle children and adults

The Kpelle are a group of people who live in the West African country of Liberia. They have their own language and traditional practices. They use neither literacy not schools of the kind that are familiar in Britain. Their traditional, tribal way of life is beginning to feel the impact of imported literacy and schooling, but the people with whom Michael Cole worked were mostly brought up in the traditional way. Indeed, Cole's main aim has been to examine, while there is still the opportunity to do so, the implications of growing up and living in traditional as contrasted with technological culture.

Cole is an American psychologist who, along with various colleagues has spent years in Liberia and got to know its peoples, languages, and ways of life. His extensive work in Liberia is reported in Cole, Gay, Glick and Sharp (1971), Cole and Scribner (1974), and Scribner and Cole (1981). The work with the free recall task is compactly and readably reviewed in Chapter 6 of Cole and Scribner (1974).

In working with traditional Kpelle children and adults, Cole used various tasks which were, of course, given in the native language. The basic free recall task was as follows. A list of twenty items was drawn up after checking that the Kpelle were familiar with these items and could group them into familiar categories. The categories (and the items) were as follows. Utensils (plate - calabash - pot - pan - cup), food (potato - onion - banana - orange - coconut), tools (cutlass - hoe - knife - file - hammer) and clothing (trouser - singlet - headtie - shirt - hat). These items were presented as spoken words, and in a sequence where items from the same category did not occur together. An individual was told to try to learn the words so as to be able to recall as many as possible in any order of the subject's own choice. After presentation and attempted recall, the list was presented again and a further recall asked for. Altogether, the list was presented five times and, after each presentation, the individual attempted recall. Thus, the individual had repeated opportunity to learn about the list.

This task was given to Kpelles in three groups: six to eight years, 10 to 14 years, and adults aged 18 to 50 years. For purposes of crosscultural comparison, an English version of the same task was given to middle-class Americans of corresponding age.

The overall finding was that the Americans showed the developmental trend that is usual in the free recall task: the Kpelle did not. With regard to number of items recalled, this increased with age among the Americans. There was also a marked increase with age in the rate at which Americans learned the list from trial to trial. With the Kpelle, older participants in the experiment recalled only slightly more than younger ones. Most strikingly, learning from trial to trial was very slow with the Kpelle; only a very few more words were recalled on the fifth trial than on the first trial. With regard to clustering, the Americans of ten years and older clustered their recall. The Kpelle showed little or no clustering at any age.

The cross-cultural findings tell us something important about memory development in children. In the free recall task, school children show an age-related developmental trend. But this trend is not inevitable. It depends on the culture in which the children develop. This dependence is further confirmed by the finding that when children, in Africa and elsewhere, have attended Western-type schools for about four years, they deal with the free recall task in the same way as Western children.

We shall return to the free recall task in Section Three. But let us now turn to the wide issue of culture specific practices.

Section Two

Cultural practices and mental development

A central point about the relation between culture and mental development can be made by referring to a study by Dube (1982). Dube presented subjects with various stories which they were asked to retell. He gave this type of memory task to Americans and to nonliterate villagers in Botswana. He found individual differences among Americans and among Africans but, overall, the Africans remembered the stories much better than the Americans. Neisser (1982) comments on Dube's findings as follows:

> Members of a culture tend to excel in the skills which that culture encourages, at least if they have the talent to do so. (Incidentally, this principle explains why Westerners usually outperform people from traditional societies in IQ tests and similar academic tasks.) Many African cultures encourage storytelling; older children are often expected to tell stories to their younger siblings. In America, storytelling is rare. Stories may be read aloud or watched on television, but they are hardly ever told. This specific difference in cultural practices turned out to affect performance [in memory tasks that require people to listen to and retell stories.]

> (Neisser, 1982, p. 275)

When a presented task shows different results in different cultures, it helps to ask: does the task relate to practices that differ between the cultures? What is the compatability between the presented task and the tasks that are common in the culture? The free recall task presents a subject with a situation that is intended to elicit learning and remembering. And there are some large contrasts between traditional and technological cultures in the practices that elicit learning and remembering. Let us consider what these contrasts are.

Schools

The contrasts can be highlighted by noting that traditional cultures do not have schools, at least not to anything like the extent of Western cultures. Schools are institutions where learning can be removed from the immediate, practical, and intelligible goals of daily life. Learning and remembering can be treated as goals in their own right, and not as serving any here-and-now, extracurricular objectives. Schools segregate learning and remembering from real life: or to be more precise, they create a new sector of real life in which learning is the main focus of interest, served by its own special, academic exercises. Schools (and in magnified form, universities) have good reasons for treating learning in this out-of-context way, although there is always the risk that decontextualisation can become excessive.

In traditional cultures, the situations which elicit learning and remembering characteristically arise as incidental to the pursuit of socially shared daily living. Learning and remembering occur because they serve and advance these pursuits. This is also the case in technological cultures with pre-school children, and with older children and adults in their life outside school. However, it is rare for people of any age in a traditional culture to meet situations which are academically contrived to elicit learning and remembering. Listen to Cole and Scribner:

> Schools represent the major cultural institution in technological societies where remembering as a distinct activity, occurring apart from the application of anything remembered, is engaged in repeatedly with a great variety of stimulus materials . . . Certainly 'deliberate memorization' does not characterize the processes by which we learn our native language, the use of elementary tools or social customs. When we turn to societies that lack formal educational institutions, when can one find such activities? The answer, we believe, is *rarely*. (Cole and Scribner, 1977, p. 269)

In brief, people in traditional cultures have little experience of learning and remembering which are provoked by academic, out-of-context situations. Nevertheless, a great deal of learning and remembering take place, and some individuals accomplish extraordinary feats of memory, such as the fluent recital of lengthy epic songs. But even such feats are not acquired in a school-like context. What is involved in reciting epic songs or genealogies is grossly misunderstood by literate Westerners who view these feats in terms of having memorized a written text by rote. Rote memory is, in fact, not involved but something much more skilful and creative (see Hunter, 1979 and 1984).

A school-like task

Let us return to the free recall task and notice how school-like it is. It has two properties that make it like an academic task of the kind likely to be familiar to school children but unfamiliar in traditional culture. First, from the outset of the task, the subject's goal is to remember the presented items for their own sake, simply because this is what the task demands, what the presenter requires. There is no further purpose evident, at least from the viewpoint of the subject. Secondly, the meaningful structure of the presented material is not made explicit, or even referred to. It is up to the subject to work out a meaningful organization that will make the material recallable.

These two properties of the free recall task seem likely to be unfamiliar to traditional people. If so, is it possible to modify the task so as to make it more compatible with cultural practices, more familiarly accessible to the subjects? This is the question to which the next section is devoted.

Section Three

When Cole and his colleagues had gathered their cross-cultural findings with the free recall task, the question arose: how are these findings to be interpreted? There were several possibilities. Perhaps the Kpelle subjects were incapable of recalling by categories. Perhaps they misunderstood some aspect of what they were being asked to do. Perhaps they were indifferent to the task and not trying to remember. Perhaps they were deliberately acting stupid. Cole and his colleagues set out to examine such possibilities by taking a new approach. They concentrated on older Kpelle children and adults, and they tried modifying the free recall task with a view to finding versions on which the Kpelle would do well. Several modifications were tried and two were found on which Kpelle subjects did well. Let us consider these two modified tasks.

The constrained recall task

In this version, the only difference from the basic task was that, on the first four trials, the experimenter would say 'Tell me all the clothing you remember'. Then, when the subject had recalled as many of the clothing items as possible, the experimenter would say 'Tell me all the food you remember'. Such constrained recall was used on the first four trials. But on the fifth and last trial, the subject was simply asked to name as many items as possible, that is, given free recall.

With this modification, the results were very different from usual. On the first four trials, the number of words recalled was very high and clustering was, of course, forced to be perfect. On the free recall trial, the number of recalled words remained high as did the extent of clustering. On this trial, the Kpelle did fully as well as Americans. The four constrained recall trials had been sufficient to lead the Kpelle subjects to adopt procedures of recalling by category, and to carry these procedures into free recall.

This finding is specially striking in the light of what happens when young Western children are given constrained recall trials. When guided to recall category by category, they do so and there is a corresponding increase in the number of items recalled. But when then asked for free recall, they usually revert to their customary recall procedures, and recall fewer items. Thus, when their recall is no longer scaffolded by the experimenter, it becomes immediately poorer – due largely to the demanding complexity of planning and controlling the procedure of recalling by categories.

However, the older Kpelle subjects do carry over the procedure of recalling by category even when it is no longer scaffolded by the experimenter. This means that these subjects have the ability to use categories as means of organizing and aiding recall – an ability that was not elicited by the basic free recall task.

The story-telling tasks

Among the traditional people with whom Cole worked, story-telling is a naturally occurring activity, which is often carried out with great skill. So, might story-telling provide a setting in which older Kpelle children and adults would spontaneously use efficiently organized procedures of recall? Such proved to be the case when the list of twenty words was embedded in stories which provided a meaningful context. The story was presented, the subject was asked questions about it and, finally, the subject's retelling of the story was tape recorded. There were two types of story.

First story 'A chief had a beautiful daughter, and many young men wanted to marry her. Each of them brought many presents for the girl and left them with the chief. One brought (name the tools). Another brought (name the foods). Another brought (name the utensils). And another brought (name the clothing).' The subject was then asked: What things did the girl receive? Which young man should get the girl? Why? The subject then retold the story to the tape recorder.

Second story (This story is lengthy, so a middle section is omitted.) 'A very handsome man, who happened to be a bogeyman, came to town one day and met a beautiful girl. The girl did not know he was a bogeyman and agreed to marry him. On the night they married, she discovered he was a bogeyman. He told her she must come with him to his farm, but she said to wait a bit while she got her things together. She knew where the bogeyman's farm was, and so she put many things on the ground in her house to show her people the way to reach his farm. She put her *plate* first, since she always ate at home. Then she put the bogeyman's *singlet* to show that he took her away. Then she put a *pot* to show that he took her first in the direction of her family's kitchen behind the house. Then she put a *knife* to show that they went past the woodcarver's house. Next was a *headtie* showing that they passed the store where she bought it. Next was an *onion* to show they passed the market, and a *cup* to show they passed the table where they sell palm wine. . . and finally a *pan* to show she was at the kitchen at the farm. The girl's people saw all these things and understood where she had gone and came and rescued her. They caught the bogeyman and killed him'. The subject was then asked to tell all the things she put on the ground and their meaning so that, if you were the girl's family, you could find the girl. The subject then retold the story to the tape recorder.

With these story-telling versions of the task, the main finding was that the way in which the to-be-remembered items fitted into the story determined, almost perfectly, the order in which the items were recalled. In retelling the first story, the items were usually recalled in category clusters. Further, within each cluster, the order of the recalled items bore no relation to the order in which these items had been presented. This showed that subjects were not just reeling off the items by rote. They were recalling the items on the basis of category membership. In retelling the second story, items were recalled more or less in the order in which they fitted into the story. In contrast to the first story, categorizing into word clusters was negligible.

Story-telling provided these traditional Kpelle people with a culturally familiar task context. They knew how to approach the task, what to do with it. They were alert to meaningful structure in the presented material. They picked up this structure and used it to organize their retelling of the story. And in the process of retelling, they recalled a large number of words that they had seemed incapable of learning when they were given a mere list to learn. These findings further reinforce the extent to which, in our own culture, the development which children show in dealing with free recall tasks has a cultural background. These developments are real enough but they are due, in part, to familiarity in dealing with academic, school-like tasks. Throughout the study of development, detailed observation and experiment are important. So too is awareness of the cultural background.

Further reading

COLE, M. and SCRIBNER, S. (1974) *Culture and Thought.* New York: Wiley.
　　Chapter 6 gives a compact and readable review of research with the free
　　recall task.
NEISSER, U. (Ed.) (1982) *Memory Observed.* San Francisco: Freeman.
　　Describes the workings of memory in natural contexts. Part 5 contains
　　several articles on recall of material in different cultures. See especially
　　the article by Dube.
KAIL, R. (1979) *The Development of Memory in Children.* San Francisco:
　　Freeman.
　　A useful introduction to the growing field of research into changes in
　　memory as children grow older.

Discussion topics

- What does the free recall task tell us about the way children remember?
- How can we account for cultural differences in memory, and other
- functions?

CHAPTER ELEVEN

Developing skills of learning
James Hartley

You may in the future be taking an examination. Presumably you will prepare for this by carrying out some revision. You will select certain topics, you will look at your lecture notes, you will read through the textbook and the essays that you wrote during the term. And, during this revision you will eventually decide when you have done enough. At this stage you will face difficult questions. How will you know when you have done enough revision? And how will you know whether you've revised the right things. As one A level student recently put it: 'The difficulty of revising is that you don't know if you know what you should know'.

How do we measure our own understanding? How do we assess whether we know what we should know? Questions such as these are typical of questions asked by psychologists interested in the field of 'comprehension monitoring'. These questions, in fact, relate to a broader issue. How do we become aware of our own cognitive processes – how do we know how skilled we are at thinking, learning and remembering?

Most people seem to be quite knowledgeable about their skills of remembering. Some cheerfully explain that they can never remember names, or dates. Others know that it is futile to go shopping without a shopping list or to a committee meeting without a diary. But in other areas of cognition people do not seem so knowledgeable about their skills or how they might support them. Technically speaking, the awareness that we have about our own cognitive processing is called our metacognition.

In this chapter we shall look at three aspects of comprehension monitoring and metacognitive development:

- We shall discuss in more detail problems involved in comprehension monitoring;
- We shall consider developmental changes in people's metacognition; and
- We shall consider whether or not it is possible to teach people to develop skills in this respect.

Comprehension monitoring

Comprehension monitoring is concerned with being aware of, waching over, and monitoring our own comprehension processes. It is concerned with assessing whether or not something has been understood. (If you had difficulty in understanding the A level student's remark given earlier and you had to re-read it once or twice, then you were indulging in comprehension monitoring.)

When we read a text we constantly make sense of it. Because of our competence and skill at reading we are unlikely to notice small errors (such as misprints). We read rapidly and we do not normally observe our monitoring processes unless we suddenly find that the text does not make sense. Then we back-track, re-read, decide the author is right and we were wrong (or vice versa). Sometimes, of course, we relax our vigilance and find ourselves at the bottom of the page without having understood a word of what was said.

We can take a specific example (based on Bransford, 1979) to illustrate how our comprehension processes operate when we are reading. Cover up the following block of sentences with your hand, and then read each sentence separately, one at a time. After each sentence try to imagine what is happening before you read the next one. Remember: cover up the sentences before you start.

> John went up to the window.
> He put down his five pound note.
> She tried to give him £2.50.
> He wouldn't take it.
> So when they went inside she bought him a bar of chocolate.

Different readers will respond differently to these sentences (especially at the early stages), but by reading them one sentence at a time, I hope that you became aware of the changes that you had to make in your own understanding at each stage in order to make sense of what all the sentences were about.

It is important to realize that all of these sentences would have been perfectly clear if you had known the context in which they were embedded (which I did not give you). If I had given a title (John and Jane at the Cinema Box Office), then you would have had little trouble in following the sentences, and you would not have questioned in your mind what was going on. Most reading is like this. A chain of inferences–reasonable inferences–is made, and the sense of the text comes as much from your brain as it does from the words on the page.

Bransford (1979) gives another example:

> The man was worried. His car came to a halt and he was all alone. It was extremely dark and cold. The man took off his overcoat, rolled down the window and got out of the car as quickly as possible. Then he used all his strength to move as fast as he could. He was relieved when he finally saw the lights of the city even though they were far away.

> (Bransford, 1979, p. 151)

If I asked you whether the passage made sense, then, according to Bransford, you are likely to say *yes*. However, I can remove this confident understanding quite easily by asking: Why did the man take off his overcoat? Why did he roll down the window? The passage only makes sense if you realise that the passage is about a car submerged in water. Without closely questioning the text, people do not realize what it is about and feel that it is quite straightforward.

Research with students shows that when confusions and ambiguities are deliberately inserted into text, many go unnoticed. While some students can and do monitor their comprehension, many do not. Moreover, there is considerable variability in how individual students respond (Baker, 1979).

Clearly we would expect young children to be less efficient at comprehension monitoring than university students, and we shall now discuss children's capabilities in this respect.

The development of metacognition

In the introduction to this chapter I posed the question: How do you know how skilled you are at thinking, learning and remembering? I also defined your knowledge of your own cognitive skills as your metacognition. Many psychologists are interested in such knowledge, how it is acquired, and how it develops from childhood to old age. Typical studies focus on how children at different ages carry out cognitive tasks that require an understanding of what one has to do in order to carry out the task effectively.

In Chapter 10, Ian Hunter described similar studies in the context of memory development. In this chapter I want to provide two more examples.

Study 1

One of the best ways of understanding a study is to take part in it yourself. Accordingly, instead of directly reporting a study, I shall first try to involve you in a similar one. You will need three different coloured pencils and about ten minutes of your time.

The instructions are as follows:

1   Read the extract reprinted in Panel 1, taken from a passage entitled 'The Life of Louis Braille'. There are twenty sentences in this extract.
2   Now underline (in one colour) *five* sentences which, in your view, are the *most* important.
3   Next underline (in another colour) the next five sentences which, in your view, are the next most important.
4   Finally underline (in a third colour) the next five sentences which are the next most important.
5   This should leave five sentences not underlined which, in your view, are the *least* important.

Panel 1

Louis Braille (1809-52)

Louis Braille's father lived in an old French village called Coupvray and worked as a saddler. He used one of the rooms in his small stone cottage as his workroom. In this room he kept an old bench and chair, and the tools and knives of his trade. There were skins and scraps of leather, and boxes of round-headed nails. There was harness, and partly finished saddles, and the smell of leather always hung upon the air.

At three years of age Louis was a bright and happy little boy, with his fingers into everything. He loved watching his father at work, and playing with odd strips of leather that fell to the floor.

His father, of course, was careful to keep the sharp scissors and knives out of Louis' reach. He liked having the child with him, and he sometimes wondered whether Louis too would be a saddler when he grew up, but this was not to be.

One day Louis had a terrible accident. No one seemed quite sure how it happened. Perhaps the child had grown tall enough to touch the tools that his father thought were beyond his reach. Perhaps he went into the workshop when no one was there. Somehow he got hold of a knife and a piece of leather. The next moment the knife slipped and he had injured his eye. Within a few months the other eye grew dim too, and by the time he was five, Louis was quite blind.

In those days little was done for blind children. When Louis went to the village school a year or two later he could only learn by listening. He listened to the teacher carefully so that he would not miss a word. He worked hard, and found that he could often answer questions more easily than the other children who had books and pictures to help them.

Extract adapted with permission from Schonell, F.J., Flowerdew, P. and Elliott-Cannon, A. (1967) *Wide Range Interest: 2*. Edinburgh: Oliver and Boyd.

This activity will immediately alert you to the difficulty of the task (and how individuals vary). If you can compare your responses with those of other people that will be helpful in this regard, but that is not our main concern here.

6 Now that you have done this, imagine next that you are to recall the Louis·Braille extract for another person who has not read it. Which five sentences do you think it would be most helpful for your to have to prompt your recall:

Sentences in category 1 (the most important)
Sentences in category 2 (the next most important)

Sentences in category 3 (the next most important)
Sentences in category 4 (the least important)
Choose one category and underline it. Do this now before reading any
further.

What we have done, in a simplified way, is to carry out a study similar to that
reported by Brown and Campione (1978). Brown and Campione asked
secondary school children to select twelve 'idea units' (from a passage
containing 50 such units) that the children thought would be most helpful for
them to have to prompt their recall of the passage. These units were then rated
by the experimenters in terms of their level of importance (using the four
categories that you have just worked with). The questions being asked were
what units would the school children pick to help them remember the passage
and what would be their levels of importance.

There was one further complication. Brown and Campione asked whether
the children would pick different units at different levels of importance if they
had to repeat the procedure. In terms of the experiment you've just done, the
question might be asked: Once you've recalled the Louis Braille extract for
your fellow student would you pick the *same* or a *different* group of sentences
to aid your recall if you had to tell the story again to another fellow student?

Now, bearing in mind the level of importance of the five sentences you
chose to aid your recall of the passage, consider the results obtained by Brown
and Campione shown in Table 11.1 below.

TABLE 11.1   Average levels of importance of units chosen to aid recall over
three re-tellings of the passage (adapted from Brown and
Campione, 1978).

Readers	1st recall	2nd recall	3rd recall
12-year-olds	1	1	1
16–17-year-olds	1	1	2
18+ year-olds	1	2	3

What do these results show? They certainly show differences in
performance with age. The older students, after the first trial, are recognizing
that to help one to recall the details of a passage you don't actually need
prompts for the most important ideas. You can recall these anyway. To
improve recall, units at level 2 and level 3 are better. Notice that the 16–17 year
olds are beginning to see that–but it is taking them longer–and that the 12-
year-olds do not perceive it yet.

In short, the older participants are more aware of what they need to know in
order to carry out the task successfully: or, more technically speaking, they
have greater metacognitive awareness.

How about you? In your experiment did you choose sentences at level 1 or
level 4? (Or in between?) When I carried out this experiment with forty

students, thirty-five chose sentences at level 1, four chose sentences at level 2 and one chose sentences at level 3. The one who chose sentences at level 3 said she thought the answer was obvious: clearly everyone, she said, knows it is easier to remember important things and to forget trivial ones, and so one needs more help to remember less important things.

Undoubtedly she was right–but do we always put into practice what we know?

Finally, in commenting on this study, we may note in line with the argument developed by Ian Hunter (Chapter 10) that you could instruct the 12 and the 16-year-olds what to do, and they would be able to do it easily. The key point is that many people can do things, but that they do not always do them. The question that arises, then, is how can we get people to be more aware of the cognitive demands imposed by certain tasks, and to be more aware of useful solutions? Some illustrations of attempts to do this will be described in the third section of this chapter.

Study 2

Meanwhile let us turn to another study of how children of different ages carry out tasks that require an understanding of what one has to do or know in order to do the task effectively. This time we shall focus on younger children following instructions. Instructions are useful tools in this respect because it is easy to see if they are carried out successfully or not.

In a study carried out in 1977, Ellen Markman asked children aged six and nine to listen to simple instructions on how to play games or perform a card trick. In both cases information was left out that was crucial to being able to follow the instructions. The children were told that Markman was testing out the instructions and that she needed their help to see if they were clear. The children were asked to tell her of any difficulties they had in following the instructions and to say if anything was omitted or was not clear.

The instructions for the card game were as follows:

> We put each of our cards in a pile. We both turn over the top card in our pile. We look at the cards to see who has the special card. Then we turn over the next card in our pile to see who has the special card this time. In the end the person with the most cards win.

There was no mention of what the special card was, or what you did if you had one.

Markman recorded the number carefully sequenced questions that she had to ask children of the two different ages before they grasped the fact that they needed more information. She found that the nine-year-olds realized that the instructions were incomplete much more readily than the six year-olds. Often it was not until the six-year-olds actually tried to carry out the instructions that they realized that they could not follow them. They *said* the instructions were clear, but obviously they were not understood in the sense that they could carry them out.

So Markman concluded that six-year-olds could not monitor their comprehension on tasks such as this, but that nine-year-olds could. In subsequent studies with passages containing ambiguities Markman and Gorin (1981) have shown developmental changes in comprehension monitoring, and that comprehension monitoring can be improved if you let children know what is required of them. Markman and Gorin found that if you told children to look for a particular kind of inconsistency they were better at detecting it than if you didn't tell them, but they also found that children would then detect the required inconsistency at the expense of other kinds. So young children could detect different kinds of inconsistency if instructed to do so, but they seemed to approach the task with specific goals rather than general ones.

Once again, then, we can see that young children can do certain tasks when instructed to do so but that they will not do them spontaneously until a later age.

Studies such as these by Markman (and now by many others) have instructional implications. They suggest that strategies can be devised to help learners develop their metacognitive awareness. We now turn to some examples of these strategies.

Learning how to learn

In this closing section of this chapter the focus of attention is on teaching learners how to monitor their metacognitive processes and thus, in effect, on learning how to learn. Two examples are given. The first one is with retarded children and the second with hyperactive children.

Study 3

Ann Brown and her colleagues (1981) distinguish between three kinds of teaching strategy:

> *blind instruction* i.e. do this, this and this. There are no explanations.
> *informed instruction* i.e. do this, because . . . The reasons for actions are given.
> *self-controlled learning* i.e. informed instruction together with instructions on how to monitor, check and evaluate one's progress.

In one study, Brown and her colleagues were concerned with whether or not mildly retarded children could assess whether they knew material sufficiently well to take a test on it. To measure this they devised a situation where the children had to memorize a sequence of pictures (e.g. cat, dog, house, fork etc.)

The sequence was too long for them to learn without using some deliberate memory strategy. The participants were asked to learn the sequences of pictures and to say when they were ready to take a test. The results indicated that the children were very poor at this task: even with unlimited study time, they were unable to remember very much.

The authors then developed a special technique which involved self-controlled learning. The learners were taught to rehearse and practice with small sequences, and to use the method of overt anticipation. This involves learners in anticipating, and saying out loud, what the next item in a sequence will be. Thus if learners have a booklet containing the pictures cat, dog, house, fork etc. and if, when looking at the first picture cat, they say that the next one is dog, they will obtain immediate confirmation of this fact when they turn over the page. Conversely, if they say 'fork' at this point, they will obtain immediate information about their error. So the method of overt anticipation allows one to monitor, check and evaluate one's progress as one learns, and it can be very useful for any list-type learning.

In Brown's study, two groups of learners were involved: a group of older children aged approximately eleven years who had a mental age of eight years, and a group of younger children aged nine years who had a mental age of six years. The older children significantly improved their performance on the task with the new method (from 58 per cent to almost 100 per cent correct) but the younger children did not benefit much from the training.

One important point to be made here is that the skills learned by the older children *transferred* to other learning tasks. The children were asked to read and recall several short stories matched to their reading ability. They were allowed unlimited study time, and they were asked to indicate when they felt they were ready to take a test on their recall of the stories. The children who had been taught the self-controlled learning techniques for the picture-memory task outperformed untrained children on the reading recall task on four measures: total amount recalled; ratio of important to trivial detail; time spent studying; and overt indices of strategy use (such as lip-movements, looking away, and self-testing).

This study shows that improvements in learning can be brought about by making tasks more structured, and by making knowledge about success more explicit. It appears that there are still age and ability effects in all of this, but that the procedures can transfer from one task to another once the learner is old or intelligent enough to appreciate them.

Study 4

This study comes from a very different source (Meichenhaum, 1977). Donald Meichenbaum is a Canadian clinical psychologist who is mainly concerned with the treatment of schizophrenic patients. In this context he has developed several self-instructional training techniques to help these patients regulate their behaviour. He has also applied these procedures to impulsive or hyperactive children (a condition described in Chapter 15).

Meichenbaum's techniques involve *talking to oneself* about what it is one has to do when carrying out a complex task. The training of impulsive children is basically done in five stages as follows:

1   The therapist demonstrates the task, talking aloud to him or herself the instructions. (e.g. 'Now what have I got to do? Let's see. First of all I've got to plug it in. Let's do that. good. Next I must see if this dial is where it needs to be. For Radio 1 it has to be . . .') The child watches and listens.
2   The child does the task, following the instructions given aloud by the therapist. (e.g. 'Now what have you got to do? First of all you've got to plug it in. You've done that. Good. Next . . .')
3   The child does the task, instructing him or herself out loud. (e.g. 'Now what have I got to do? First of all I must plug it in. I've done that. Good. Next I must . . .')
4   The child does the task, instructing him or herself in a whisper. (Very quietly. 'Now what have I got to do. First . . .')
5   The child does the task, saying the instructions to him or herself silently.

The instructions for the task consist of a set of questions, the answers to which are given in the form of anticipation and rehearsal. Each stage is punctuated by guiding statements (e.g. be careful here, watch it, remember to do this before that) and by self-rewarding statements (e.g. good, doing fine so far, its coming on, done it!).

The evidence from Meichenbaum's studies suggests that impulsive children can use self-controlled learning techniques: they can learn to regulate and control their impulsivity by using such techniques, and they are able to transfer their skills to different tasks.

Conclusion

This chapter examined three things: comprehension monitoring, the development of metacognitive skills, and learning how to learn. It seems that not all readers fully monitor their comprehension when they are reading (although this may depend upon the nature of the text and the reader's purpose), and that the skills of comprehension monitoring and metacognition are acquired slowly. Nonetheless, instructional techniques have been devised to help children develop and use such skills. These techniques makes tasks more structured and ensure that learners monitor, check and evaluate their comprehension as they learn.

Further reading

BRANSFORD, J. D. (1979) *Human Cognition.* Belmont: Wadsworth.
A basic text in this area. Chapter 5 in particular examines the role of prior knowledge in learning.

BROWN, A. L., BRANSFORD, J. D. FERRARA, R. A. and CAMPIONE, J. C. (1983) 'Learning, remembering and understanding'. In Mussen, P. H. (Ed.) *Handbook of Child Psychology*, Vol. 3. New York: Wiley.
A long, difficult chapter but full of detailed information for the really interested reader. Incidentally this Handbook contains review chapters on most of the topics in this text, so it is worth having a look at if you are interested in other topics as well.

HOWE, M. J. A. (1984) *A Teachers Guide to the Psychology of Learning.* Oxford: Blackwell.
A more readable text devoted to explaining the implications of recent work on metacognition for instruction. Useful if you are writing an essay on this topic.

Discussion topics

- How do reading skills improve as children get older?
- Outline a list of behaviours that you think it would be helpful to check off (mentally) whilst reading for learning.

CHAPTER TWELVE

The development of children's drawing ability
John Pigram

It is a puzzling question as to what children are doing when they draw and paint. Are they trying to express the way they see the world or are they merely manipulating pens and crayons across the paper in whatever physical way takes their fancy? When children begin to scribble on paper, they produce very similar shapes and symbols, but are these expressions of an idea in their minds at the beginning or does the idea only evolve as the 'doodle' progresses? Undoubtedly these aspects of children's drawing interact and what children draw, and the way the product appears, are influenced by ideas or plans that the child has for the drawing together with the ability of the child. Research on children's drawing has investigated both *what* it is that children draw and the question of *how* they execute their drawings.

Common patterns and symbols in children's drawings

Kellogg's well-known book (*Analyzing Children's Art*, 1969) was a compendium of individual examples of young children's art-work gathered from her vast collection of paintings, drawings and photographs. These examples were formed into categories that made up a loose developmental structure illustrating what sort of patterns and symbols the young child would typically produce at each of a number of age-points, rather than *how* or *why* each type of pattern occurred. Kellogg's account is therefore descriptive, rather than analytic.

The appearance of regular patterns occurs from about the age of 18 months, though the majority of children are not capable of anything other than an apparently uncontrolled scribble at this age. For Kellogg, however, even these early 'Scribbles' are capable of categorization both in terms of the *type* of scribble produced and in their placement on the drawing surface (not all drawings at this age are made on paper!). Scribbles at this age are often produced with free hand movements in the form of to-and-fro, zigzag or roving lines. At the age of two years the child is not capable of making the finer co-ordinated movements found in the more intricate patterns of later ages. Kellogg found that the positioning of a Scribble on a page usually fell into one of 17 'Placement Patterns', for example those occupying a half or quarter-page, or forming an arc or pyramid shape. Even at this early stage we can see that a not inconsiderable level of organization is present in the child's artistic output. Figure 12.1 gives examples of Scribbles and Placement Patterns, as well as the patterns that occur later.

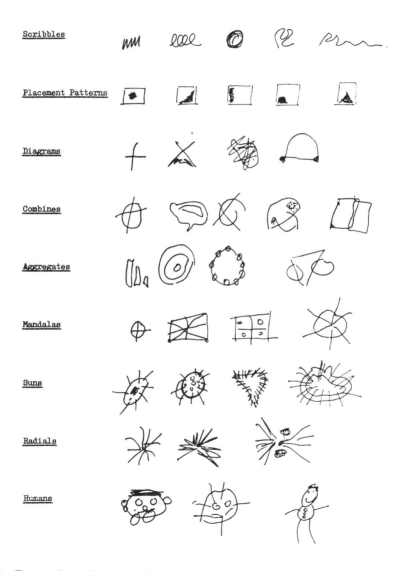

12.1   Types of drawings described by Kellogg.

Between the ages of two and three years, Kellogg claimed that 'Diagrams' emerge from earlier Scribbles. Diagrams are usually formed from unbroken lines, but may include extra scribble added for elaboration. Five Diagrams are clearly recognizable as containing geometric figures (rectangles, ovals, triangles and diagonal and square crosses). Children require little external motivation to practise drawing these repetitive forms; the will to draw and paint is intrinsic and to be found both in the act of creation itself as well as in the final result. Perhaps one reason why certain figures are so readily and repetitively produced is that they are inherently simple and pleasing shapes, capable of minimal yet endless modification.

The next type of pattern that Kellogg found was 'Combines'. These are combinations of two or more Diagrams brought together in a number of ways, for example by being placed side by side, overlapping or one Diagram enclosing another. Between the age of three to four years, 'Aggregates' (three or more Diagrams drawn together) appear. Behind Kellog's terminology lies the simple fact that with age the child both draws and prefers more complex configurations of essentially simply elements.

The drawing of 'Mandalas' is, for Kellogg, a key stage in the emergence of representational images from abstract patterns. This balanced, stable form often consists of a cross within a circle, although elaboration on this basic theme is common. 'Suns', appearing at around the age of four, are similar in shape to Mandalas, but possess single lines that extend beyond the perimeter of the central unit. Elaboration within a Sun often represents the child's first attempt at drawing a face or human figures. However, before the child devotes a larger amount of drawing time to these human images, one further type of pattern was found to emerge in the drawing repertoire. 'Radials', a combination of crossing straight lines, are typically attempted at around the age of three years, but only successully drawn at five years. Although Kellogg does not discuss why successfully-drawn Radials appear so late, one hypothesis is that a higher level of motor and perceptual co-ordination is needed to draw the lines of equal length in a number of horizontal, vertical and oblique orientations, all of which must intersect at a single point.

The transformation of Suns into faces and then into complete human figures is discussed more fully by Kellogg (1979). The transition from patterns to representational drawing is not, however, a fixed boundary line over which the child will never return. Rather, as Figure 12.1 shows, patterns drawn at the age of two to three years contain elements that reappear when faces and humans occupy a greater part of the child's effort. These early elements include small circular and other shapes within enclosed units that are destined to return as facial detail. Similarly, the single strokes emerging from these units can justifiably be claimed to be early attempts at arms and legs, even though the child may not choose to name the complete drawing as a human. It is the manner in which these strokes become fewer and placed in certain typical positions around the central body (or head-body unit) that has lead to the conclusion that they are early attempts at limbs.

A classificatory scheme like Kellogg's is interesting but there are at least two problems with it. First, although Kellogg's work centres on the classification of qualitatively different patterns, she presents no evidence to show that her classification system is either correct or indeed the only one possible. It may well be that, for example, Combines and Aggregates are not qualitatively distinct forms of pattern, but rather merely different types of a similar pattern. The second criticism, brought forward by Gardner (1980), is related to this first point. Although Kellogg describes drawing and painting development in terms of classes of symbols, she also fails to present evidence that children are actually using higher-order concepts (such as that represented by the term Mandala) when they draw. As such, Kellogg may be attributing a greater level of cognitive development than the child is in fact demonstrating. Finally, Kellogg's account remains a descriptive one, and developmental psychology has concerned itself with understanding and explaining developmental change, rather than merely recording it.

Drawing rules and strategies

Kellogg's work focused on the content of the drawings and their meaning but this has proved a difficult line of enquiry because of the problems in knowing what a child intends by the drawing, and to what extent the aims for the drawing were formulated when it began. These are not issues that can be easily answered by questioning children and they do not lend themselves to experiments. An alternative approach to the study of drawing development is to ask specific questions about underlying skills and abilities and to control strictly the experimental environment so that these skills may be rigorously examined.

When studying the development of drawing skills, it is advantageous to ask children to reproduce abstract designs or figures set by the experimenter, rather than of the child's own choice. One reason for this approach is that, by noting carefully how children of different ages actually go about copying a range of set figures, one can hypothesize about the *strategies* or *rules* that are being employed in this non-representational drawing task. We are thus concentrating on *how* the child draws, rather than *what* is drawn, and can go on to note whether drawing strategies change with age or with the nature of the drawing task.

One study exemplifying this approach is that of Goodnow and Levine (1973). This study drew an analogy between the development of linguistic and graphic skills, where the latter is controlled by a 'grammar of action' in the form of drawing rules. The authors asked groups of children aged between four and seven years, as well as a group of adults, to reproduce a series of 15 simple geometric figures. Each of these stimuli (see Figure 12.2 adapted from Goodnow and Levine, 1973) remained in view whilst it was being drawn.

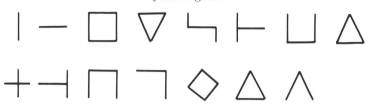

12.2   Geometric figures for children and adults to copy.

Goodnow and Levine invoked a number of 'rules' to describe the order and sequence of individually drawn strokes. There were two types of drawing rule: 'Starting Rules' (i.e. start at the *top* of a figure, at the *left* or with a *vertical*) and 'Progression Rules' (draw all verticals *top-to-bottom*, horizontals *left-to-right* or drawn with a continuous line or *thread*). As can be seen, not all of these rules could apply to each of the 15 stimuli in Figure 12.2, and conflict between drawing rules could occur where the use of one rule was incompatible with another. For example, Figure 12.3 shows one possible drawing path taken when drawing a square, and the drawing rules that this path employs. This shows that for this particular copy, two out of each of the three Starting and Progression Rules were employed, with neither the vertical start nor the thread rule being used.

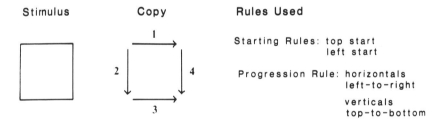

12.3   Path taken in drawing a square and the rules employed.

How does the use of drawing rules change with age? It was found that with increasing age there was more use of four of the six rules, until by adulthood the top and left start, and top-to-bottom and left-to-right rules were being employed in over 80 per cent of individual reproductions. This increasingly consistent use of rules with age was seen as reflecting a higher level of organizational and planning ability that is also to be found in other areas of the child's cognitive development, for example that of language. It has been found (Goodnow, 1977) that these drawing rules possess different inherent strengths, and are susceptible to the external influence of script direction in a particular culture. For example, Arab children of nursery school age drew a single horizontal line from left to right on 75 per cent of occasions. Once these children were formally exposed to the native right-to-left script, however, the direction of drawing single horizontal lines reversed to 70 per cent right-to-left. This finding neatly demonstrates how an analysis of simple drawing 'rules' can reveal just how the young child goes about executing simple graphic tasks.

The way in which children draw more complex figures than those shown in Figure 12.2 confirms the higher level of organization and planning of older children. For example, when older children within the range six to nine-years-old made mistakes in drawing complex figures, they tended to do so in a regularized manner by omitting the lines that do not form a central part of the figure (i.e. the lines that make the least number of joins). Similarly, even when a figure was correctly drawn these 'least attached' lines were left until the last part of the reproduction. The six-year-olds, however, displayed neither of these effects, organizing and executing their drawings in a less structured, more haphazard manner. This finding confirms that certain types of drawing are to some degree planned before commencement.

Is there any evidence of strategy and planning in young children's representational drawings, for example of humans? This area of research has been looked at in detail by Norman Freeman, and is reviewed in his 1980 book. One of Freeman's studies typifies the method he used to examine the development of representational skills. The subject matter of the study was the phenomenon of 'tadpole' humans, which are very commonly drawn by pre-school children. Figure 12.4 shows typical tadpole figures.

Why do these drawings appear perfectly satisfactory to the child artist, but decidedly strange to the adult onlooker? Both of the tadpoles given in Figure 12.4 have legs and arms extending from a central circular shape. Freeman decided to investigate what this central shape represented for the young artist. Does the child really believe that humans look like this, or is this strange form due to specific problems the child is experiencing with the drawing task itself? If the central unit represents the head, then a trunk has been omitted and the

12.4   'Tadpole' drawings of people.

arms and legs placed, as a matter of expediency, on the head. Conversely, the central shape may represent an undifferentiated head/body amalgam that includes the facial features. Freeman hypothesized that these two options could be tested by asking children who spontaneously drew tadpoles to complete the unfishished drawings of humans given in Figure 12.5. The relative size of the head to the body was systematically varied across the five stimuli. If tadpole drawers truly believed arms were to be drawn onto heads, then they should draw like this regardless of the size of the head in relation to the body.

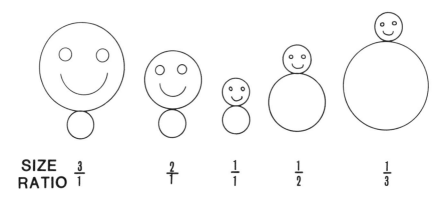

SIZE $\frac{3}{1}$ $\frac{2}{1}$ $\frac{1}{1}$ $\frac{1}{2}$ $\frac{1}{3}$
RATIO

12.5 'Tadpole' figures varying in proportions of head to body.

The results from this study did not resolve the question posed. It was found that tadpole drawers tended to add the arms to whichever was the larger of the head or body segments. What, then, can we conclude about the significance of tadpole humans in the artistic endeavours of children? According to Howard Gardner (1980), the central amorphous shape is seen as initially forming the child's early attempts at the human figure, and as something from which to 'hang' the various limbs and in which to draw the critical facial details. With time and practice, however, this head/trunk unit is seen as inadequate for the task in hand. Eventually it is separated out into the individual components of head and trunk, onto which arms and legs can be more accurately placed and drawn in greater detail.

Drawing in relation to other processes of thinking

How does the development of drawing, as we have described it in this chapter, relate to other mental skills? This more global analysis has been attempted by Howard Gardner and his co-workers at Harvard University's Project Zero. Their analysis is based on observations of children's activity in a number of 'symbolic media', such as language, drawing, building with clay or blocks, music, gesture and dance, symbolic play and the use of number. Gardner and Wolf (1983) examined the development of a number of *symbolic skills*, both in terms of features unique to each skill and in the ways in which developmental paths may be common across skills.

They suggest there are four stages in the development of symbolic skills in drawing, and that these stages can be found across several domains of children's activities. These stages reflect the preoccupation of the child with some newly acquired ability in handling the world. The first stage they label as 'event or role structuring'. Here the child focuses on the roles and activities that the people around engage in. The child talks in two or three-word utterances about events and roles e.g. 'Mummy makes cake'. In drawing the main importance may be the very fact of engaging in that activity: 'the child is drawing' and it may not matter much what or how.

The second stage is referred to as 'qualitative or topological mapping' and occurs at the age of about three. It is marked in the area of drawing skills by the first recognizable attempts at human representation, as Kellogg has noted. The preoccupation is with physical similarities between objects, which Gardner and Wolf suggest becomes almost a fetish at this age. Children find meaningful shapes and figures in all manner of random patterns such as branches that look like aeroplanes. In drawing, the marks on the paper now all stand for something or somebody. Missing at this stage, however, is any precise concept of quality. Although drawings of people will often have such peripheral features as fingers, far too many (or few) fingers will be drawn. It is as if it is sufficient that the child knows that fingers are to be included: how many is an irrelevancy. 'Quantitative or digital mapping' is the following stage at about the age of four. It is mainly characterized by greater accuracy, particularly with numbers. However the stage is marked generally by a literalness and compulsiveness which in a drawing of someone running, for example, makes it more important to get the number of limbs right than try to depict the movement.

The fourth stage is called 'notional symbolization' and centres on ways in which children of five or six devise their own notations to help them accomplish a task. Some children were found to spontaneously make marks on a piece of paper to try to help themselves remember a tune, which they were going to have to recall a week later. Drawings may also be used to help unfold a story or to relive a past event.

Through the approach of Gardner and Wolf we can begin to see some of the functions that drawing has for the developing child's intellectual skills. The study of children's drawing clearly illustrates one feature that is fundamental to a whole variety of mental abilities. This is the way in which children's thinking and expression become progressively more complex and differentiated, but this greater complexity is built on the combination of simple elements that have been practised at an earlier stage.

Further reading

GARDNER, H. (1980) *Artful Scribbles*. London: Jill Norman.
A thorough attempt to assess different approaches to the study of children's art. Contains a number of insightful examples from the drawings of children.
GOODNOW, J. J. (1977) *Children's Drawing*. London: Fontana.
An excellent introductory text, though it is in need of some updating now.

Discussion topics

- What are the main principles that characterize the way children's thinking develops as suggested in this, and other chapters?
- What are the strengths and weaknesses of different approaches to studying the development of children's drawing ability?

PART III

The personal domain

Introduction

The previous two sections of this book have examined the way children interact with the world about them, the increasing sophistication of these interactions, and how these interactions foster the development of the child's abilities through active experience.

In this section we aim to look at the individual child and consider such things as what makes children differ, how they perceive and interpret their experiences, and how they express themselves.

This section illustrates the forces shaping the character and personality of different children. Broadly these influences are either 'biological' or 'environmental' although the first chapter in the section (Chapter 13) argues that there is a third factor related to self-determination. That is to say, the character of children is not just shaped by outside influences, for which they are simply passive recipients, but is also shaped from the inside by the interpretation and meaning which is put on external experiences and through the choice and preference for gaining some experiences and rejecting others. This is not to suggest that the mechanisms behind choosing and selecting particular kinds of experience could not ultimately be explained in terms of other biological and environmental influences, but it does serve to emphasize that the developing child actively participates in the formation of individual personality through selection of experience.

Some aspects of the environmental 'data' from which children develop their character and outlook are illustrated in Chapter 14. From the mosaic of information about the characteristics of each sex and society's stereotypes of sex differences, the child can acquire an identity based on being a 'boy' or a 'girl'. As ever, this is a complex process involving perception, imitation, trial and testing, assessment of reactions and satisfaction (or otherwise) with the effects achieved. Chapter 14 describes the environment of sex stereotypes and attributions surrounding children. However, one should note that while this provides an interesting description of the climate for development, the description is sometimes based only on the researcher's own impression and insight. This can be misleading unless that impression is typical of interpretations generally. The effects on individual children will depend on their subjective perception and interpretation of these outside forces. Adopting a gender identity is not a passive process in which the child has an appropriate identity thrust upon him or her, simply according to the way he or she is treated. We saw this aspect in Chapter 4 in the way children reacted to the categorizations of 'black' and 'white' that are placed on them and the effects this had for self-esteem. Individual children differ in whether they find being a 'boy' or a 'girl' satisfactory and there is often a fusion of various aspects of each identity (as suggested at the end of Chapter 14) in a way which is not always possible with racial identity.

Chapters 15 and 16 illustrate the contribution of biological influences, in particular to the variations in intelligence and personality found in different children. These chapters explore some of the ways in which an individual's development can be abnormal and the consequences for their abilities and personal characteristics.

Finally in this section, we take a brief look at the ways in which children express themselves through play. We discover that play can serve a variety of functions such as exploration, manipulation, rehearsal, practice and the expression of fantasies and other ideas. These different purposes are found in different episodes of play, though children may concentrate more on a particular function of play at a particular time in their lives. Fantasy play, for example, may be more important when there are social and emotional crises in a child's life. However, there is little evidence of any developmental progression in the purposes for which play is used and the functions it serves. Rather, play incorporates the interests and preoccupations of children to explore, predict and control their environment and other people throughout their development. It is also a universal activity of children found in all cultures when children have free time to express their own inner worlds.

Methods of research in the personal domain

The study of individual characteristics and personality poses interesting problems for research which might be borne in mind while reading the chapters of this section. In essence one is moving from looking at the average or typical response to looking at the range and variation between individuals. There have been two classic methods for doing this which are described in Chapter 13. One method assumes that individuals have the same character- istics but differ in the strength or amount of that characteristic which they possess. So we all have 'intelligence' but we may differ in the amount. Individuals can then be compared relative to other individuals. The other approach suggests that individuals differ qualitatively in having particular characteristics which make them unique. These two approaches lead to rather different ideas about the nature of individuality and the best methods for assessing it, as described in Chapter 13. The one method favours standardized tests where people's responses can be precisely graded relative to others; the other favours an open-ended search for the characteristics that typify the individual's manner of handling experiences. This method depends heavily on individuals' verbal insights into themselves, which brings us to another methodological point.

It is the interpretation of experience, rather than the environment itself which is important in influencing individual attitudes and behaviour. This is why the description of the environment as seen by a researcher is of only limited interest: even if it were objective and free from personal biases, it would not tell us how the environment is perceived and interpreted by particular individuals, which is what influences them. Much of what we can learn about individual experiences has to be through verbal reports. Verbal reports yield data that cannot usually be obtained by other means but they pose certain methodological difficulties which have to be overcome. First, adults, let alone children, cannot always monitor their own experiences or be conscious of the ways in which experiences were processed internally. Secondly, their reports may be distorted accidently because, for example, they cannot find the right words to express what they mean or feel; or because memory for distant or trivial events may be inaccurate: or the reports may be deliberately distorted because they wish to give a particular (more desirable) impression of themselves. For these reasons verbal reports, especially from children who are easily biased by suggestions from adults, have to be collected using skilled and experienced interviewing. This involves, among other things, setting the right context for the interview, establishing a good relationship with the interviewee, and asking questions in an appropriate way. As far as possible, corroborating evidence should be sought in different parts of the verbal report or in behaviour, and the topics approached by various lines of questioning to control the influence of the interviewer and check the reliability of the account. Given proper attention to these points, it is possible to conduct meaningful interviews with children as young as three (Gelman and others, 1983).

CHAPTER THIRTEEN

Individual differences and the development of personality
John R. Hegarty

The fact of individual differences

There are over 50 million people in the United Kingdom. One might imagine that, purely on the basis of chance, one might find at least two who were identical in character, ability and temperament. However, I think it likely that such a search would fail. There are no two individuals who are psychologically identical. Even identical twins, who appear to share the same genetic make-up, begin to differ psychologically as they grow older. And if we were to look to a larger number of people to find two who were psychologically the same–perhaps to the population of the world–I think that we would find greater diversity, not less, as the effects of a wider genetic pool and of greater cultural diversity were brought into play.

For disciplines that study people (medicine, biology, anthropology, sociology as well as psychology) the fact that each one of us is unique is both exciting and depressing. Exciting because it suggests a tremendous richness of subject matter but depressing because it complicates any search for general principles and laws.

In this chapter, I want to stress the fact of individual differences. I shall look at some of the forces which give rise to individuality and shape our personality. Finally, I shall describe two of the ways in which psychologists have tried to understand the growth of individuality.

What determines individuality?

While the whole of this chapter has a bearing on this question, I would like to tackle the issue explicitly now.

(i) *Biological factors*

It is likely that individual differences are, quite simply, a universal fact of nature. An article by Sir Peter Medawar entitled, 'The Uniqueness of the Individual' (Medawar, 1957) considered exactly this question in relation to the difficulty surgeons faced in making skin grafts. Medawar noted that it was quite straightforward to graft skin from one part of an individual to another but not from one individual to another. Individuals appeared to be immunologically unique. Medawar suggested that it is biologically advantageous to a species to encourage diversity amongst its members for the greater this diversity the greater the likelihood of some individuals adapting to radical changes in environment and thus continuing the species.

The diversity Medawar is referring to stems from diversity in genetic information within a species. This diversity in genetics might also give rise to diversity in temperament and other psychological processes, in which case one might expect human infants to show marked individual differences in temperament in the first few months of life and for these to persist into later life.

An interesting study by American psychologists Thomas, Chess and Birch (1970) appears to bear this out. They were interested to find out how far infants as young as two to three months of age would display a characteristic individual temperament and how far this would remain with them as they grew older. They developed a method for rating the babies' behavioural characteristics (for example, level of motor activity, response to a new object or person, general mood, degree of distractibility) and proceeded to study a number of babies using the method. Babies did indeed show marked individual differences on these variables, as they had expected. They then followed the children over a period of 14 years, observing them periodically at home and school and interviewing their parents and teachers. Their general findings were that,

> Children do show distinct individuality in temperament in the first weeks of life, independently of their parents' handling or personality style [and] the original characteristics of temperament tend to persist in most children over the years.
>
> (Thomas, *et al.*, 1970, p. 352)

This study suggests that individual differences in temperament are marked, even in infancy when the mind has had few environmental influences. The origins of such temperamental variations between individuals must be largely genetic, although variations in the infant's uterine environment will have a part to play.

It was at one time fashionable to debate the relative influence of 'heredity' and 'environment' in the formation of personality and ability. This will be described in more detail in Chapter 19. We now realize that the two influences interact in complex ways to form personality. We have innate tendencies towards particular patterns of feeling and thought, which life-experiences facilitate or inhibit the expression of. Animal studies, which cannot be directly extrapolated to people (as argued in Chapter 18) but which are nevertheless suggestive, show more clearly some of the hereditary influences on behaviour. One example is the breeding of dogs. Modern domestic dogs have the wolf as a common ancestor and yet it has been possible to breed dogs with a tendency towards specific behavioural traits. Retrievers are easier to train as gundogs; collies for working sheep. In the psychological literature, a well-known study by Broadhurst (1960) showed how a tendency towards responding anxiously to fear-provoking stimuli could be bred into a strain of rats. Over ten generations, two strains were produced. Members of one strain showed high anxiety in the presence of bright lights and noise while the individual members of the other strain were markedly less anxious. The results of the study show that the least anxious individual in the 'highly anxious' group was nevertheless more anxious than any of the other group. Even so, it is interesting to note that there was still considerable individual variation in behaviour among the individuals in each group, despite the in-breeding, which is a common finding in other in-breeding studies. Some other examples of the influences of heredity on behaviour can be found in later chapters. (See chapters 16 and 19).

(ii) *The influence of the environment*

Whatever the strength of hereditary influences on our behaviour and personality, environmental effects are clearly extremely important. Many psychological studies exist which document the effects on the developing personality of an individual's sex, his social class, the cultural traditions into which he is born and the specific ways in which his parents and others relate to him. Some of these are described in other chapters (e.g. the chapters on Psychosexual Development and Social Communication). Here I would like to give one further example of the way early life-experiences may form personality and persist through much of the individual's life, until a personal crisis forces the individual to appraise, and perhaps change their habits of feeling, thought and behaviour. This example is the pioneering work of Lawrence LeShan (1977), a psychotherapist who has worked extensively with adult cancer sufferers. His work is interesting and it has practical significance, but for our purposes here it illustrates the influence of environment on the developing personality.

LeShan worked with cancer patients over many hours, interviewing them and listening to their accounts of their early life and current worries and concerns. This method of gaining data in psychology has advantages and disadvantages compared to carrying out experiments or observing naturally occurring behaviour. Because the interviews are unstructured and free-ranging, they lose something in terms of rigorous scientific control. The interviewer is not a passive observer and recorder of the person he is studying but actively engages in discovering their ideas and emotions. The method thereby gains in subtlety, complexity and depth of understanding. It allows people to express themselves in their own way and emphasizes what they believe to be important for them. For some problems it is the only way to investigate complex inner beliefs and feelings, although often it is used as a preliminary method of investigation to generate hypotheses which are later verified by more rigorous and objective methods. A recurring theme in the interviews was that many cancer patients had experienced a loss of their 'reason for being'; this loss of their sense of purpose in life had often pre-dated the first noted symptoms of cancer. A second theme was the frequent inability of his clients to express anger or resentment before and after cancer symptoms appeared.

LeShan was tempted to believe that these personality characteristics had something to do with the onset of the cancer. A comparison of cancer sufferers and a control group of people without cancer showed a markedly higher incidence of these two aspects of personality in the cancer group. But what had caused people to lose their sense of purpose in life and why should they not want to express anger? LeShan studied the emotional life history of his clients and an explanation began to emerge. In 76 per cent of all the cancer patients he studied (and in 95 per cent of those undergoing intensive psychotherapy) but in only 10 per cent of non-cancer control patients, LeShan found a typical emotional life-history. It had three parts: first, a childhood or adolescence marked by feelings of isolation caused by the experience of painful personal relationships, perhaps with parents; second, the experience, later in life, of a secure and meaningful relationship which seemed to bring great happiness and a meaning in life; and, third, a sense of utter despair when that relationship was lost. Sometime after that third phase, the first symptoms of cancer would be noticed.

Whether this personality pattern predisposes an individual towards cancer cannot easily be proven to the satisfaction of all workers in this field. Nor can it be proved that the personality pattern LeShan has found is not the individual's inevitable destiny, given their particular pattern of genes. For LeShan and for others who have found a similar pattern, however, it is early life-experiences which establish the individual's personality, making them emotionally vulnerable to later stress. These experiences are not, however, immutable; LeShan describes how some of his clients found a will to live and conquered their disease in the course of psychotherapy.

(iii) *Self-determination and individuality*

Man's individuality is not, however, caused solely by his biological nature and by the vagaries of his life-experiences. Rather, I believe that individuals have a measure of free will which allows them to make decisions and choices in their life. This is a principle underlying psychotherapy, that an individual's autonomy may be strengthened within a relationship between therapist and client so that he can make meaningful choices in his life without feeling forced to feel and do certain things by outside pressures. The work of LeShan described above is to do with exactly this. Another example from my own use of psychotherapy shows the power of self-determination.

A young woman, aged 30, had suffered from a progressive skin complaint since the age of 14. It meant that her skin had hardened progressively over most of her body so that she could not walk and was disfigured (although her face and the backs of her hands were largely unaffected). When I visited her, she spoke of having nothing to live for. She was dependent on her ageing parents for her personal needs and was confined to bed on account of her severely ulcerated feet and contracted muscles. She told me that the doctors had told her that the condition would heal of its own accord and that *all she could do was wait* (I believe this statement to be highly significant) for this to happen. My concern was that Anne had no belief that she could help herself. Indeed, she had not been encouraged to do anything for herself. My view was that she should come to believe that she had power within herself to change her life and her condition and my counselling was aimed at that. I suggested she practise daily meditation and relaxation exercises, since these appear to strengthen self-resolve, and that she begin to set herself personal goals. I met with her weekly at first and at longer intervals thereafter to encourage her in meditation and goal-setting.

The remarkable thing (even when one believes in such an approach) is that within three months Anne's ulcerated feet had healed sufficiently for her to be able to walk on them. Within six months she had begun to go out, was no longer dependent on others for her physical needs and, at the time of writing, lives a normal life, even though her basic skin disease remains unchanged.

I think it important to realize that the role of the counsellor or therapist in this case, and in many others, is not to 'treat' the condition but to assist in the individual's self-treatment. Anne improved, in my view, as a direct result of her own hard work and by the exercise of her will. Environmental pressures had combined to suppress her will, giving rise eventually to depression and hopelessness. Thus one sees the possible deleterious effects on personality of relationships and life events as well as the optimizing effects of other relationships and experiences. Environment serves to enhance or inhibit the individual's autonomy and will.

Individual differences and psychology

Psychologists recognise that individual differences exist and that they are extensive, but they do not agree on how best to regard them as part of a scientific study of the mind.

Broadly, there are two schools of thought on this matter. One school favours the measurement of human characteristics using tests of various kinds on large numbers of people in order to obtain representative data for the general population. In order to facilitate the description of common trends, statistical techniques have been used. In such studies, the individual only matters insofar as he contributes to the data of a group of people. One individual is considered unrepresentative of 'people in general' so that results from single individuals would be disregarded. Individual variation is only of interest in terms of how close or far it is from the average. Individuals are described relative to other individuals rather than in terms of their own particular characteristics. This is known as the 'nomothetic approach'.

There are others, espousing an 'idiographic' approach to the study of Man, who believe that a valid study of human beings can be gained only by recognizing individuality. Reducing people to statistics and obscuring individual differences in group trends, they would argue, deprives human beings of their person-hood. An idiographic approach would seek to understand and highlight the uniqueness of individuals, not to minimize it.

Neither of these approaches is more correct than the other and one is not right and the other wrong. They are merely different. The nomothetic approach has strengths when one wishes to make general statements about defined groups of people; an example would be the use of psychological tests to assist in the diagnosis and remediation of developmental handicaps in children (see Chapter 16). Here one needs to know what is the average ability of a particular age group of children to assess whether a particular child is falling substantially below what can be considered normal. The idiographic approach helps us to understand people as individuals and it helps us to work with individuals if they wish to make changes in their life, as happens with those who seek psychotherapy. Even so, there is not one idiographic approach within psychology but many. Each approach tries to help us in understanding the way an individual's particular personality has developed, though different approaches emphasize different factors in the formation and growth of personality. We can show this in two brief examples.

Sigmund Freud's (1856–1939) theory stressed that the major force in shaping personality was the manner in which early conflicts and tensions were resolved. Freud considered the most important conflicts involved, on the one hand, instinctive urges to seek pleasure and immediate gratification of needs such as hunger, warmth, physical and bodily comfort. These instincts he located in part of the primitive, unsocialized mind he called the 'id'. These instinctive urges are in conflict, on the other hand, with the constraints of other people (parents, social norms) and the limitations of the environment to supply and gratify these needs, for example, the availability of food, the time and patience of a parent to cuddle a baby. The developing child internalizes these external constraints and restrictions as the 'super-ego'. Both the id and the super-ego were thought by Freud to be mainly unconscious. The role of mediating and reconciling the demands of the id and the constraints of the super-ego was the function of the conscious mind, which Freud termed the 'ego'. The way in which these three components of our minds function and the extent to which a balance is achieved, gives rise to particular personalities.

When the opposing forces of the id and the super-ego cannot be reconciled, the individual experiences anxiety which the ego tries to find ways of reducing. The mechanisms adopted by the ego to reduce anxiety may produce patterns of thought and behaviour which are maladaptive in the long term and give rise to particular aspects of personality such as obsessions, phobias or psychosomatic illnesses.

A contrasting explanation of some of the factors shaping individual personalities is provided by the humanistic approach of Carl Rogers. For Freud, the individual's personality is shaped by experiences of early childhood and forces that are largely outside awareness and individual control. Carl Rogers (1902–) takes the view that everyone is born with the capacity to develop into a psychologically healthy human being, believing in themselves, open to new experiences, rational, taking responsibility and having the potential for good personal relationships with others. Individual personality arises from the manner in which each of us conceives of ourself and interprets our experiences of reality, together with the ways in which we seek to develop and enhance our experiences. The optimum conditions for personal growth arise when the individual's relationships with others, from early childhood onwards, show positive regard and are accepting and unrejecting. Rogers believes that individuals need positive regard from others to grow and mature, which leads them to desire acceptance and love from other important figures in their lives. To the extent that this acceptance is conditional (say, on being clean, or not being aggressive) then the person's view of themselves is restricted and qualified so that their view of themselves as worthy and competent may be diminished.

Personal growth in children or adults can be assisted by 'counselling', the term used to describe Rogerian psychotherapy. The task of the counsellor or therapist is not to analyse, diagnose or treat, as in the Freudian approach, but to accept the individual as a person in his own right, to value him as a person, and to encourage him to regard himself in the same light. As the person succeeds in becoming psychologically mature (and autonomous), anxiety and distress disappear, to be replaced by inner confidence and sensations of harmony.

Conclusions

It seems reasonable to suppose, as I have argued, that individuals are indeed individuals. It appears not at all controversial that this uniqueness arises out of our genetic constitution and out of the vagaries of life's experiences. It is probably not surprising, either, that different psychologists have adopted different stances in viewing people. What, then, is being stressed in this chapter?

First, I feel it important that one does not *ignore* the fact that people are individuals.

Second, I think it important that psychology has something to say about the origins of that individuality. A study of biological and environmental factors on personality is, therefore, important. It is also necessary to encourage the formulation of contrasting models or paradigms which offer descriptions and explanations of *individual* psychological processes; the ideas and findings of Freud and Rogers are good examples of such contrasting models.

Third, I think that psychology should have something to offer each individual who wants to change; this necessitates methods of study that will discern the idiosyncratic nature of individuals and methods of therapy flexible enough to be effective with each individual.

Further reading

MACKAY, D. (1975) *Clinical Psychology: Theory and Therapy*. London: Methuen.
    A short and readable account of clinical approaches within psychology that contains a fuller description of Freudian and Rogerian approaches to the individual.

Discussion topics

● The reader might like, as an exercise, to review their life and note what influences (genetic, environmental, or arising from self-will) appear to have shaped their personality. Does this 'self analysis' throw any light on the actual influence of these three factors in determining personality?
● Is it possible, through psychotherapy or any other means, to change an individual's personality?

CHAPTER FOURTEEN

Psychosexual development
Helen J. Graham

You may have better things to do on a Sunday than ponder the riddle of whether or not Joan of Arc was really a man. Yet this is precisely the question that was posed to readers of the *Observer*, on 20 September 1981. Moreover, it was revealed that for Robert Greenblatt, Emeritus Professor of Endocrinology at the Medical College of Georgia, this was no matter for idle speculation but the subject of lengthy and painstaking research.

Greenblatt's investigations have led him to the conclusion that Joan of Arc was affected by a rare condition known as 'Testicular Feminization'. This syndrome is one of a number of sexual anomalies in which there is an incongruity between the genetic sex of an individual and the sexual identity suggested by the appearance of the external genitals at birth. These individuals are termed pseudo-hermaphrodites.

Testicular Feminization arises as a result of abnormal foetal development in a genetic male. In the course of normal foetal development the sexual organs of the male develop in response to the hormone testosterone. Some male foetuses, however, have an insensitivity to this hormone, which is thought to be because of a genetic defect. Consequently in these foetuses the penis fails to develop, and the testes remain in the abdominal cavity so that at birth these individuals have the physical appearance of a female. Subsequently, the individual develops like a female, usually proving to be most attractive, with good skin and complexion and well-developed breasts, but having no uterus they cannot menstruate or bear children.

Greenblatt's theory that Joan of Arc was affected thus, if correct, would mean in effect that the Maid of Orleans, genetically speaking, was a man. Greenblatt is reported as claiming that given this possibility

> It is perhaps easier to understand her eccentricities, her derring-do, impetuosity, fearlessness, utter self-confidence, her tendency to cross-dress, and her religious zeal and avowed virginity.

> (Greenblatt in the *Observer*, 20 September 1981)

144

Perhaps . . . On the other hand, it is altogether simpler and much less eccentric, albeit somewhat dull, to accept, as most people have throughout history, that Joan of Arc was female. Why, therefore, should Greenblatt seek to do otherwise. The answer that suggests itself would seem to be that Greenblatt finds the behavioural traits manifested by Joan of Arc inexplicable in a woman, but not in a man; arguably a view almost as archaic as Joan herself.

Gender attributions

Traditionally it has been assumed that males and females differ not only physically but also behaviourally and psychologically, and that such differences are biologically determined and innate, and thus 'natural'. Accordingly, characteristics such as emotionality, passivity, nurturance, caring, fickleness, irrationality and the like, have been deemed to be 'feminine' traits, and viewed as the consequences of femaleness. While 'masculine' traits such as aggressiveness, dynamism, rationality, bravery and independence have been deemed to be the consequences of maleness, in other words, as facts of biology. Thus when psychologists began to study psychological factors relevant to sexual development they also focused on the ways in which males and females differ behaviourally, cognitively and emotionally, ignoring to a great extent similarities between the sexes, and also the wide diversity of behaviour in members of the same sex. Indeed Hutt (1972), having reviewed the research on psychosexual development, concluded that 'The evidence strongly suggests that at the outset males and females are wired up differently' (p. 18).

During the past ten years or so, however, a major shift was discernible in much psychological thinking when it began to be recognized that many characteristics, which comprise masculinity and femininity, are socially constructed stereotypes rather than features intrinsic to males and females, and they are independent to a great extent of biological sex (although there are exceptions as described in Chapter 22). Ironically, much of the change in attitude arose from the study of sexual anomalies of the kind that concerned Greenblatt. Money, Hampson and Hampson (1957) concluded, on the basis of studies of matched pairs of pseudo-hermaphrodites who were of the same genetic sex but had been assigned to different sexes at birth, that psychosexual identity is established more in accordance with the sex in which the individual is reared than on biological sex. Thus they argued that social conditioning appears to be a far stronger determinant of psychosexual identity than biology. Money and Tucker (1977) restated this argument on the basis of further research, and claimed that human beings are 'wired, but not programmed for gender' and that the expression of their potentialities is determined less by biological factors than environmental influences. Subsequently, Money and Ehrhardt (1972) reviewing the clinical data on a number of sexual anomalies found the evidence to be consistent with this conclusion, and noted that individuals affected with the syndrome of Testicular Feminization were found to have a high preference for the feminine role and to be fully content with it. Money and Ehrhardt thus went on to suggest that the effects of social learning on psychosexual identity are so powerful that the social influences of early childhood can shape, and even reverse the biological contributions to gender.

Evidence for their claims was provided as the result of bizarre and tragic circumstances involving a set of identical male twins, one of whom had his penis almost completely excised as the result of a surgical accident whilst undergoing circumcision. The medical opinion was that this boy would be able to function more adequately as a female than as a disabled male, and consequently the child was reassigned as a female at the age of seventeen months; a decision that involved the surgical removal of the testes, construction of a vaginal opening and canal, and sustained hormone treatment. This child and its twin have been studied extensively throughout childhood and reported on by Money and Ehrhardt (1972), and Money (1974) who claim that the 'female' twin is fully adjusted to her psychosexual identity, and that this provides strong evidence that most of the components of what are considered to be biologically determined sex differences are socially conditioned, and that reversal of sex is possible if it takes place early enough and subsequent rearing is consistent. These claims were made on the basis of evidence available prior to the onset of puberty in these children, and observations made subsequently have cast some doubt on Money's conclusions. Nevertheless, despite considerable medical, psychological and ethical controversy surrounding the issue, this and related research has served to indicate the importance of social factors in the development of psychosexual identity, as a result of which it is widely accepted that masculinity and femininity are largely learned behaviours. Thus in most recent psychological literature the term sex is reserved for the biological contribution to psychosexual development, whilst the term gender is used to denote the socially determined or learned aspects.

Social factors in gender development

The process of social conditioning is set in motion at birth. Money and Ehrhardt (1972) claim that the assignment of a child to one or other sex on the basis of the appearance of its sex organs at birth activates a whole set of responses in others which differ quite dramatically depending on whether the child is classified as male or female. Moreover, they point out that the difference in response is one of the most universal and pervasive aspects of human social interaction.

Adams and Laurikietis (1976) have likened the process to a recipe which goes much as follows: take any newly born baby, any race any colour, assign it a sex, then dress it in pink, give it a doll, encourage its passivity, don't expect too much of it, protect it, teach it about 'femininity', encourage its incompetence, discourage its independence, instruct it in domesticity and subservience. This, they claim, will produce a 'real' woman. Whereas, if a 'real' man is required, take the baby as instructed above, but dress it in blue, give it a toy gun, encourage its activity, expect a hell of a lot from it, make it independent, make it protect itself, encourage its confidence and assertiveness, and train it to earn a living. This recipe works, not because it is natural and inviolable, but because it is known to all and passed on from generation to generation thus ensuring that everyone learns what are the limits of appropriate and permissable behaviour for individuals who have been categorized as members of a given sex.

Given that these limits define what might be thought of as 'sex roles', it is appropriate to think of the process by which individuals learn their gender identity in theatrical, or dramaturgical, terms. This analogy brings out several aspects of the process.

Casting

In the theatre, roles are most usually allocated or 'cast' on the basis of the physical attributes of the actors, and the performance demanded by the roles scripted in advance, this being the 'play'. The casting of roles thus give rise to certain responses in the production team and other members of the cast, who have expectations as to how any given part should be played. Similarly, at birth when an individual is assigned to his or her sex role this sets in motion responses in parents and others. It is often not realized that the sex assigned to the child is the first cue others have as to how to behave in relation to it. As Money and Ehrhardt (1972) have pointed out a baby is never simply that, but a baby-boy or baby-girl and despite minimal differences between them at birth, parents treat them differently according to sex. Research has demonstrated that mothers look and talk more to their infant girls than to their boys from the first to the twelfth week of life (Lewis, 1972). During the first three months of life, but not thereafter, boys are touched, kissed and cuddled more than girls but after the age of six months, girls are encouraged to touch and remain nearer to their mothers than boys, who are encouraged to play at a distance, and to be more active and curious in their play. Moreover, there is a clear difference in the toys offered to boys and girls (Rheingold and Cook, 1975), boys being given significantly more vehicles such as cars and aeroplanes and girls significantly more female dolls, and boys being provided with objects that encourage activities away from the home, while girls are given objects that encourage activities directed to the home and caring for children.

The script

On being allocated a role in a play one is usually also provided with a script, or written copy of the play. The manner in which children absorb their gender roles seems to be in some ways similar, in that gender differences pervade the mass media and even the language children learn. Individuals are acutely sensitive to information regarding their roles and appropriate behaviours, and they pick up cues in conscious and unconscious ways. For the most part they are unaware of learning the script, and others are not necessarily aware of teaching it, or prompting. Hence their belief that the ensuing performances are 'natural' rather than learned. Yet these ways of acting are learned from parents, teachers and the society as a whole.

(i) *Language*

Beattie (1979; 1980) has drawn attention to the extent to which everyday language reflects sex stereotypes. He argues that ordinary language has a very strong sex bias, and that these linguistic biases have enormous psychological and social significance, and are especially powerful because they are both widespread and inconspicuous. He points to the different uses of terms such as man, woman, lady, gentleman, boy and girl, which appear to be simple male-female equivalents but in common usage are not.

The term 'men' is by far the most common for males, the term 'boy' being used almost exclusively for the male child and signifies immaturity and lack of status. Hence its derogatory connotations when used to refer to adult males in the American South and elsewhere. The term 'girl' however is frequently substituted for 'woman' in contexts where 'boy' would not appear for man. Osgood and others (1975) found that across twenty-three different language groups, the word 'girl' is perceived as being more positively evaluated than 'woman' but far less potent, being highly stereotyped predominantly in respect of physical qualities such as smallness, beauty, prettiness, and loveliness, but also traits such as weakness and dependence. The term 'woman', however, elicits responses of maturity and unattractiveness, and whereas a boy greatly increases his status when he becomes a man, a girl loses status on becoming a woman. Lakoff (1975) also points out that whereas the term 'gentleman' is rarely used except on toilet doors, the term 'lady' is very commonly applied to women. Lakoff suggests that the term is in fact a euphemism for woman and is resorted to because the concept woman requires ennobling as it lacks inherent dignity of its own. Hancock (1963) has demonstrated that the less status and dignity a woman has, the more her status is likely to be enhanced by recourse to the term 'lady', hence 'cleaning ladies', 'char ladies' and 'serving ladies'.

(ii) *Stereotypes in the mass media*

Many studies have documented the existence of sex stereotypes in children's picture books, textbooks, comics, television programmes, films, advertising and magazine fiction. Thus, Adams and Laurikietis (1976) point out that in fairy tales lovely maidens and princesses abound, all young, beautiful, dependent and incredibly dim, waiting for some handsome, brave, dashing prince or knight to rescue them. The storyline is beauty = youth = success (equivalent with marriage). This constitutes 'romance', after which life effectively ends, albeit continuing happily ever after. Any woman demonstrating the slightest intelligence or independence is by definition old, and either a hag, harridan, spinster, witch or stepmother. Women who are not stereotypically submissive, cowardly and dull are invariably depicted as being odd, or queer (e.g. 'George' in Enid Blyton's 'Famous Five'). Men, by comparison, come in only two forms–good and fantastic–and it goes almost without saying that they are all brave, brainy, strong and handsome. These myths are perpetuated in comics, in Hollywood productions such as 'Star Wars', 'Superman' and 'Flash Gordon', and in romantic fiction and popular magazines. Heeley (1983) points to the insidious implications of this genre by drawing attention to the cult of violence which pervades contemporary boys' comics, both in their content and form. He suggests that these help to inculcate a particular definition of violence, 'one which sees it as normal, natural and inevitable, the fate of the enemy, and the lot of weak and the poor' (p. 18).

Even textbooks portray different images of adult males and females. Males are shown as jobholders *and* fathers, while females are shown as jobholders *or* mothers (Unger, 1980). Moreover, women in children's textbooks are rarely depicted in roles outside the home. Adams and Laurikietis (1976) point to books from which generations of British children have learned to read, the 'Ladybird' series. Once again the message is clear: e.g. 'Peter has to help Daddy with the car. Jane has to help in the house'.

Of course, it is not sufficient merely to demonstrate that stereotypes exist in the communications media, it is necessary to show that children are affected by them. Studies by Deutsch (1975) and Jennings (1975) have shown that even pre-school children are aware of sex stereotypes in stories, and there is also evidence (DeFleur, 1964) that children learn about their roles in society from media content.

Similarly, many studies of children's television (see Dohrmann, 1975) have shown that children accept and imitate what they see on television, and various studies confirm the power of sex-role stereotyping on children's behaviour and attitudes. Recent analyses of sex role portrayals in a variety of programmes suggest that by emphasizing the domesticity of women and the independence of men, television provides role models that reinforce sex stereotypes, which define femininity in passive-dependent terms and masculinity in active-masterful terms and serve to enhance the male image and diminish that of the female.

A review of television advertising by Busby (1975) reveals that women are predominantly depicted in domestic situations, as dependent on men, as sex objects or household functionaries. Men are significantly more likely to be shown outdoors and in business settings, and men over the age of fifty outnumber women by a factor of two. Similarly, 87 per cent of all adverts using voice-overs employed male voices. Indeed throughout the media men greatly outnumber women, being depicted, particularly in 'soap operas', as powerful, violent and smart, while women tend to be either sex objects or domestic functionaries. Unger (1980) concludes on the basis of research into media stereotypes that sex-role stereotypes may be characterized as stable constructs that reappear in every context, in all age groups, and across a wide variety of situations. Thus, to return to the theatrical analogy, it would appear that the psychosexual 'script' is very easily absorbed from the social environment even in early childhood. Nevertheless, knowing the script is not the same as enacting a part. How then does the child learn to play its gender role?

Role playing

While there are many different ways in which an actor might interpret any role, even within the theatre, there are frequently constraints that restrict the individual to certain kinds of performance. Those performances that have received wide critical acclaim tend to be held up as 'classic' or standards against which all others are judged (e.g. Olivier's Hamlet). Young actors thus tend to imitate these models. Similarly, children learn how to play their gender roles through imitation, and their performances are maintained by reinforcement contingencies in the immediate environment, that is, by being rewarded for appropriate sex-stereotypical traits, and punished for inappropriate behaviours. Green (1974) points out that imitation of gender roles involves two processes: identification with members of the same sex, and complementation of members of the opposite sex. Theoretically, therefore, the two models for gender-role development are provided within the nuclear family. Green argues that where a role model of either sex is absent, or present but passive, the child will tend to identify with the dominant parent. Thus where the male model is absent the male child will identify with the mother rather than complement her. Green suggests this could, under certain circumstances, lead to the development of effeminate behaviours and failure to respond appropriately to other females. The absence of the male model may also affect girls in that they have no role to complement, which may give rise to later difficulties in relating to males. However, even where a male parent is absent, it is relatively unusual for a child to have no exposure to male models in the form of older siblings, relatives, neighbours and teachers, or via the television.

If, however, a child is to identify with members of the same sex and complement those of the opposite sex it is essential that it can discriminate one from the other. One of the first ways it learns to do so and thus to discriminate gender, is through dress. Indeed, this discrimination is regarded as so fundamental to cognitive and social development that intelligence tests invariably include this sort of discrimination item.

Costume

Costume, or dress, has a dual function, as any actor knows. On the one hand it helps the audience to identify the role of the wearer, and as such it can be extremely precise. In theatre, great attention is paid to costume because it is realized that if it is not correct the audience will not be convinced by the role. Similarly, dress or costume helps to identify social roles and determines to a large extent the way others respond to a person. From the point of view of the observer it is very convenient as it indicates the kind of response appropriate to that person. The other aspect of costume is that it also gives the wearer a sense of identity. This aspect is often ignored by psychologists but by comparison, actors have always been aware of the importance of costume in the successful playing of a role. Many actors, most notably Sir Laurence Olivier, claim that they commence to learn their part 'from the outside in', gaining the 'feel' of the role from their costumes.

Dress thus has important psychological significance. Where roles are well-defined such that very different patterns of behaviour are expected of them, this is reflected in different forms of dress. Girls' clothes tend to emphasize the wearer's uselessness, delicacy and vulnerability, whereas boys' clothes emphasize the wearer's strength and dynamism. Moreover, these character-istics are reflected in the names given to clothes – Wranglers for 'men', 'Tuf' boots, 'sweat' shirts. Thus, while one cannot too easily climb a tree or change a car tyre in a party dress and open-toed sandals, so in the functional garb of the male it is difficult to look decorative. Consequently, it is difficult for the female, dressed in a traditionally 'feminine' manner, to express the practical side of her nature, or for a male in 'masculine' attire to express the aesthetic side of his. In spite of almost twenty years of 'unisex' patterns of dress, sex-typed differences in dress are very often maintained by parents, and insisted on in many schools and work situations.

Equipped therefore with a detailed script, role models, costume, and prompters in the wings, the child learns to perform its primary role in society. Rehearsals during childhood provide feedback on the acceptability or otherwise of the performance, and subsequently the audience adds its praise or condemnation, cat-calling and hissing, and declaring as 'queer' those who fail to play their parts acceptably, and applauding those who meet with their approval. Thus it is that each of us develops our psychosexual identity.

With this in mind, therefore, we can now return to Joan of Arc. How are we to view her under the spotlight of this dramatic analogy? All the evidence on the development of psychosexual identity would seem to suggest that Joan of Arc, whether afflicted by the syndrome of Testicular Feminization or not, would have developed a female identity and experienced herself as feminine to the extent that her rearing and socialization were consistent with that of a female. That is not to say, however, that she, or indeed other women throughout history, necessarily accepted the limits imposed thereby, for as Oscar Wilde observed: 'Most men and women are forced to perform parts for which they have no qualifications . . . the world is a stage, but the play is badly cast' (The Picture of Dorian Gray). Casting solely on the basis of physical attributes would ensure that most people fail to develop their full potential and to develop as fully balanced persons. In recognition of this Bem (1972) introduced the concept of androgyny. Androgyny refers to the coexistence of 'masculinity' and 'femininity' in the same person. Bem pointed out that many people not only appear to be androgynous, but even think of themselves as such. Such evidence as is available (Bem, 1975) appears to suggest that androgynous individuals are more functionally adaptive than traditionally sex-typed individuals, and thus androgyny is increasingly being claimed as a model for well-being.

Further reading

ARCHER, G. and LLOYD, B. (1982) *Sex and Gender.* Harmondsworth: Penguin.
     An uptodate and fairly comprehensive evaluation of biological and social contributions to gender development.
UNGER, R.K. (1980) *Female and Male: Psychological perspectives.* Harper and Row.
     An excellent review of mainly American research about gender development with a feminist perspective.

Discussion topics

- How appropriate and useful is the theatrical metaphor to understanding psychosexual development?
- How, if at all, might the breakdown of the family influence psychosexual development?

CHAPTER FIFTEEN

Abnormal personality development
Andrew B. Hill

In this chapter three main points will be discussed. First, what is meant by the term 'abnormal' in the description of people? Secondly, we will examine some important distinctions in the use of the term 'abnormal'. Finally an account will be given of two major types of abnormal personality development.

The nature of abnormality

The term 'abnormal', taken literally, means 'away from the norm', that is, away from what is usual or common. Thus when the term is used it implies a deviation in some respect(s). When applied to people, or to features of a person, the term is usually taken as having perjorative connotations and its meaning is not always clear. Actually the term 'abnormal' does not necessarily carry implications of negative evaluation. To say a child has developed an abnormal level of intelligence is not necessarily to assert something bad or undesirable. It would be quite as abnormal for a child to have an IQ of 180 or an IQ of 20. Both are substantial deviations from the norm of 100 which is the average level of intelligence. However, the *particular nature* of the abnormality may carry implications of undesirability. Given the choice of having their child's IQ boosted to 180 or reduced to 20 most parents would choose the former as more desirable because a very high IQ would be more useful to the child than a very low one.

But if what is meant by the term 'abnormal' is a deviation from the norm, two questions arise immediately. First, which norms are being referred to and second, how substantial must a deviation be before it is considered as truly 'away from the norm'?

Social and psychological norms

If it is said that a child has an abnormal personality it is quite reasonable to ask how this conclusion was arrived at. One response to this question might be that the child's behaviour, including speech and apparent emotional reactions, have been observed in a variety of situations either at first hand (by literal observation) or at second hand through talking with the child and examining responses on formal measures of personality. From observations of behaviour, inferences may be drawn about personality. If the child is ultimately considered to be abnormal in personality this is presumably a conclusion based upon observations that his behaviour is, at least in some respects, abnormal, and here lies a pitfall for the unwary. The behaviour may be abnormal in the sense that it represents a deviation from *social* rather than psychological norms, yet it does not seem wise or desirable to consider social deviancy as necessarily indicating psychological abnormality. In the West we rightly condemn Eastern Bloc countries where people who display social and political attitudes at variance with government policy are detained in mental hospitals on the grounds that they are suffering a psychiatric disorder. Yet some forms or degrees of deviation from social norms of behaviour might reasonably be said to reflect psychological abnormality. How, therefore, can a decision be made as to whether a deviant behaviour is merely socially deviant with no implication of psychological abnormality, or whether it truly reflects psychological abnormality?

Any piece of behaviour is the end product of a good many psychological and physiological processes and the most important of the psychological processes are those of perception, learning, memory, emotion, motivation, thought and intellectual abilities. Deviations from the normal (i.e. usual and adaptive functioning) of these processes represent deviations from psychological norms and such deviations define psychological abnormality. If a particular piece of behaviour results from functioning in one or more of these basic processes that deviates appreciably from the psychological norm, it would be considered as psychologically abnormal whether or not it was also socially abnormal.

An example may help to make the distinction between social and psychological abnormality clearer. A child who steals a toy, but who has learned the conventional moral value that stealing is wrong and who shows no appreciable deviation from normal levels of psychological functioning, is abnormal only in the social sense. The child has departed from social norms of conduct (as discussed in Chapter 5). However, if the child had not been able to learn that stealing was wrong despite adequate opportunities to learn and despite having been punished in the past for stealing, then this deficiency in ability to learn would indicate that the stealing behaviour is a result of psychological abnormality.

Notice that the question of culpability (i.e. blame) comes into the distinction between social and psychological normality. It can be argued that the child who is merely socially deviant cannot be excused his deviant behaviour on psychological grounds while the child who is socially deviant as a result of a psychological abnormality may be so excused, though the psychological abnormality must be clearly relevant to the behaviour.

Personal and interpersonal norms of psychological functioning

When considering deviations from psychological norms a further useful distinction can be made between deviation from the child's own *personal norms* and deviation from *interpersonal norms*. An example may clarify the distinction. Roger is a seven-year-old boy of good intelligence, normally of calm and placid disposition who is usually independent, sociable and cooperative but who is going through an *episode* of crying and clinging to mother. He refuses to go to school and starts to wet the bed again after being dry at night since the age of four. Roger is clearly showing *regressive signs* in his behaviour (i.e. behaviour appropriate to a much younger child) and these suggest not merely that he is unhappy but that he has departed in dysfunctional ways from his own personal norms of psychological functioning. He now clings where before he was independent, he cries though formerly he was emotionally calm and placid and he is nocturnally enuretic after being dry for three years.

Now consider Gerald, another seven-year-old who, since he was a baby has been anxious in many situations where he was away from his mother, has always tended to cling to mother and shown little inclination or capacity to try to cope with any novel situation on his own. Gerald is not going through an episode where his psychological functioning has departed from his own personal norms, he has always been very timid, anxious and dependent. Rather he has consistently shown a deviation from *interpersonal norms* in that he has consistently deviated from the usual levels of anxiety and dependence shown by most children of the same age and has deviated in personally unhelpful or maladaptive ways.

Having discussed the first question raised earlier concerning the types of norm from which an individual may deviate, we can now use the idea of psychological norms, both personal and interpersonal, to examine how sizeable deviations have to be before they are considered abnormal. This relates to the different ways in which children can exhibit abnormality. There are at least two important distinctions which can be made here based on Foulds (1976) work.

The first distinction involves whether the abnormality is a deviation from personal or interpersonal norms. Psychiatric disorders can appear as short-term episodes during which an individual exhibits signs of disturbance (blushing, stammering, trembling in social situations, lack of eye contact during conversations) or symptoms of distress. At other periods of his life, he does not show these signs. Thus, signs and symptoms represent deviations from the individual's normal psychological and physiological functioning, that is deviations from personal norms.

Other individuals show deviation from interpersonal norms in terms of having extreme positions on personality traits and attitudes. This type of abnormality involves a continuing and relatively constant disorder.

A second important distinction involves the extent to which the individual can cope. Deviations are said to be maladaptive if they impair the individual's happiness and ability to cope with the demands of everyday life. Foulds, for instance, distinguishes two types of deviation from interpersonal norms. If the deviation is manageable either by the individual himself or by parents or indeed society, Foulds calls this a *maladjusted personality*. If the deviation is so great as not to be manageable by the individual or his family or society, and requires treatment, Foulds considers it to exemplify a *personality disorder*.

While Foulds' view is interesting and potentially useful it has certain weaknesses. First, he takes a rather narrow view of personality by defining it only in terms of traits and attitudes, and secondly he does not allow for the fact that deviations in psychological functioning from personal norms can be of the same nature and severity (though not duration) as in personality disorders that are deviations from interpersonal norms. For example, Roger's anxiety levels during his episode of disorder can be of the same nature and severity as Gerald's, though Gerald's anxiety has been long lived and Roger's has not.

Examples of abnormal personality development

Personality is, of course, still developing in children and it is often not possible to diagnose specific forms of abnormal personality in the early years of life, for example psychopathic personality in which wrongdoing does not seem to be associated with feelings of guilt. However, personality can obviously develop abnormally in children even if specific forms cannot be diagnosed reliably. In the remainder of this chapter an account will be given of two major psychiatric disorders that clearly reflect abnormal personality development, and which tend to be present from a very early age and have rather poor prognoses. These are Infantile Autism and the Hyperkinetic Syndrome.

Infantile autism

Infantile autism is a psychotic disorder which fortunately is quite rare, appearing in only about 0.02 per cent of children. It is often detectable at birth and always becomes apparent before the child attains the age of 30 months. Indeed it must be evident by this age for the diagnosis to be made. There are three major features in addition to age of onset which define the condition. These are: (i) a particular kind of failure to develop social relationships, (ii) a particular kind of impairment in language development, and (iii) a very marked dislike of change in the environment with a tendency to enage in routines and 'ritual' repetitive behaviours. In the psychiatric literature this is referred to as an 'insistence on sameness'.

(i) *Impaired development of social relationships*

Children who develop normally form strong attachments to the adults who take care of them, usually the mother and father. They enjoy being picked up and cuddled and run to the accustomed caretaker adult for comfort and protection when they are hurt or frightened. Autistic children do not form attachment bonds of this sort. They do not show a welcoming response to being picked up and cuddled and may as babies react aversively to this, crying and arching away from the adult who picks them up. They tend to approach strangers as readily as parents or their usual caretakers but do not readily approach adults or other children much at all. They appear as aloof and largely uninterested in forming social relationships. When of an age where cooperative play with other children would be seen in the normally developing child (see Chapter 5) this is clearly absent or poorly developed in the autistic child, and they generally prefer to play on their own with toys or other inanimate playthings. They seldom make friends with other children although they may, as time passes, develop a more affectionate relationship with their parents. A particularly striking feature of the autistic child is that he or she does not use eye contact with others in the way the normally developing child does. Overall autistic children seem rather self-contained and lacking in the warmth and emotional responsiveness of the normal child.

(ii) *Imparments in language development*

Michael Rutter, who is one of the foremost authorities on infantile autism in Britain, regards the language impairments and associated cognitive deficits of the autistic child as being the core feature of the condition. Autistic children show a marked delay in the acquisition of speech and about half never acquire speech capabilities that allow them to communicte adequately for day-to-day living. Those who do develop useful speech by the age of five years have a very much better chance of outgrowing their autistic disorder and adjusting more or less normally to life as adults. From the time at which speech begins to develop towards the end of the first year of life, autistic children often show abnormalities. They frequently display oddities in the sound pattern of pre-speech babble and usually do not use gestures as an accompaniment to attempts at speech to the same extent as normal children.

If speech does develop, the autistic child shows a curious tendency to reverse personal pronouns such that sentences which refer to self tend to start with 'you' rather than 'I' (e.g. 'You go to school' rather than 'I go to school'). This appears to be related to another curious feature of the speech of autistic children, namely echolalia. This is a tendency to repeat back sometimes immediately, sometimes after the passage of a few minutes, hours or even days, phrases that have been spoken to the child. Just as production of speech tends to be impaired so does comprehension. In fact, if anything, comprehension tends to be more impaired than production. The autistic child typically has difficulty in understanding what is said, particularly if sentences are complex, that is, contain more than one idea.

The language deficits of the autistic child are almost certainly a function of impairments in particular cognitive processes. Contrary to a rather early view taken of infantile autism, which considered autistic children to have normal, or even superior, levels of general intellectual abilities (intelligence), it now seems clear that about three quarters of all autistic children show some degree of mental retardation. However, children in the other quarter do not necessarily display a better development of language and the cause of the language deficits cannot be wholly ascribed to general mental retardation. The memory capabilities of autistic children are very interesting because they appear normal in some respects but distinctly impaired in others. Immediate memory for sounds (e.g. memory for digits spoken aloud at the rate of about one per second) is generally about as well developed as in normal children, but longer term memory for words, which requires words to be encoded into memory in terms of their meaning, shows a quite marked deficit.

(iii) *Insistence on sameness*

The dislike of change in familiar surroundings, activities, diet, even clothing is very pronounced in autistic children. They seem to like routine and almost welcome sameness or monotony in their experience. Much of their behaviour has a stereotype quality with a good deal of repetition of the same activity. They tend to be fond of collecting things and often become attached to objects that will be carried around by the child wherever he goes. Removal of these objects or interruption of repetitive play routines is likely to provoke a substantial tantrum in the child. Of course normally developing children respond with bad temper or aggression to frustration induced by removing favourite toys, but the attachment to inanimate objects shown by autistic children seems appreciably stronger than that of normal children, and it is tempting to speculate that this attachment serves some of the purposes that attachments to people serve in normal children. That is, inanimate objects seem to provide emotional satisfactions for the autistic child of the sort provided by people in the case of normal children. However, this is a speculation which goes well beyond available evidence.

The course of the disorder and outcome in infantile autism
It was once thought that infantile autism was not a specific syndrome of disorder but that it existed as a form of childhood schizophrenia. This is no

longer accepted and it is currently believed to be a form of abnormal development in its own right. Unlike schizophrenia, which tends to show periods of remission and relapse, autism is a continuing disorder. This is not to say that it never remits. In fact about a sixth of all autistic children improve to the extent that they can lead relatively normal, independent, lives. A further sixth, perhaps slightly more, improve quite materially but do not develop fully normal social and linguistic competencies and continue to require sheltered and protective conditions of living to some extent. Unfortunately, about six in every ten autistic children, on average, do not outgrow their psychological problems and never become adequately adjusted in a normal fashion to the demands of daily living, and so require special care either by parents or by an institution. The best indicators of whether an autistic child is likely to develop normal modes of functioning are first, level of intelligence and, secondly, the possession of useful speech by the age of five. It has been found that of children who do not have useful speech at five years of age, only between 3 per cent and 20 per cent will go on to develop adequate speech by mid-teenage. Similarly, the prognosis is poor for autistic children with IQs below 70 (approximately three quarters of autistic children) and especially poor if the IQ is below 50.

Cause and treatment

The cause of infantile autism is, as yet, unknown. There are some indications that the condition may be associated with damage to the brain, especially in autistic children who are also mentally handicapped. There is also some evidence of genetic involvement though autism is definitely not simply the result of genetic factors. The electrical activity of the brain revealed in electroencephalograms (EEGs) is sometimes abnormal, though not invariably so, and the abnormalities are not found to be of a consistent type from one research study to the next.

One interesting research finding has been that autistic children seem to have highly selective attentional processes. That is, they attend to one particular feature or group of features in the environment and appear to 'filter out' a good deal of the stimulation impinging upon them. This may go some way towards explaining their difficulty in understanding language. If they filter out a lot of stimulation then perhaps insufficient attention is paid to speech for understanding to develop. In turn, this possibility would be consistent with the impairments of memory for material that requires semantic encoding. However, this is merely speculation and in any event does not explain why the autistic child has such selective attentional processes.

Medical treatment in the form of drugs has proved of little value in the treatment of infantile autism. Rather more success has been obtained with psychological treatments, particularly those involving the use of operant training procedures. Operant training usually involves the selective use of rewards to develop a particular behaviour. For example, an autistic child may be trained to engage in spontaneous speech to a greater extent by providing a valued reward immediately after the child speaks. Initially the reward may be given after every occasion the child speaks, even if only a single word or sound is made. The reward acts to reinforce the response of speaking, that is, make it more likely the child will speak spontaneously in the future. Later a partial reinforcement schedule may be used. In this the reward is given intermittently rather than after every single utterance. Partial reinforcement schedules have the advantage of establishing behavioural responses that are more durable, that is, the response tends not to be 'forgotten' easily. An interesting review of psychological techniqes and their effectiveness can be found in an article by Margolies (1977), but sadly it must be concluded that, at present,* the abnormalities in personality development apparent in autistic children remain very difficult to remedy.

The Hyperkinetic Syndrome (Attentional Deficit Syndrome)

This childhood disorder is known in Britain as hyperkinesis (or more formally, the 'Hyperkinetic Syndrome') while in the USA it has become known as Attentional Deficit Syndrome. More than almost any other psychiatric disorder of childhood, hyperkinesis has stirred up controversy about its *prevalence* (i.e. the number of children in the population who display the disorder). In the UK one large-scale study found clear evidence of the hyperkinetic syndrome in only about 0.01 per cent of children while studies in European countries and the USA have found between 5 per cent and 20 per cent of children show the disorder. The wide discrepancy in prevalence rates can almost certainly be attributed to the use of rather lax diagnostic criteria, particularly in America. A great many normal children appear from time to time, or even for most of the time, to be behaviourally overactive but do *not* show other central features of the hyperkinetic syndrome, and are thus not properly to be considered as suffering psychiatric disorder. The condition appears much more frequently in boys than in girls; estimates of sex prevalence suggest somewhere between four and nine boys display the disorder for every one girl. Like autism, the Hyperkinetic Syndrome is not, strickly speaking classified as a personality disorder, but also like autism it may reasonably be thought of as reflecting abnormalities in personality development. The reasons for this are that it appears at a very early age, tends not to be episodic in nature, involves disturbance in development of important psychological functions and is frequently associated with (i.e. seems often to be a precursor of) genuine personality disorders in adult life–particularly psychopathic personality in men and hysterical personality in women.

Major clinical features

There are four 'core' features of the Hyperkinetic Syndrome. First, the children display *behavioural overactivity*. As babies, and indeed later in childhood, hyperkinetic children seem to sleep less than is normal and they are fidgety, over-talkative and generally inclined to display a great deal of energy. It is often claimed they are 'always on the go' but some research has questioned whether the hyperkinetic child is actually more active than normal. Suggestions have been made that it is overactivity of an aimless, rather than purposeful, sort which characterizes the hyperkinetic child. Second, hyperkinetic children are very *distractible*. Their attention span is very short and they appear unable to concentrate on a particular activity for any length of time. They seem to daydream and are easily distracted by events irrelevant to a task in which they might be engaged. Thirdly, hyperkinetic children are inclined to be very *impulsive* and do things on the spur of the moment without a thought for possible dangers that might follow from an action. For example, a non-swimmer might jump into the deep end of a swimming pool with no thought of how he would manage to get out. In speech, hyperkinetic children are likely to blurt out embarassing statements or say things with a degree of tactlessness inappropriate to their age. Finally, hyperkinetic children tend to be very *excitable*. They have a low tolerance of frustration and often show temper tantrums of some ferocity. It is interesting that distractibility, excitability and impulsiveness are all, in more moderate degrees, components of the normal personality trait of extraversion, but it would be quite incorrect to consider that hyperkinetic children are simply excessively extraverted.

Academic attainment and intelligence

Almost always hyperkinetic children have academic difficulties at school. At one time it was thought this was likely to be due to generally low levels of intellectual abilities. But it now seems from more recent research that, although hyperkinetic children do generally have lower IQs than normal children, their academic attainment levels are usually below those expected for normal children of the same IQ. In other words, it appears that the academic difficulties are specific deficits which cannot be wholly accounted for by deficiencies in general intelligence. The reasons for the difficulties hyperkinetic children have in learning at school are not clear but they may be a function of the difficulty they have in concentrating and sustaining attention on tasks for any length of time. However, there are some suggestions of neurological impairment, which possibly could account for the academic difficulties, though this seems unlikely as the weight of evidence is not great, and where neurological impairments are found they tend to be of a variety of types rather than being consistently of one sort.

Course of the disorder and prognosis

To some appreciable extent the course of the hyperkinetic syndrome shows a change over time in its major features. As babies it is the overactivity features that predominate. At the toddling stage, while overactivity continues to be evident, the attentional difficulties become more obvious. Later, during the early and middle school years, the focus often becomes problems in academic learning, though in quite a few cases aggressive, uncooperative and generally antisocial behaviour begin to emerge as central features. However, it should be emphasized that not all hyperkinetic children show antisocial conduct. In adolesence, antisocial conduct and educational retardation become the dominant features and behavioural overactivity tends to lessen, though during this period a number of hyperkinetic children begin to show features of depression and low self-esteem.

The prognosis for hyperkinesis is generally poor, and adults who suffered from hyperkinesis as children tend to be appreciably more susceptible to psychotic disorders and also show more antisocial and aggressive tendencies than adults who did not suffer hyperkinesis as children.

There seems also to be something of a link between hyperkinesis in childhood and later psychopathic personality in adult life. One study found almost 40 per cent of hyperkinetic children later received the diagnosis of psychopathic personality. However, psychopathy is notoriously difficult to diagnose reliably and one must take this finding with some caution.

Causes and treatment

Like autism, the causes of the hyperkinetic syndrome are, as yet, unknown. There is some evidence of a genetic component and children born to fathers suffering psychopathic personality disorder or displaying alcoholism, show an increased risk of suffering hyperkinetic syndrome. But the disorder is definitely not wholly genetic. A number of studies have provided evidence that the hyperkinetic child tends to 'seek stimulation' and this has been interpreted as suggesting they suffer low levels of 'non-specific arousal' in the central nervous system. Such a suggestion is, to a limited extent, consistent with electroencephalographic (EEG) studies, which have tended to find that about a third to a half of hyperkinetic children have abnormal EEGs, with the most common type of abnormality being an excess of slow wave activity. This type of abnormality would be expected if the children were under-aroused neurophysiologically. However, this still leaves a half to two-thirds of hyperkinetic children with no abnormal EEGs. Thus it might be safer to conclude that hyperkinesis is not a unitary disorder, but that there may be several varieties of it, only one of which is associated with low arousal.

Perhaps the most striking support for the under-arousal theory comes from studies of treatment. About two-thirds to three-quarters of hyperkinetic children show improvement in their condition when treated with stimulant drugs (methylphenidate or dextroamphetamine). This type of treatment does not cure the condition because when the drugs are discontinued the problems re-emerge, and in fact this treatment has given rise to much of the controversy surrounding the hyperkinetic syndrome. Antidepressant medication is effective in a proportion of cases particularly with adolescents, but this type of therapy also fails to provide a lasting cure.

Psychological, and particularly behavioural, treatments have met with some success. A behavioural treatment called 'time out' has sometimes proved helpful in reducing the frequency of temper tantrums and aggressive behaviour in hyperkinetic children. 'Time out' simply involves removing the child from the (usually social) situation in which the tantrum or aggression has occurred and leaving him/her alone in another room for up to ten minutes. This has the effect of removing the child from social stimulation that might reinforce the undesirable behaviour. If carried out consistently the lack of reinforcement brings about a weakening of the tantrum behaviour because responses that are not reinforced tend to 'extinguish'. The use of 'time out' has recently become controversial on ethical grounds and many British psychologists now refuse to use it. For more information on behavioural treatments, the interested reader is referred to papers by Mash and Dalby (1978) and Loney (1980). But psychological treatments have not proved more effective than drug treatments and they too fail to effect a lasting cure though they can provide temporary improvement.

Further reading

MORRIS, R. J. and KRATOCHWILL, T. R. (1983) *The practice of child therapy.* New York: Pergamon.
This gives an account of a variety of different treatment methods, including those used for the disorders discussed in this chapter.
RUTTER, M. and HERSOV, L. (Eds) (1977) *Child Psychiatry: Modern Approaches.* Oxford: Blackwell.
Those interested in making a more detailed study of abnormalities of child development will find this a useful reference book.

Discussion topics

● In what ways is a child with an abnormal personality more than just a child who is considered socially unacceptable?
● What are some of the ways in which development can become abnormal?

CHAPTER SIXTEEN

Abnormal development leading to mental handicap
Nigel Beasley

As explained already in this section (Chapter 13) it is widely recognized that biological and environmental factors play a part in the development of the individual. They also play a part in the development of abnormalities.

The biological contribution to mental handicap

Each of us begins life as a single fertilized cell. This cell contains all the information necessary for the development of a single cell into a human being. Such information is contained in 23 pairs of chromosomes. Twenty-two of the pairs are common to both sexes, but the twenty-third pair differs between the sexes, females having two similar looking X chromosomes and men having an X and a much shorter Y chromosome. During the course of development, copies of these chromosomes will be included in each of the trillions of cells that are produced. The chromosomes contain the basic units of heredity known as genes: every chromosome contains many thousands of them. The single cell at the beginning of life divides and redivides with each division doubling the number of cells. The genes provide the information, in a manner that is not yet understood, for cells to differentiate to produce the extremely complex physical bodies that we have.

The information given in the genes is our biological heredity. The ovum and the sperm each contain one-half of the chromosomes of the mother and father. Different ova or sperms produced by an individual receive different combinations of chromosomes, and which sperm will unite with which ovum to produce a new individual is a matter of chance.

Chance combinations of genes, and damage to chromosomes during the process of biological development, sometimes leads to malformation. Much of the severe mental handicap in children and adults is caused by such harmful genes and aberrant chromosomes.

Harmful genes

Harmful genes that produce mental handicap may be either dominant or recessive. A dominant gene means that the abnormality will always manifest itself when that gene is present. It can be transmitted by either one of the parents and it will appear in half the children on average, as demonstrated in Figure 16.1. (Remember that the pair of chromosomes in the parents' reproductive cells split, and each parent contributes one to the offspring, who thus ends up with a pair of their own.)

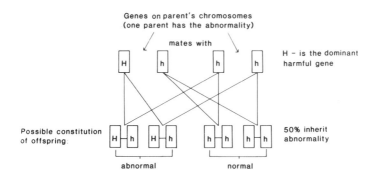

16.1   A dominant harmful gene (H) causes abnormality in 50 per cent of the children on average from these parents.

One example is called Epiloia which gives rise to tuber-like nodules in the brain. The incidence of this gene is estimated to be about one in 30,000. The effect is usually to produce severe mental handicap, but because the relationship between brain anatomy and mental functioning is not a simple, straightforward one the handicap may not appear for a number of years or may go unnoticed. Another condition produced by a dominant gene is Neurofibromatosis, which is more common in that one in 3000 of the population may be affected. It gives rise to disorder characterized by the formation of nerve tumours and the growth of such tumours in the brain may lead to mental handicap. Because this depends on the location and size of such tumours, only ten per cent of people with the gene are mentally retarded to any degree. We can see from these examples an important point, that mental retardation does not follow automatically from the mere presence of a particular gene abnormality.

Conditions caused by recessive genes which are associated with mental handicap are far more common than dominant gene conditions, because the carriers of harmful recessive genes are not necessarily affected themselves and are more likely to be fertile. The effects from recessive genes only manifest themselves if they happen to combine with a similar recessive gene from the other parent. As this is more likely to happen if the parents are related and share a common ancestry, there is a higher incidence of abnormality among

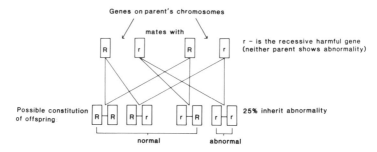

16.2   A recessive harmful gene (r) causes abnormality in 25 per cent of children, on average, if both parents are carriers of the recessive gene.

children of related parents. When both parents have the recessive gene, there is a one in four risk of the child inheriting the gene in duplicate, as shown in Figure 16.2.

Phenylketonuria is an example of a condition caused by recessive genes. The incidence is approximately one in 14,000 babies. The genes give rise to a metabolic malfunction due to the absence of a specific enzyme in the liver. This in turn leads to brain damage. However the condition can be detected in early infancy and a special diet can prevent brain damage.

Some harmful recessive genes are located on the X chromosomes and so their effect is different for each sex and there are two X chromosomes in females but only one in males. A male with this type of harmful gene would certainly be affected, whereas females with the gene on one chromosome would be carriers but would not manifest the condition unless it were also present on their other X chromosome. Therefore these conditions manifest themselves more frequently in males than in females. Haemophilia is perhaps the best known X-linked condition but it is not associated with mental-handicap. An example of X-linked abnormalities that give rise to mental handicap is Lesch-Nyhan syndrome where an enzyme deficiency leads to an accumulation of uric acid in the blood, which causes brain damage. (Note that not all recessive sex-linked genes are necessarily harmful: see Chapter 22.)

Chromosomal abnormalities

Normal development can be disrupted if there are more, or fewer, than the usual complement of 23 pairs when the ovum and sperm fertilize. Chromosomes can also become damaged so that parts are missing. Such chromosomal aberrations can lead to mental handicap, and are probably the largest cause of severe handicap. Down's Syndrome (which used to be called 'mongolism') is the most common of these conditions, found in about one-third of all severely mentally handicapped people. Normally, this condition is due to the presence of an extra chromosome identical to the normal pair 21. A small proportion of cases result from the extra chromosome being attached to another chromosome, belonging to another pair, to produce a larger combined chromosome.

There are other similar abnormalities, although they are less common, which result from the presence of an additional chromosome, or a small defect in the chromosome where part of the long or short arm is missing.

Congenital handicap of environmental origin

The birth of a child with damage to the central nervous system that will result in some kind of mental handicap can also be caused by environmental factors that impair development of the foetus in the womb. Cowie (1981) gives the following list of environmental dangers in the antenatal period:

Deficient maternal diet–animal experiments have shown that malformations of the central nervous system can occur if the pregnant mother is fed a deficient diet. Vitamins, particularly Vitamin A and vitamins of the B group, appear to be of special importance. In man, the evidence rests on carefully monitored application of some of the animal findings, and on observations following famines, some of which are reported in Chapter 20. The vitamin supplements given to mothers during pregnancy and the advice given by the primary health care team to ensure an adequate diet perhaps go beyond the conclusive scientific evidence, but the number of congenital malformations can be reduced by an adequate diet.

Irradiation–there is conclusive evidence that following the bombing of Hiroshima and Nagasaki pregnant women who were near the explosion gave birth to children with an increased incidence of defects, including mental handicap. It has been suggested that the incidence of congenital malformations might be higher in regions with greater background radiation, but the evidence is inconclusive at present.

Infection–the placental barrier provides a defence against most forms of infection but there are exceptions. It has been known for some years that the apparently mild infection from the *rubella* virus (German measles) can have catastrophic effects on the developing foetus, with the effects being particularly severe in the early weeks of pregnancy. In late 1983, a £2 million campaign to reduce the number of handicapped babies by immunizing all women against rubella was announced by the Department of Health with the active backing of the Princess of Wales. Although immunization is offered to all schoolgirls, only 83 per cent take it up and many older women are still unvaccinated. There are other viruses and parasites which can infect the mother and cause mental handicap such as toxoplasmosis, a parasitic infection acquired from eating raw and undercooked meat. In England and Wales, about one baby in 20,000 is affected but it is more common in warm areas of the world, especially among people who have much contact with animals.

Drugs–the thalidomide tragedy of the early sixties focused attention on the problem of possible harmful effects of drugs taken in pregnancy. Between 1959 and 1962 some 500 children were born in this country with limb and other deficiencies after their mothers had taken thalidomide for morning sickness during early pregnancy. More recently, the effects of nicotine and alcohol on the developing foetus have been examined. The National Child Development Study showed that maternal smoking in pregnancy resulted in a significant increase in the death-rate of infants at the time of birth, and a four-month lag in reading age at seven-years-old (Butler and Goldstein, 1973). Maternal alcoholism has resulted in infants displaying a number of abnormalities that have been termed *foetal alcohol syndrome* (Dowdell, 1981). It is not yet known how a moderate or light intake of alcohol during pregnancy affects development but the general feeling among researchers and health educators is that alcohol consumption on any one occasion should be strictly limited during pregnancy. The same kind of advice applies to all kinds of drugs: extreme caution is recommended in both prescribing and using any drug in pregnancy (Jobling, 1975). Closely related to drugs, and with similar effects, are harmful chemicals taken in food from a polluted environment.

Endocrinological factors - maternal diabetes is well-known as a potential risk to the foetus. Disorders of the thyroid and pituitary glands in a pregnant mother may also be a potential danger to her unborn child.

Blood group incompatibility - in most cases this is due to rhesus incompatibility and severe jaundice may be caused giving rise to neurological damage. Nowadays the management of rhesus incompatibility has eliminated these severe effects.

Maternal Phenylketonuria - this is primarily an environmentally induced condition in contrast to the genetically transmitted condition of phenylketonuria. The high phenylalanine level in the mother's circulation has severely damaging effects on the developing embryo.

Natal and post-natal causes

The development of the central nervous system does not stop at birth and many of the environmental factors already mentioned can operate after as well as before birth. This will be explained in more detail in Chapter 20. Difficulties and injury at birth resulting in lack of oxygen and cerebral haemmorrhage may cause mental handicap; childhood infections such as meningitis can cause severe mental and physical damage. Lead-poisoning is less of a risk now with a reduction in the number of lead water pipes and lead-based paints but lead is still put in petrol and some researchers argue that it causes a degree of mental handicap in children living in areas of concentrated motor exhaust fumes. Some children have a reaction to whooping cough vaccine but the number is small. Perhaps the most common cause of mental handicap post-natally is brain damage caused accidently, as in a car crash, or deliberately, as in the case of battered babies and children.

What is mental handicap?

The causes mentioned above that have led to damage or malfunction of the central nervous system commonly result in some degree of mental handicap. In other words, the development of the mental abilities of such children is abnormal. In Chapter 15 we read that the term 'abnormal' means 'away from the norm', away from what is usual or common. The most common method of measuring the normal pattern of mental development is by intelligence tests and the result is usually expressed in terms of an intelligence quotient. Most (68 per cent) of the population has an intelligence quotient of 100 plus or minus 15. A person is regarded as having a mental handicap if his or her intelligence quotient is less than 70. Approximately 2.5 per cent of the population have a quotient between 50 and 70 and 0.4 per cent have a quotient of less than 50.

A quotient of about 70, if it remains consistent over a number of years, means that a child is developing at about three-quarters of the normal rate. An IQ of 50 would represent a rate of development of about half the normal and so on. A child with mental handicap not only has a slower rate of development than the average; he or she also has a correspondingly lower ceiling of development approximately corresponding to say the normal 12 or 8-year-old in the above example.

In Chapter 9, the contribution of Piaget to our understanding of cognitive development was discussed. Piaget divided the course of cognitive development into four major stages. According to Piaget, there must be an invarient order in the emergence of these stages. The question then arises as to whether mentally handicapped children pass through these stages in the same order, at least to the point at which their development reaches a plateau. The answer seems to be yes: mentally handicapped children do follow the same course of development through the first two stages, although the evidence is sometimes limited. For example, a study reported by Cicchetti and Sroufe (1976) examined the relationship between cognitive and emotional development in Down's Syndrome infants living at home. Fourteen infants were examined on 30 test items, grouped into four categories–Auditory, Tactile, Social, Visual. Normal children laugh at earlier ages to tactile and auditory stimuli than to visual and social stimuli (see Chapter 3). This study aimed at examining whether the same order of development occurred in Down's children. Cichetti and Sroupe found that infants with Down's Syndrome lagged well behind the normal infants in the onset of laughter–the median age was 10 months, compared to 3–4 months for normal infants. Despite differences in onset and frequency of laughter, the order of items producing laughter was the same as for normal infants. Smiling was much more frequent than laughing with Down's Syndrome infants, but developmental changes in the categories of items eliciting smiling were parallel to those of normal infants' laughter.

Achenbach (1973) included mentally handicapped children in a study of the development of conservation to determine whether their performance would show developmental trends similar to those of normals. (Conservation was described in Chapter 9.) Sixty-one mentally handicapped children, mean IQ 47, took part in the study. The experimental tasks included:

> *Conservation of quantity* – 1.45 litres of water dyed blue was poured from a translucent jug into a 0.45 litre translucent jug. A hidden drain allowed the small jug to accept all of the liquid while being filled only half way.
>
> *Conservation of number* – two toy Indians on horseback were presented. After being asked how many there were, the child placed the Indians in an opaque box while keeping the horses as a reminder. The bottom of the box was opened releasing the original Indians plus a third Indian hidden in a false bottom.
>
> *Conservation of colour* – the child inserted five white marbles into a hole in a wood box. The box was turned around and five black marbles were emptied into the child's hands from a hole in the opposite side of the box.

The responses of the children to these situations was assessed in terms of the expression of surprise or suspicion, verbal or nonverbal, that was shown. It was predicted that surprise responses to a contrived change of colour would developmentally precede surprise responses to contrived violations of conservation of number and quantity. Achenbach found that across all levels of mental ability there was no difference in the frequency of surprise responses to colour and number. Surprise responses to both colour and number exceeded those to quantity.

Our knowledge of the cognitive development of mentally handicapped children is still incomplete, particularly of those functioning in the 2–5 year mental age range. The use of intelligence tests as a measure of mental ability can be criticized, and it is wise not to rely solely on this measure when describing the level of a person's mental development. Our behaviour is not only governed by our level of cognitive development and understanding, but by our experiences and emotions. As adults in everyday life, a measure of adaptive behaviour is perhaps more representative of our capabilities. So it is now more common to use a measure of adaptive behaviour as well as IQ in defining the degree to which an individual can meet the standards of personal independence and social responsibility expected of his or her age and cultural group.

Mental handicap in the family

The birth of a child with mental handicap comes as a tremendous shock to parents. Many writers have likened the emotions felt to those experienced on the death of someone close. It is a death of the normal child expected with its potential for life stretching out into the future; the emotions of grief and anger at this loss are frequently experienced. Such emotions are not confined to the parents as a child is born into a wider family than the nuclear unit. Grandparents, particularly, feel the loss but aunts, uncles and siblings of the parents can also have strong emotional reactions. This emotional turmoil does not make adjustment easy in the months following diagnosis. In some ways the experience is worse than death as the future is uncertain. It is not possible to say how severe the mental handicap will be. One can estimate if the child suffers from a particular syndrome but one is guessing into the future particularly if it is being done in the first two years of life. Families need a lot of support from professionals, such as doctors, nurses, psychologists, at this time but it is not easy to give, as the professionals can also experience very similar emotional reactions to the birth of a child with mental handicap (Newson and Hipgrave, 1982).

Most children with a mental handicap grow up with their families. Placing children away from the family is now not thought good for the child's development nor for the family's needs. The philosophy of care is that each handicapped person should live with his own family as long as this does not impose an undue burden on them or the child. Advice and support is needed from health, education and social services but it is important that there is collaboration between professionals and parents as the skills and resources of each are needed to aid the development of the child with mental handicap (King's Fund Centre, 1976). One such scheme for collaboration is known as the Portage model. The scheme involves weekly visits by a Home Teacher who works with the parents in deciding what skills to teach and how to teach them. The Home Teacher also shows parents how to observe and record behaviour. The basis of the teaching system is a Developmental Checklist, which lists behaviours from birth to five years of age, and a set of cards, which suggest teaching activities, to match each of the 580 behaviours on the checklist. The basic premises underlying the scheme are (Weber and others, 1975):

1   Parents care about their children and want them to attain their maximum potential.
2   Parents can, with instruction, be effective teachers of their own children.
3   Socio-economic, educational or intellectual levels of parents do not determine their willingness to teach their children nor the extent of the gains children will attain as a result of parental instruction.
4   The method suggested for teaching mentally handicapped children is the 'precision teaching method' which breaks down the task to be learnt (such as pulling on a sock) into very small steps. Each step is taught in turn and each step is mastered before proceeding to another one. For instance, by starting at the end (e.g. pulling the sock up over the ankle) and working in small steps, the precision teaching method provides ready feedback and encouragement for both children and parents.

The home-based precision teaching method has inherent educational advantages (Weber and others, 1975):

1   Learning is occurring in the parents' and child's natural environment; the problem of transferring back into the home what has been learned in the classroom does not occur.
2   There is direct and constant access to behaviour as it occurs naturally.
3   If instruction occurs in the home there is more opportunity for full family participation in the teaching process.
4   There is access to the full range of behaviours, many of which might not occur within a classroom, such as temper tantrums that are shown in the home.
5   Since the home teacher is working on a one-to-one basis with parents and child, it is possible to set individual instructional goals.

The Portage Model is an example of a positive approach to parent and professional collaboration that helps the family in caring for and adjusting to their handicapped child and gives the child a good start in its development to full potential.

Further reading

FOSS, B.M. (1966) *New Horizons in Psychology.* Harmondsworth: Penguin. Chapter 17 presents a readable, short introduction to some broad issues in the study of the psychology of backwardness and severe subnormality.
CARR, J. (1980) *Helping your handicapped child.* Harmondsworth: Penguin. This is a practical book designed for anyone who has, or who works with, mentally handicapped children. It tells you how to see what your child can or cannot do and how to break down into manageable steps what you want to teach.

Discussion topics

*   Why does development sometimes go wrong?
*   What are the consequences of mental handicap on the development of children?

CHAPTER SEVENTEEN

Play–a child's eye view
Glyn Prosser

In a chapter on play it seems appropriate to adopt a somewhat playful approach. In this vein I have chosen as headings to the different sections, quotations taken from answers given by my grand-daughter, Helen Steady (personal communication) to the question 'What do you mean by play?' The authority I attribute to her in this field is that at the time when we engaged in this scholarly discussion she was seven-years-old. Her answers were:

'Doing something you don't need to'.
'It makes me happy'.
'You want to feel grown up'.
'Not real: you want to feel like somebody else'.
'You've got nothing else to do'.

In this chapter I shall look at the role of play for the individual and what it means for the child. In spite of a vast literature on the subject (e.g. Peter Smith's 1982 review and the compilation of papers in Bruner, Jolly and Sylva, 1976) it is difficult to find a definition of play that really satisfies. So I will begin with Helen Steady's definition.

'Doing something you don't need to'

The force of this definition, which is admittedly an over-simplification, is that play behaviour has no clear immediate benefit. Smith (1982) refers to this as the functional criterion, which excludes from being play those behaviours necessary to survival and reproduction, e.g. eating, escaping a predator, or copulating. I suspect that little Helen's catalogue of necessary behaviours would differ from this, apart from the need to eat; and even in connection with this activity there have been a few unnecessary behaviours from time to time. She would, however, understand Mussen, Conger and Kagan's (1965) characterization of play as 'behaviours that are not reactions to pressing environmental demands and are not concerned with realistic problems' (p. 269) even if she might jib at their further statement that 'In these situations the child is freed from behaving sensibly'. The pressing environmental demands that the authors have in mind are sleeping, eating, seeking help with problems, reacting to frustration and attack, solving realistic problems, and meeting the socialization demands of adults. In the last category, Helen might also include answering her grandfather's questions.

Referring back to Smith's functional criterion, play may be of future use, but it does not serve an immediate end. We might add to this that if the one who plays can discern a future use in the activity then something of the element of play is lost. When, at school, the mathematics teacher, trying desperately to make the subject interesting, announces to the class that they are about to play an exciting game, the children may or may not be excited. What is certain is that they do not perceive it as playing a game. They know, in fact, that it is not a game, even if the attempt to make the learning situation less unpleasant is successful. One also wonders how many children are really deceived by the developmental researcher who begins his or her experiment or session of controlled observation by saying, 'Now we are going to play a little game'. Of course, the child-subject who is being observed may enjoy the activity, but this is not the same as saying that the child is playing. It is possible, for example, to enjoy eating Marmite sandwiches without cutting them into 'soldiers' or putting them face down on the tablecloth. Necessary activities, for both children and adults, can be enjoyed without them being play.

Corinne Hutt (1979a) quotes with approval a distinction made by Dearden (1967) between the usual serious activities of the adult, and the less constrained activity of the child. To re-quote, 'play is neither the pursuit of purpose dictated by common prudence nor is it the fulfilling of an obligation to anybody . . . a child at the sink, for example, may or may not be playing, depending on how he regards his activity. If he does as he pleases, then he is playing . . . Play is a non-serious and self-contained activity which we engage in just for the satisfaction involved in it.'

Hutt adds the comment, 'Above all, play is *fun* and, like virtue, is its own reward'. With this thought and continuing to bear in mind Bruner's (1976) stricture, 'psychologists and other students of behaviour are often given to an excessive sobriety in dealing with play' (p.23), I am led on to Helen's next statement.

'It makes me happy'

This is essentially the position taken by Michael Lewis (1982) who invites us to concentrate on the internal, affective (i.e. emotional) nature of play.

However there are difficulties with this approach. We cannot observe happiness directly from the outside, we can only infer it. In rough-and-tumble play between the young of certain species the animals give and recognize a 'play face', which is a particular kind of open-mouthed gesture having some visual likeness to a foolish grin. Associated with this there is a slack and exaggerated gait and a marked 'galumping' in movement. This looks like a kind of happiness, but it would be impossible to say whether or not it is. With human beings, of course, we can ask them–but even such verbal behaviour is not always completely reliable as a guide. Lewis acknowledges that the task of distinguishing between play and play behaviours is not an easy one.

This does not prevent Lewis from inviting us to concentrate on the internal, affective nature of play. We can recognize happiness within ourselves and we have our ways of recognizing happiness in others. It would, therefore, be better for us to focus our attention on those aspects of behaviour that indicate that the organism–human or animal–is having fun, rather than try to classify behaviours into play and non-play on the basis of some hypothesis regarding their function. Indeed, his argument goes, fun and whimsy may be the primary function of play and, from an evolutionary perspective, play could be seen as adaptive. To use his words 'happy organisms are healthier, smarter, and more likely to reproduce' (p. 166).

Schwartzman's approach is somewhat similar. She puts forward the suggestion (Schwartzman, 1982) that play may be regarded as a mode or process. She is not satisfied with the either/or thinking which seems to characterize writers and researchers intent upon drawing a line between work and play. She complains that writers tend to say either that play matters or it doesn't; that 'play is either very serious and consequential or it is frivolous and inconsequential'. By questioning the assumption that play is a distinctive behaviour category she is led to consider play as an attitude or frame of mind that can be adopted towards anything. It is the way certain objects are regarded that indicates whether or not humans or animals are playing with them; and this also applies to attitudes that are held toward individuals, activities and events. On this view, typical everyday activities such as fighting, feeding, mating and parenting, may be undertaken playfully, and it is possible for a switch to occur from playful to serious and vice versa.

In our study of Sri Lankan children, (Prosser and others, in preparation) we found that children were sometimes observed to be playing 'family at meal'. The children were not necessarily training for the parental role, nor were they under any instruction to do so. They were playing. However, in the course of play, it sometimes happened that role conflicts emerged and real problems arose. The children became genuinely annoyed and, strictly speaking, could no longer be regarded as being at play.

Readers will also be familiar with those occasions when 'play fighting' gradually–or even suddenly–became serious. Smith (1975) in his description of rough-and-tumble play notes that nursery or playground staff sometimes confuse the 'play-fighting' or 'play-hunting' of 3–4 year olds with actual aggressive behaviour. Incidentally, this may contribute to the unreliability of observers' reports on playground aggression after children have been exposed to violence on television or film. Nevertheless, over-reaction and misunderstanding can cause the switch from play to true aggression, particularly with children lacking experience of rough-and-tumble play. Both animals and humans can fail to read the 'play face' signal.

An example of the way in which the switch can be made from serious to non-serious is given by Corinne Hutt (1966) in her study of exploration and play in children. Thirty nursery school children between the ages of three and five years took part. They were taken to a small room in their nursery and invited to play for a few minutes while the observer finished off some work. Five familiar toys were available for the children to play with, and there was in addition a specially devised object which consisted of a red metal rectangular box on four brass legs. A lever at the top of the box could be moved in four directions marked by Post Office digital counters, and either a bell or a buzzer could sound, depending on the direction in which the lever was moved. Conditions were varied by the experimenter who could arrange for the counters to be covered and/or the bell and buzzer to be switched off. In this way the children were exposed to four conditions of relatively increasing complexity, i.e. from the condition where there was no sound (of bell or buzzer) and no vision (of counters) through vision only and sound only to the presentation of both sound and vision.

17.1. Are you *sure* that's his play face?

In her results, Hutt reports that the children would look at the object as soon as they came into the room and, as they approached i·, often asked the observer what it was. Then exploratory behaviour began as they carefully inspected it or handled it, usually holding on to the lever. Finally, they engaged in active manipulation of the lever. Over a series of six trials, the amount of investigative or exploratory activity decreased, particularly under the no sound and no vision conditions. Eventually, as the children became familiar with the object, a variety of behaviours followed, e.g. patting the lever repeatedly, leaning on the lever making the bell ring continuously, using the object together with some of the other toys in a kind of 'game', and running around the room with one of the toys viz. a truck, ringing the bell each time the object was passed.

During this experiment, then, children who had been presented with a novel object switched from investigative exploration to playful activities. While investigating the object, the children's attention was fixed upon it. They were taking it seriously. Once they had become familiar with it, their attitude was more relaxed or, as Hutt put it, 'the receptors were desynchronized (i.e. vision and manipulation were no longer simultaneously directed towards the object) and the behaviour towards the object might almost be described as "nonchalant" (p. 210).

Granted that play is engaged in for its own sake and that there is a significant element of fun in it, there still remains the possibility that long-term benefits will accrue from play. What has Helen to say on this one?

'You want to feel grown up'

One of the main functions of play, according to Mussen, Conger and Kagan (1965), is to practise new skills. The example they give is that of a girl who sews a napkin. She is motivated by the desire to acquire and perfect a new skill. The assumption is that young chilFen have a basic need for mastery and competence. Associated with this is a desire to participate vicariously in the life of adults. Some role model is selected, e.g. a nurse or mother, and the child seeks to create some perception of similarity to the model. Traditionally (see Chapter 14) the girl played being a nurse or a mother; the boy played cops-and-robbers. Roles may be reversed nowadays, although one suspects that most parents feel less anxiety if their children follow the older pattern, and Helen herself actually gave me the example of dressing a doll. Be that as it may, her answer 'You want to feel grown up' nicely illustrates the motivation for a certain kind of play.

Motivation for activity that in fact prepares the child for adult life looks like being adaptive. In evolutionary terms it should contribute to survival of the species; and this is the argument that Smith (1982) has developed at some length, with full illustrations from observation of play behaviours in animals. He states quite categorically that 'the primary function of animal play is to provide indirect practice for certain skills when direct or optimal practice is unlikely or unsafe' (p. 139). He lists the functions of mammalian play as follows:

(i)   Physical training–young animals are prepared to spend energy in active physical play in order to develop their muscles and increase their fitness.

(ii)   Learning competitive social skills–this includes social play which largely consists of play-fighting and serves the two purposes of (a) rehearsing the ability of males in particular to fight seriously later with members of the same species when defending territory or competing for a mate, and (b) giving practice in the competitive area of predation. Some species are more liable to be predatory, e.g. cats, and need practice in stalking, pouncing, seizing, biting, gnawing and shaking. Others which are potentially the prey, e.g. squirrels, will benefit from practice of predatory-avoidance behaviours such as jumping, running and jinking.

(iii)   Learning non-competitive social skills–it is possible that social bonding, social rank and social communication are enhanced by play, but the evidence for this is weak and Smith considers that the learning of social skills is an incidental benefit of play.

(iv)   Learning cognitive (environmental) skills–there is evidence that behaviours involving the use of tools by e.g. chimpanzees are rehearsed during play. This is sometimes referred to as trial-and-error play, and has advantages over simple observation and direct practice.

Our main concern is with the play of children. However, an interesting link between animal and human studies is provided in a paper by Sylva, Bruner and Genova (1976). They start from the point of view that play in both animals and humans may be a matter of borrowing bits of behaviour from non-play modes and assembling them into unusual sequences. The most famous animal example is that of Sultan, one of Kohler's (1957) apes. Apparently, when a banana was placed outside the animal's cage and beyond his reach, Sultan grasped a bamboo stick and used it to rake in the banana. The main interest centres on the next stage in Sultan's development. If the stick was not long enough to reach the banana, and two or more bamboo sticks were available, Sultan suddenly joined the two sticks together by telescoping one into the other. Psychologists refer to this as insight learning. This interpretation was questioned by Birch (1945) who experimented with six young chimpanzees. Until these animals were given the opportunity to manipulate or play with the sticks, they failed to solve the stick-as-rake problem.

Taking their cue from Birch's work, Sylva and her colleagues presented 90 children with variations on the stick-as-rake problem. Given three sticks of length 15, 13 and 4 inches respectively, and two clamps, their task was to get a piece of chalk from a transparent plastic box, which could only be reached if the sticks were clamped together. There were three main preparatory conditions viz: (i) After seeing the experimenter tighten one clamp on to the middle of one long stick, the child was allowed free play with 10 blue sticks and 7 clamps; (ii) The child observed the experimenter tighten one clamp on to the middle of one long stick then construct an elongated tool by rigidly joining two long sticks with one clamp; (iii) The experimenter only demonstrated one clamp tightened on to the middle of one long stick. There were two measures, (a) The number of children who spontaneously solved the problem, and (b) The number of hints per child required before the problem was solved.

Results showed that the children who had been given opportunity to play with the sticks and clamps were more likely to reach a spontaneous solution than those who only observed the experimenter using the clamps. The probability of chance occurrence of the difference between conditions (i) and (iii) (39 per cent and 9 per cent respectively) is less than one in a hundred.

The authors conclude from this, and a further development of the experiment, that solving problems requires self-initiation, opportunity to test out different sequences of action, and an absence of the stress that goes with fear of failure. Play provides all of these.

'Not real: you want to feel like somebody else'

What did Helen mean by this? It is possible, if not probable, that she was referring to what psychologists call fantasy or symbolic play–the terms are roughly synonymous. A brief reference to the classification scheme used by Corinne Hutt (1979a) might help to make the point that not all play is the same, but there are different types of activity that would all loosely be called play. The classifications are as follows:

1 Epistemic behaviour–this includes problem-solving, exploration (e.g. the early behaviour of her subjects with the novel object described above), and skill acquisition.
2 Games with rules–this includes street games such as hide and seek, and marbles (see Chapter 5).
3 Ludic behaviour–this includes playing that tries out new ways of dealing with things (innovative play), play that involves repeating certain actions over and over (perseverative play), and fantasy or symbolic play.

In our Sri Lankan study, we were especially interested in the amount of fantasy or symbolic play engaged in by the children. Forty children between the ages of four and five, 20 of whom lived in each of two villages, were observed at play. The villages differed in socio-economic terms and it was expected that the children who were better off and had access to toys would use play materials in the way they were intended, i.e. as representational objects, more than the poorer children. The latter were also expected to indulge in more physical play.

The results supported our predictions. The better off children indulged in more symbolic play including the use of objects to represent something else (fantasy objects), the use of props to represent crockery, cutlery or food (fantasy food) and the playing of familiar roles (fantasy person). They also played more with non-toy materials e.g. sand, water and clay, and various non-toy objects, e.g. pieces of wood, old tyres and boxes.

The poorer children did more running, jumping, dancing, throwing things and singing action songs. As a matter of interest, boys fitted the stereotype as far as physical play is concerned, and their rough-and-tumble play occasionally became more serious.

'You've got nothing else to do'

At this point, Helen is possibly hinting at the most significant thing of all with regard to play. She is bringing together the two global factors we have been discussing: function and motivation.

For Helen, as for most children, and for many adults, play comes as an opportunity to relieve boredom. Psychologists sometimes refer to this condition as under-arousal, and a strong case can be made for the view that organisms, both human and animal, aim at an optimal level of arousal. Hutt (1979b) has proposed such a theory in connection with children's play and although, as Smith points out, it may not be clear why arousal level should be functionally important, such a theory is most helpful as we move higher up the phylogenetic scale. The organism, particularly the human organism, has 'spare capacity' for the greater part of the time, and this may be 'used' at a lower level by rehearsing familiar or unfamiliar routines. Levels of use may change from moment to moment, switching from serious to non-serious, but it is just as well for most of us that play is available as a viable option.

Further reading

BRUNER, J.S., JOLLY, A. and SYLVA, K. (1976) (Eds.) *Play: its role in development and evolution.* Harmondsworth: Penguin.
   A comprehensive collection of articles by different authors, covering a wide variety of different aspects of play.
GARVEY, C. (1977) *Play.* London: Fontana.
   A short, readable introduction to research on the many different kinds of play.

Discussion topics

- What is play?
- What can we learn about the nature of play from observation of animals?

PART IV

The biological domain

Introduction

The relationship between biological processes and psychological events–between body and mind – has for many years been a contentious one. This is equally true in development. There are at least two important issues that are worth bearing in mind while reading the chapters in this section.

First of all, although it is common to think of biological and environmental influences on psychological development as separate and distinct, in fact this turns out to be too simple, and needs refining. Environmental events can affect the biological system and sometimes biological effects only take place under particular environmental conditions. The obvious cases in which the environment can be seen to affect biological aspects of development are those in which something goes wrong, though the effects can in fact be beneficial as well. Some of the environmental influences that have adverse consequences on the biological system were described in Chapter 16, and further examples are given in this section. Chapter 20 describes the consequences of undernutrition on biological and mental growth: it turns out that the brain is particularly vulnerable during early development and that this can have long-term effects for mental growth. Very often the expression of biological influences depends upon a suitable environmental climate. For example, there appears to be a tendency for language to be represented in the left hemisphere of the brain in humans, but of course this biological disposition requires appropriate linguistic experience to manifest itself.

Secondly, to say that there is a 'biological' basis to some phenomenon does not mean that it is unalterable. This issue arises in different guises in several chapters in this section. Chapter 19 shows that the effects of genes may not always be manifest if appropriate environmental circumstances do not arise; while conversely, a 'genetic' difference between two strains of rat, which has been inbred over many generations, can be completely masked by massive environmental stimulation. Chapter 22 shows that a particular difference in intellectual functioning between males and females probably has a biological basis, but that this interacts with, and is overlaid by, the expectations that culture has for the kinds of jobs appropriate to males and females. Finally in Chapter 21 it is pointed out that, while in the normal case particular parts of the brain are specialized to perform particular functions, if brain damage occurs early in life, other parts of the brain can take over these functions.

Methods of research in the biological domain

One might have thought that it would be relatively easy to conduct experiments and other types of investigation into the biological side of development, but this is not the case for several reasons.

First, whether working with animals or humans one can only infer the effects of – for instance – genes or hormones from observations of behaviour, and from differences in behaviour between different populations. These inferences are often difficult because many factors, including social ones, may contribute to the differences. Secondly, complex forms of behaviour are likely to be affected by many different genes. It is relatively easy to see the effect of a single gene – an effect is present or it is not – but when many different genes are contributing, the effects may again be difficult to distinguish from those of other factors. Thirdly, genes do not affect behaviour directly, but simply contain information that determines the proteins that a cell manufactures. The effects on behaviour are thus indirect, so that again it is seldom clear whether, or in what way, there is a genetic basis for some difference, or whether this difference is due to experience. Fourthly, much of our knowledge of the ways in which the biological substratum works arises from animal studies. This is necessary because detailed study of biological mechanisms often requires strict control over environments, and strict control over breeding. Fortunately it is not possible to perform research of this kind on humans. However, it does mean that some issues, which are of most interest to humans, are unavailable for detailed study: sometimes because animals do not display a particular kind of behaviour (for example, talking); sometimes because differences between humans and other animals produce profound effects on the way in which development proceeds (for example, children can make a great deal of use of the experience of others through language, which is not possible for other species).

Because of these difficulties, the conclusions drawn from research in the biological domain depend on making inferences from the results to the underlying mechanisms. These inferences are often contentious and open to alternative interpretations. This is clearly the case with much of the research into the relative influence of genes and environment in determining IQ as described in Chapter 19, where almost every study seems to have been criticized for one reason or another. The scrutiny which these studies have received reflects their social controversy and the political debate surrounding whether differences in IQ are innate or environmental.

Studies of the effects of biological processes also demonstrate the difficulties of controlling variables in research so that unambiguous conclusions can be obtained. This is particularly so since much research on humans necessarily makes use of 'natural experiments' where the conditions are created for other reasons than research (e.g. studies in Chapter 20 of malnourished children or split-brain patients in Chapter 21). Often the differences between the groups being compared in the research are confused and confounded by extraneous variables (e.g. the effects of undernourishment are combined with effects from an understimulating environment, which the children often also experience) so that an unambiguous interpretation of the results is impossible.

Awareness of these difficulties for research in this area is having some desirable consequences. On the one hand, there seems to be more caution about making policy decisions on the basis of a small number of studies of a restricted number of variables; on the other hand, psychologists are displaying more conceptual sophistication in that there seems to be less tendency to accept simple conceptual schemes into which results are forced, so we no longer believe, for example, that if something is apparently 'not learned' then it must be instinctive.

CHAPTER EIGHTEEN

Animal behaviour and child development
David F. Chantrey

People often look to the behaviour of animals to throw light on the behaviour of humans, in the apparent hope that by learning about 'simpler' animals we will understand something of the bases underlying human behaviour.

There are two traditional approaches to the study of animal behaviour. In one, careful laboratory studies were performed mainly to investigate the learning capacities and perceptual abilities of animals. Usually the animals for these investigations (principally rats and pigeons) were specially bred in the laboratories. The findings were open to criticism on the grounds that the results were the consequence of unrealistic environmental conditions. This approach is often known as comparative psychology.

In the other approach, known as ethology, a careful study is made of the behaviour of animals in their natural surroundings. The difficulty here is often that the conditions under which the studies were conducted were hard to control precisely, so that extraneous variables were always likely to affect the data collected, and the past experience of the animals was not always known.

Learning and instinct

The two styles of approach obviously had their own special concerns and interests. Comparative psychology tended to emphasize the role of learning in behaviour, while ethology has often emphasized the role of instincts in producing behaviour. It was not until recently that the two streams of thought began to come together (see Hinde, 1970). But one question to which they both sought answers was, 'How does the behaviour we observe in adult animals arise?' In other words, what causes behaviour to develop in the way it does?

The answer that came most readily from the comparative psychologists' approach was that all behaviour is learned. That is, adult behaviour is the product of past experiences. The extreme form of this approach is epitomized in the notion of the *'tabula rasa'*, or blank slate–this is the hypothesis that when animals are born they have a completely blank, unformed mind, which is unprepared for behaving in specific ways. The animals' behaviour is then, as it were, moulded on to this *tabula rasa* as a consequence of its earliest experience.

Ethologists were not convinced by this argument. They pointed to the fact that insects, for instance, will often perform species-characteristic behaviour without the benefit of previous relevant experience. They could also detect some non-experiential elements in the higher animals. Some birds will peck at objects almost as soon as they leave the egg (though Kuo (1932) was able to show that there were some experiential elements occurring even within the egg). Young mammals suckle and even seek the nipple very shortly after they are born. And how, it was asked, were we to account for behaviour that was common to all members of a species despite their having very different experiences? For instance, all black-headed gulls use the same behaviour during courtship (Fig. 18.1), and all greylag geese use the same method to retrieve eggs that roll out of their nest (Fig. 18.2).

18.1 Courtship display of black-headed gulls.

These were the kinds of arguments that led to the term *innate* being used to describe such behaviour patterns, which were called *instincts*. Behaviour patterns such as egg retrieval by the greylag goose were described as *fixed action patterns* (FAPs), which were said to be elicited by the action of *innate releasing mechanisms* (IRMs)–in the case of the greylag goose, the sight of the egg outside the nest is the IRM. As it turns out, these simple-looking behaviour patterns are often more complex than is apparent at first sight. The full egg-retrieval response involves not only pulling back the bird's beak, but also moving it from side to side to control the egg as it rolls over uneven ground. If the egg is pulled away just after the bird has begun pulling in its beak, the beak continues to be pulled right back, but the side-to-side movements do not occur. Perhaps the side-to-side adjustments are subject to development as a consequence of experience, while the beak-pull is not.

A   B

18.2   Egg retrieval by greylag goose.

If even comparatively simple-looking behaviour may be developed in complex ways involving the interaction of various developmental mechanisms, then it seems that to call behaviour 'innate' or 'instinctive', and to suppose that it is 'inherited' or 'hard-wired', may be too simplistic. In fact, the terms innate and instinct have fallen into some disrepute and, at least for some authors, disuse. For they came to be used glibly of a variety of phenomena which may or may not be related to each other. The evidence used to show that a behaviour pattern was innate included, that it developed in the absence of experience, that it occurred in all members of a species, that it survived deprivation from specific (or 'all') experience. Yet, while these lines of evidence may appear to establish a basis for saying that a behaviour pattern is innate, in fact they each establish something subtly different about behaviour, and at best they only establish that the behaviour is not learned. A negative criterion for a developmental cause, such as this, is never very satisfactory. (See Hinde, 1970; 1974).

Inheritance of behaviour

What this suggests is that it may be unsafe, or unhelpful, to call a behaviour 'instinctive'. But this is not say that there are no genetic inputs to behaviour. There is good evidence that behaviour is, indeed, affected by genetic changes and, further, that it can and does evolve. For instance, Ewing (1963) used a series of connected funnels in an experiment designed to select for activity in the fruit fly, *Drosophila melanogaster* (Fig. 18.3). Ewing bred together flies that moved quickly through the apparatus ('fast line') and flies that moved slowly through the apparatus ('slow line). After ten generations of this selection, nearly all descendants of the 'slow' flies moved slowly through the apparatus, while nearly all descendants of the 'fast' flies moved quickly through the apparatus.

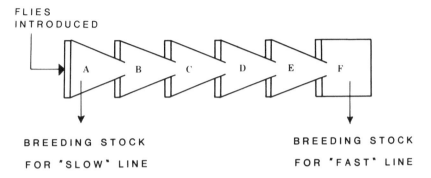

18.3   Diagram of apparatus used by Ewing.

Experiments such as this have been used as evidence that behaviour is at least partly grounded on genetic factors, and that it is subject to evolution by natural selection. The nature of this genetic input is, however, by no means well understood. It is not sufficient to suppose that single genes 'control' single behaviour patterns. All such 'phenotypic' effects are also subject to environmental inputs, and the nature of the interactions between such gene and environmental effects is not a simple matter. (For a detailed treatment of behaviour genetics, see Plomin and others, 1980.)

An example: parent–offspring interactions

Unless we are to be over-simplistic, we cannot say that a particular behaviour is innate or learned. What we must do is to keep an open mind about how behaviour develops, and look in detail at the precise course of its development. Let's look at an example of a situation where this has been attempted.

There have been many studies of the parent–offspring behaviour of animals. Perhaps the best-known kind of process studied in this area is *imprinting*. The first person to study imprinting in detail was Lorenz in 1935, but the phenomenon had been described over 60 years earlier by Spalding. They noticed that young birds of some species followed their parents very soon after hatching. This was particularly true of the so-called *nidifugous* species in which the young are feathered and mobile soon after hatching: they generally require a few hours for drying out and the development of some motor coordination. These are birds such as chickens, ducks, coots and moorhens. The young of *nidicolous* species, on the other hand, are featherless and unable to follow their parents; these are species such as blackbirds, sparrows and robins. The difference between them is that the young of nidicolous species are protected from predators by special mechanisms such as nests, and their parents feed and defend them. The young of nidifugous species, which are often ground-nesting, must follow their parents for protection and food.

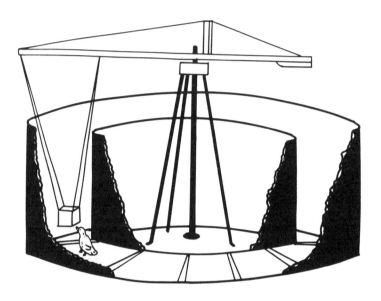

18.4   Testing imprinting reactions in chicks.

Lorenz was interested in this phenomenon of imprinting principally because of its rapidity. The young birds were quickly learning the characteristics of their parent, for they would only follow the parent and would avoid other things. It turns out that chicks will imprint with a large number of objects, though there are some limits to the kind of object they will learn to follow. Using apparatus such as that shown in Figure 18.4, it is possible to show that chicks will learn to follow a red block, for instance, and will approach it, twittering gently, when it comes into sight. When a blue cylinder appears which they have not previously seen, they will flee from it, peeping loudly.

This learning takes a very short time. Lorenz claimed that it happened almost instantaneously. That was why it was called imprinting (*'Prägung'*, a term that implies a stamping in). This was thought to be a feature of learning unique to imprinting, as was the fact that it was said to be limited to a short period in the animal's life. Chicks are susceptible to imprinting from a few hours after hatching until a few days after hatching. These and other features of imprinting led Lorenz and others to suggest that imprinting was a special sort of learning.

Imprinting clearly does involve learning, but one aspect of it which has only more recently been emphasized is the active part played by the chick. In the absence of a conspicuous object to become imprinted with, chicks actively search for one. Furthermore, imprinting is not really a special sort of learning, as it now appears to be a form of perceptual learning (see Bateson, 1973). The chick is learning the features of the object on which it is being imprinted. Experiments have shown that domestic chicks' ability to learn to distinguish between objects is affected by their previous (imprinting) experience with them (see Chantrey, 1972, for instance). The same kinds of effects are seen with rhesus monkeys (Bateson and Chantrey, 1972) and mongolian gerbils (Chantrey and Waite, unpublished). Part of the imprinting process does resemble what has been called perceptual learning, and one of the effects is the development of perceptual abilities (see Chapters 6 and 7).

Imprinting, then, can tell us something about perceptual development, in general. Can it, though, tell us anything about the development of the human parent–offspring bond as some people have suggested? Regrettably, the answer is probably not a great deal. Human children do not follow their parent in quite the same way as chicks and ducklings follow theirs, though human children do develop preferences for particular people (usually their parents). As described in Chapter 3, they will then smile preferentially at them, and cry when separated from them (which may encourage the parent to 'follow' the child!). Externally, then, there are only some superficial similarities between imprinting and the formation of the human child–parent bond. It is tempting though to suggest that internal processes may be similar (or even the same). I have said that imprinting may involve perceptual learning, and clearly the time at which the human child is developing her preferences for a parent is also a time of rapid perceptual change and development (described in Chapter 6). Further than that, however, we may not safely go. People are not ducks! Children are not chicks! The gross anatomy of the brains of people and of birds are sufficiently different to make us extremely wary of assuming any similarity in detailed developmental mechanisms between them. Such similarities, if they exist, must be demonstrated experimentally in each case.

If the study of imprinting in birds is of little help to our understanding of the details of child development, perhaps the study of closer relatives among the non-human animals would provide a better understanding. There have been a number of studies conducted on captive primates (usually rhesus monkeys) which have looked at the issue of the role of the young animals' social companions (especially the mother) in the development of its behaviour. For many animals, it must be said, the mother is the more important parent. Very often, it is only the mother who can be sure which offspring are hers, especially in species where the female mates with several males. In any case, the male is often the animal who has the opportunity to leave parental care to his mate, and this is especially true of mammals, where the female is specially developed to feed the young (for a discussion of parenting strategies, see Maynard Smith, 1977). The same is not, of course, necessarily true for humans, and in the matter of who should care for the young, as in all other cases, the behaviour of animals should not be taken to be prescriptive of human behaviour.

Several workers have looked at the effects of separating young rhesus monkeys from their mothers. (This work is also referred to in Chapter 2). Harlow and his co-workers (see summary in Hinde, 1974, from p.234) separated young monkeys from their mothers, or from other young monkeys, or from both for long periods (up to one year). The results are summarized in Table 18.1.

TABLE 18.1   Results of Harlow's experiments on long-term social
deprivation in infant rhesus monkeys.

| | | *Separated from mother:* | |
		No	Yes
	No	(controls) normal behaviour	almost normal behaviour
Separated from peers:	Yes	Lack of 'affection' Highly aggressive	(Total isolates) All social abilities destroyed

These results are surprising. They suggest that infant monkeys develop almost normally even if they grow up without a mother, as long as they have other young monkeys to interact with. Moreover, their development may be abnormal if they are separated from other infants even though they are with their natural mother. In other words, Harlow's experiments suggest that it is interaction with *peers* that is the essential determinant of normal development in monkeys. Although these experiments are sometimes said to show the importance of the mother in development, they in fact suggest that she hardly counts at all.

Other results suggest this may be a rash conclusion, though no one would deny that interacting with other (same-age) infants is important. Hinde and his colleagues (again, see in Hinde, 1974) had a colony of captive rhesus monkeys in as near normal a social mix as was possible. They tried the effect of removing the infant from the colony for very short periods (a few days). Such infants, they found, behave differently from infants who have never been separated when they are returned to the colony, and these differences can sometimes be detected for several years after the separation.

Surprisingly, the effects are even more marked if the infant is left in its familiar social setting, but the mother removed for a few days and then replaced. It is likely that this is a reflection of the disruption of social ties that occurs when the mother is taken out of the colony and then replaced. She has then to spend time re-establishing relations with all other members of her social group and can give less attention to her offspring. (It is worth asking yourself whether you would expect a similar effect in human families.) Rhesus monkey societies are complex, and this complexity is reflected in the results of social deprivation on the subsequent behaviour of the infants. For details of this research, see Hinde's (1974) summary.

Now it is tempting to suggest that these results have implications for human behaviour. For instance, it might be said that parents should not leave their children even for short periods (for instance, for hospital treatment), and that if they do, this might have a bad effect on the children. In fact, it has to be said that we are again not entitled to draw such conclusions for human behaviour directly from evidence derived from work with rhesus monkeys. Just as people are not ducks, they are not rhesus monkeys either. Although the evidence is suggestive, it cannot be taken at face value; for these ideas to be applied to people, evidence must be gathered *from* people to confirm or deny the effect.

Observational techniques and evolutionary perspectives

Ethology and comparative psychology have arguably had their greatest impact on the understanding of human development in generating ideas (hypotheses) and providing methods for studying behaviour (as seen in Chapter 6). However, the ideas do need testing on people before we can be sure that the effects in animals do indeed have human applications.

The methodology developed for observing animal behaviour has been applied to the observation of child behaviour. There have been a number of studies in this area (see Blurton-Jones, 1972 for a review; and Hinde, 1979). Of the most recent studies, there is research into behaviour of pre-school children at home by Davie and her colleagues (1984). Children were observed in the course of their waking day wherever they went, using a technique of direct observation. By this means, it was possible to learn a great deal in detail about the daily life of children, their families and friends. It was found, for example, that commercial toys, even though readily available, played a smaller role in children's activities than everyday domestic items. Using these observational techniques it was possible to quantify fantasy play in various ways. The results suggest that working class children indulge in as much, and as complex, a form of fantasy play as middle class children at home. Observation of social interaction revealed potent effects of family position: last born children received much less attention from their parents, particularly their fathers, compared to first born. All these studies rely on techniques developed in the study of ethology.

Finally, although I have tried to instill a degree of healthy scepticism for the generality of theoretical insights gathered from work with animals to understanding human behaviour, there has been one recent development which for some gives hope for a more general theory of behaviour. This is sociobiology, a term used for many years, but popularized by Wilson (1975; see, too, Dawkins, 1976). This way of thinking about behaviour adopts an explicitly evolutionary approach and attempts to take into account facts known from a wide range of disciplines.

Several workers have claimed that this approach provides insights for human behaviour. For instance, it has been shown that altruistic behaviour towards closely related individuals (as in maternal behaviour) may serve to perpetuate genes of the altruistic individual. Few would disagree with the belief that early in our history, human behaviour was evolved largely by evolutionary mechanisms based on genetic changes. Our view of the extent to which such mechanisms are still important will depend on the extent to which we believe that the evolution of language has led to a stronger emphasis on cultural mechanisms for the evolution of human behaviour today.

Further reading

DAWKINS, R. (1976) *The Selfish Gene*. London: Oxford University Press.
A well written introduction to the ideas of sociobiology, which suggest that evolution and genetics influence social behaviour.
HINDE, R.A. (1974) *Biological bases of human social behaviour*. New York: McGraw Hill.
A thorough review of the many ways in which the study of animals may be relevant to understanding human behaviour. The chapters in Section D are especially relevant to child development.

Discussion topics

- What use is the study of animal behaviour in understanding human development?
- What are the difficulties in extrapolating from animal to human behaviour?

CHAPTER NINETEEN

Genes and environment: the case of intelligence
S. J. Hutt

The question of whether heredity or environment is more important in determining mental characteristics is one of the oldest problems in psychology. Yet despite at least one hundred years of research in the study of individual differences, the nature–nurture controversy remains . . . a controversy. There are at least two reasons for this. In the first place, there are still no agreed ways of determining the relative effects of heredity and environment in the development of mental characteristics, such as intelligence. In the second place, many scientists are worried about the social policy implication of findings purporting to throw light on the relative contributions of heredity and upbringing in human development.

The ways in which notions about inheritance of psychological characteristics have affected social policy have been well summarized by Kamin (1977), and by McClearn and DeFries (1973). These surveys contain examples that occasionally are humorous, but generally are tragic. Amongst the former is Bartolommeo da Vinci's attempt to find for a wife a peasant wench whose physical and psychological characteristics closely matched those of his step-mother (Leonardo's mother), in the hope that offspring from such a liaison would produce a child of Leonardo's genius. Less happy is legislation based on the principle that socially undesirable characteristics may be controlled by limiting the progeny of people who possess them. The 1935 Nuremburg laws forbade intermarriage between German Jews and non-Jews; other laws have prevented the immigration of certain groups to the USA, have prevented mixed racial marriage in South Africa and have imposed compulsory sterilization on epileptic and educationally subnormal women in the USA.

The IQ and race controversy

Perhaps the most recent controversy was whether the observed differences in intelligence between black and white Americans can be attributed primarily to genetic differenes between the two groups, rather than differences in social conditions and educational opportunities. The matter is no longer as inflammatory as it was a decade ago. It may nevertheless be worth considering, as it could give a useful focus to some of the theoretical issues which I wish to raise in subsequent sections. That there is a marked difference between the two groups in terms of performance on IQ tests is incontrovertible. The mean IQ for black Americans is some 15 points lower than that for whites. Now, granted that the differences in social, economic and educational opportunities of blacks and whites in America are so great, there follows a very practical question: could this difference in IQ be bridged simply by improving the quality of life for blacks? Around 1970, a number of thoughtful, rigorous and liberal scientists gave their attention to this question and answered it: No. Arthur Jensen (1969) was the most articulate exponent of the argument that differences in intelligence could not be substantially reduced by improving the environment.

In genetics, 'genotype' is the name given to the genetic constitution of an individual. 'Phenotype' is the observable and measurable characteristics such as eye colour, height and intelligence. The phenotype results from an interaction between genotype and environment (see Figure 19.1). The variation in intelligence between people is due both to differences in genetic make-up and to variations in environment which can either foster or inhibit the expression of this genetic potential. The genotype determines the potential phenotype of the individual. An 'impoverished' environment can depress the physical or psychological characteristics (phenotype) attained; an 'enriched' environment can enable the phenotype to attain the upper limit set by the genotype, but no more.

Jensen claims that 80 per cent of the variation in intelligence is due to

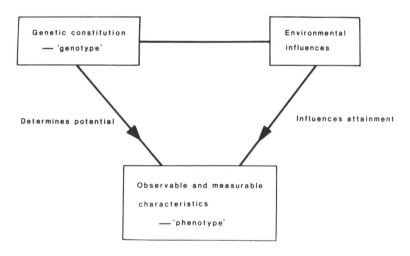

19.1   The relationship between genotype and phenotype.

heredity and 20 per cent to environmental influences. He calculates that if we could abolish overnight all those environmental influences that disadvantage people in peforming IQ tests (for example poor education, poor nutrition) we would only reduce the IQ difference by 1.6 points. Thus, even the most radical legislation abolishing those educational and social disadvantages of blacks that depresses the IQ they achieve, would not be sufficient to raise their IQ by the 15 points necessary to bring it to the level of the average for whites. An accessible explanation of why a 20 per cent reduction in environmental variance produces such a small change in IQ is provided by King (1971).

There are all sorts of problems with this kind of argument. Some psychologists have questioned whether the IQ tests used are valid and fair when applied to people with different cultural backgrounds. (Remember that we saw in Chapter 10 the effects cultural differences can have on the way different people perform in psychological tests.) Others have pointed out that much of the argument rests on the claim that the distribution of IQ scores in the population is similar to the distribution of other 'polygenically' determined characteristics, such as height and weight (i.e. ones determined by the interaction with the environment of a large number of genes, each with a small effect). These characteristics are distributed in the population so that there are large proportions of people around the average and progressively fewer towards the extremes of the scale (a 'bell-shaped' distribution such as the one shown in Figure 19.2 for height).

With regard to intelligence scales, the fact is that they are ingeniously constructed to give a similar bell-shaped distribution of scores (see Figure

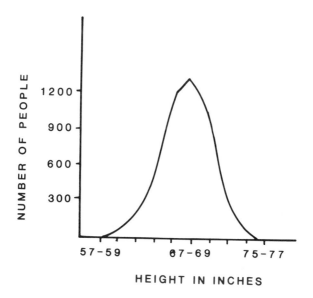

19.2 Numbers of men of particular heights.

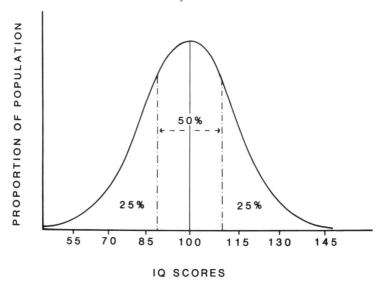

19.3   Proportion of population at various levels of IQ.

19.3) for the population, but this distribution does not just 'naturally' happen as with height and weight (Layzer, 1972), Therefore, even though intelligence test scores *appear* to follow a similar pattern to height and so on, it is such an artifact that we cannot make assumptions that this is determined by a similar set of gene-environment controlling mechanisms.

Nevertheless, if we concede that intelligence can be validly measured by IQ tests, and that the observed bell-shaped curve of ability could have an underlying distribution of genotypes for intelligence in a particular population, what can be said about the crucial estimate that 80 percent is inherited?

Heritability and IQ

There are three main ways to study the effects of inheritance on psychological characteristics. They are: studies of adopted children; studies of family pedigrees; and–a special case of the latter –twin studies.

(i) The study of adopted children

The study of adopted children is potentially a very powerful tool for analysing genetic influences in behaviour. What happens is that a measurement is made of the particular characteristic in each of three people: a person who was adopted shortly after birth; her/his natural parent; her/his adoptive parent. It is preferable if the comparisons are made between same-sex parents and children. The assumption is that if there is a strong resemblance between an adoptee and the natural parent, from whom the child has been separated from birth, inheritance has been a major factor in development. Conversely, if the resemblance between adoptee and adopting parent is stronger than that between adoptee and natural parent, it is likely that environmental influences have been the more important.

Until fairly recently, the most widely acclaimed study of intelligence in adopted children was that of Skodak and Skeels (1949). Though a number of methodological problems have been identified in this study (Kamin, 1977) it remains, at least, of considerable historical interest. The study included 100 children born to single women in the mid-West of the USA in the 1930s. The children were adopted within six months of birth. The mothers' intelligence was assessed by their length of schooling (length of education correlates highly with IQ, and in fact it was also possible to test directly the IQs of the majority of the mothers). The IQs of the children were measured on several occasions from age two until age fourteen. These IQ scores were then correlated at each age point with estimates of intelligence for their natural mothers (whom, of course, they had not seen since birth). A second series of correlations was carried out between the children's IQ scores at each age point and the number of years of education enjoyed by their adoptive mother (remember that number of years of education is highly correlated with IQ). The results are shown in Figure 19.4 (based on Honzik, 1957.)

The diagram shows the correlations for children and natural parents who live in the same household. The correlation between a child's IQ and measures for the natural parent becomes greater and greater until in adolescence it reaches about 0.4; there is no such correspondence between the IQs of adopted children and measures for their adoptive parents. Moreover, the correlations between the IQ of an adopted child and measures for the natural parent at each age point are very similar to those between children and their natural parent who grow up together in the parental home. Skodak and Skeels' study was of especial interest to behaviour geneticists. Jacob and Monod (1961) (see also DiBeradino and others (1984) for an intriguing updating) had suggested that genes do not have all-or-none effects. Rather, there are 'regulator' genes, which are concerned with the transcription of information from 'structural' genes, which in turn produce the enzymes that serve as catalysts of organic activity. Regulator genes are able to 'switch on' or 'switch off' structural genes, their action being determined in part by the local environment, such as hormonal concentrations. What is intriguing is the thought that if intelligence is governed by a number of different genes, the genes may not all come into operation at the same time; rather, more and more genes from the natural mother may be switched on by the time the adoptee reaches adolescence (McClearn and Defries, 1973, p. 175). Since the offspring inherits 50 per cent of genes from each parent, the correlation between child and mother's IQ would be 0.5 at most. The correlation of 0.4 with the IQ of the separated natural parent seems to indicate a high level of genetic

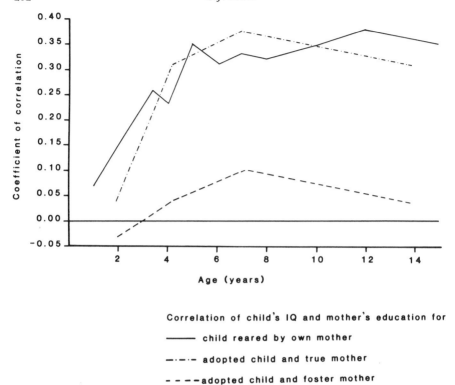

19.4   Correlations at different ages between child's IQ and educational level of own or of adoptive mother.

determination for IQ, of the order of 80 per cent. It should be noted however, that authors such as Kamin (1977) and Munsinger (1975) have raised many practical and methodological difficulties about studies of adopted children in general, and the conclusions that legitimately may be derived from them.

(ii) The analysis of family pedigrees

The second main method for studying genetic influences upon psychological characteristics is by the analysis of family pedigrees. The rationale is that if inheritance plays a major role in determining such characteristics, the more genes a person shares with another family member, the more similar the two of them will be psychologically.

   Probably the best known study of family pedigree and intelligence is that of Erlenmeyer-Kimling and Jarvik (EKJ) (1963). The authors collected some 52 studies carried out over a period of 50 years in which the IQs of different groups of individuals were correlated with each other (Figure 19.5). The groups varied between those where there was no genetic relatedness, through

Category	Correlations 0.00 0.20 0.40 0.60 0.80	Groups included
Unrelated people:		
– Reared apart	────────	4
– Reared together	─────	5
Fosterparent–Child	──────	3
Parent–Child	────────────	12
Siblings:		
– Reared apart	──	2
– Reared together	────────────	35
DZ twins:		
– Opposite sex	──────	9
– Like sex	────────	11
MZ twins:		
– Reared apart	──────	4
– Reared together	─────	14

19.5   Correlations between the IQ scores of people of different degrees of family relatedness. Horizontal lines show range of correlations.

studies of parents and children, to studies of groups of twins, either fraternal or identical. Although there are few examplars in some of the categories and the range of correlations is wide, an overall pattern does emerge. As genetic relatedness becomes closer, the correlations become higher. Environmental influences may also be discerned. Unrelated people reared together provide correlations generally higher than those for unrelated people raised apart. Identical twins raised together provide higher correlations than those for identical twins raised apart. However, the message we are meant to derive is clear:

> The composite data are compatible with the polygenic hypothesis which is generally favoured in accounting for inherited differences in mental ability . . . We do not imply that environment is without effect upon intellectual functioning; the intellectual level is not unalterably fixed by the genetic constitution. Rather, its expression in the phenotype results from the patterns laid down by the genotype under given environmental conditions (p.1479).

The EKJ study has been subjected to much criticism: there are wide age, sex, ethnic and socio-economic differences between the subjects in different studies; a wide range of intelligence tests was used; and the time span of the different studies was one during which large social changes were taking place (these criticisms were anticipated by the authors). The twin data may have been especially flawed because of uncertainty in determining whether they were identical or fraternal twins in the days before a reliable method, using blood groups, had been discovered. Kamin (1977), even more tellingly, has pointed out that the identity of some of the studies was difficult to determine, that where it was possible to determine the studies, EKJ wer guilty of selective reporting (i.e. reporting from within a single study those correlations that best fitted the polygenic hypothesis), and that the full analysis promised in the short Science article has never appeared. Thus, the EKJ study must be approached with caution and this appears to be a general caution in relation to pedigree studies of IQ. An excellent review of parent–child resemblances in IQ has been published by McAskie and Clarke (1976).

(iii) Comparisons of twins

The third main method for studying genetic factors in behavioural development is that of twin comparisons. Monozygotic (identical) twins are two individuals derived from division of a single zygote (fertilized ovum) at some stage in the development of the embryo after fertilization. Generally, they are wrapped at delivery in the same chorion (in effect, a biological cellophane wrapper). Such twins are genetically identical. Dizygotic (fraternal) twins are people derived from the independent release and fertilization of two ova. They have separate chorions at birth. They are no more alike genetically than brothers and sisters born at different times, i.e. they share 50 per cent of their genes. Where they are different from ordinary brothers and sisters is that they share the same birth date, the same birth order in the family (if there are other brothers and sisters) and they are subject to similar environmental experiences. Monozygotic (MZ) twins of course are of the same sex, whereas dizygotic (DZ) twins may be of the same or of different sex. The proportion of European twins who are monozygotic is 30 per cent. Zygosity is determined by analysis of blood groups; if twins are monozygotic all their blood groups will be the same.

There are several reasons why comparisons of identical (MZ) and fraternal (DZ) twins are of particular fascination to psychologists. It could be argued that twins who grow up in the same home are experiencing the same environment. Therefore, any difference between MZ and DZ twins should be due to the greater genetic similarity of monozygotic twins. Unfortunately, this argument runs into trouble if we concede that parents and others are more likely to treat identical (MZ) twins similarly than they are fraternal (DZ) twins (Smith, 1965). Scarr (1968), however, has noted that in the small number of cases in which parents guess wrongly the zygosity of their twins, they tend to treat them according to their *actual* zygosity, i.e. more similarly if they are biologically identical, though the parent thinks them to be fraternal twins, and vice versa.

Some twins, for social reasons, become separated shortly after birth and are perhaps fostered or adopted by different families. If we can trace such twins in later life, measurements of their psychological characteristics will be of particular interest. If MZ twins raised apart were more similar to each other than DZ twins reared together, this would seem to provide good evidence that the characteristic under examination is inherited. However, it can be argued that adoption agencies do not place children in homes taken at random; particular care is taken to place children in 'good' homes, whose characteristics are likely to be similar.

The IQs of MZ twins raised apart correlate around about 0.8. This is the median correlation coefficient of the four most widely quoted studies of MZ twins raised apart, those of Newman and others (1937), Juel-Nielsen (1965), Burt (1966) and Shields (1962). Sadly, as readers may know, there have been accusations of fraud relating to the studies of the late Sir Cyril Burt (Hearnshaw, 1979) so that these studies have to be disregarded. Moreover, there are methodological problems with both the studies of Newman and others (1937) and Shields (1962), whilst the Juel-Nielsen study sampled a mere twelve twin pairs. The twins raised apart in the Newman study were identified through newspaper and radio appeals. They are therefore likely to be a highly selected sample: who listened to particular programmes or read particular newspapers; who shared a comparable level of education; who were similarly motivated. To their credit, the Newman study gives sufficient detail to enable a dispassionate reader to assess the difference in social and educational advantage (DSEA) between twins. If we divide the DSEAs into 'large' and 'small' and the difference in IQ between co-twins into 'large' (more than 10 IQ points) or 'small' (less than 10 IQ points) an interesting picture emerges (Layzer, 1972). The twins with small differences in their IQs are mainly those who have small DSEAs; the largest discrepancies between the IQs of twins are found when there are large differences in DSEA (in four cases, over 20 IQ points). In other words, even for MZ twins, large differences in social and educational environment are associated with large IQ differences. Shields (1962) is also helpful in providing considerable detail about his subjects. What becomes evident, as one reads through his protocols, is how often the tag 'MZ raised apart' has to be interpreted with scepticism. Not only do such twins tend to get allocated to homes with very similar socio-economic conditions, but as Kamin (1977) noted, some so-called separated twins may be fostered by members of their own family, may go to the same school and may regularly play together.

Newman and his colleagues were among the first developmental psychologists to employ, as well as correlations, a statistic called H², an estimate of 'heritability'. This attempts to estimate heritability by comparing variations in scores for identical twins with those for fraternal twins. Both types of twin may share common environments (i.e. a twin is brought up with his co-twin), but in addition, identical twins have identical genes. The idea of using fraternal twins as representatives of those members of the general population brought up in similar environments runs into difficulties though, since of course fraternal twins have 50 per cent of their genes in common with one another as well as living in similar environments. There have been a number of attempts to produce a formula for heritability that takes account of this difficulty (Mittler, 1971), none of which is totally satisfactory. Jensen's formula for computing heritability was devised to take account of the important factor of assortive mating (people marry people like themselves). This looked particularly impressive until Vetta (1977) noted that one of the terms in the formula presupposed that the answer was already known and was of the order of 0.8. Depending upon what assumptions are made in calculating H^2, recent studies of non-separated twins (all of which, predictably, have been criticized) have come up with estimates of heritability of between 0.3 (Adams and others, 1976) and 0.5 (Loehlin and Nicols, 1976). (The latter authors also provide a useful review of the field.)

IQ and race reconsidered

What, then, may we conclude from the above discussion of human heritability studies? On the one hand, it would be overstating the case to say that heredity plays no part in the determination of IQ. On the other hand, the figure of 80 per cent for the contribution of heredity to intelligence is based upon much shakier evidence than previously thought because of the unreliability of the studies, disagreements as to how heritability should be computed, and the difficulty in replicating the findings.

Hirsch (1967) defined heritability as:

> the proportion of the total phenotypic variance which can be attributed to genetic variation *in the same population, at a single generation under one set of conditions.*

This definition contains important qualifications which I have italicised, and will consider more closely now:

(a) *In the same population*

Can an estimate of heritability obtained from white, caucasian populations, be generalized to a population whose gene pool is different? Bodmer (1972) has cautioned that whilst differences in skin colour have a genetic basis, the similarities between blacks and caucasions in terms of (say) blood group distributions are not all that striking. Human beings, be they caucasians, negroes or asians can all interbreed successfully-they belong to the same species. Nevertheless, there *are* some genetic differences between people with different coloured skins. It is important to enquire whether IQ heritability estimates are similar for the various subgroups. A study of particular interest is that by Scarr-Salapatek (1971). She measured heritability in black Americans and white Americans, who were also divided by social class ('high' and 'low' socio-economic status–SES). What is interesting is that she obtained quite high heritability estimates for the whites in her sample (about 0.8) whilst the estimates for blacks were low (about 0.5). This seems to vindicate those (such as Hirsch) who said that you cannot generalize heritability estimates from one population to another. Even more interesting, however, was that there was a social class difference. Much higher heritability estimates were obtained from high SES twins than from low SES twins, irrespective of colour. One of the ways in which Scarr-Salapatek interpreted her data was by emphasising that phenotypic characteristics, such as IQ, are the result of *interaction* between environment and genotype. The more 'enriched' the environment, the wider the range of phenotypes. Middle class people, irrespective of whether they are black or white, are exposed to more enriched social and educational experiences, so that the variances of IQ distributions are going to be much greater for middle class than for working class people. It is the wider variances that ensure high heritability estimates. On the other hand, in 'disadvantaged' environments genotype–environment interactions are more limited, and the variances of IQ distributions are going to be much smaller; hence heritability estimates are going to be smaller. Now, because in general, the black population and the working class population are likely to be co-extensive, it is to be expected that heritability estimates for blacks will be lower than those for whites. Thus, estimates of heritability differ for different populations.

(b) *At a single generation*

Bodmer and Cavalli-Sforza (1975) have noted that 'heritability' has two quite distinct meanings, depending on whether we are talking about, firstly, animals (or plants) that can be systematically interbred, with proper control over their environments; or secondly about people, over whose lives we cannot exercise such control. Estimates are heritability obtained under the former conditions are referred to as heritability 'in the narrow sense'; ones obtained under the latter conditions as estimates 'in the broad sense'. Even when geneticists are able to control both the environment and the interbreeding of animals selected for some phenotypic character, such as exploratory behaviour, they do not expect to get a constant value for 'narrow' heritability across generations (Plomin and others, 1980). It seems even more unlikely that 'broad' heritability estimates (which attempt to take account of all sources of phenotypic variation) will remain constant across generations, when nutrition, education, and social opportunities may change (Hirsch, 1967).

(c) *Under one set of conditions*

As we mentioned above, it is possible to breed animals for behavioural characteristics (see Chapter 18). In one such study (Cooper and Zubek, 1958), rats were bred for maze-solving ability ('maze brightness' or 'maze dullness') for thirteen generations. By this time, the two groups showed no overlap in maze-running performance. Sub-groups of maze bright and maze dull animals of the thirteenth generation were then reared in one of two possible post-weaning environments: a 'restricted' environment or an 'enriched' environment. In the restricted environment there were no moveable objects and the cage faced a blank wall. In the enriched environment the rats had a large number of moveable objects in their cages, which were placed facing a wall painted with 'modernistic' designs. Whilst subgroups of maze bright and maze dull animals brought up in laboratory cages retained their customary difference in performance, animals reared in one of these experimental environments behaved quite differently when confronted by the maze learning task. Maze bright animals reared in the enriched environment performed slightly better than the corresponding group of maze dulls, but *both* groups performed significantly better than either dulls or brights raised in ordinary laboratory cages. Conversely, both dull and bright rats raised in the restricted environment performed very poorly; both groups performed at the level of the animals who had been so carefully reared to be maze dull! What Cooper and Zubek's study shows is that an animal's genotype may contribute a relatively minor part of the phenotypic variance compared with the animal's upbringing. This leads to a more general proposition: any single genotype may develop a different phenotype depending on the environment in which it develops. To this may be added two riders: first, animals of only slightly different genetic strains may perform quite differently from each other on (say) a maze learning task, having been exposed to the same enriched environment post-weaning (Henderson, 1975). Secondly, even quite small differences in testing conditions, for example the temporal spacing of trials, may completely transform the performance of animals of different heredities, so that differences, which have been carefully bred for over many generations, may be apparently 'washed out' (McGaugh and others, 1962). Thus, 'heritability', even in animals whose environment and breeding can be systematically controlled, is very volatile; phenotypic expression is not merely a function of genes and the environment in which those genes are nurtured, but of the very measuring conditions we are employing. And if this is true for animals, how much more true is it likely to be for people, whose environments are so diverse and whose mating patterns so idiosyncratic?

Let us conclude with two human analogues. The first was presented by Benjamin Bloom in answer to Jensen's original thesis (1969). Bloom (1969) measured the IQs of two groups of Israeli children, each one from a different ethnic background: one group were the children of European immigrants; the other group were the children of the indigenous mid-Eastern population. Each of these larger groups were then subdivided according to their pattern of upbringing, that is, whether they had grown up in a conventional nuclear family, or on a *kibbutz*. The average IQ of the home-reared children was 105 for those of European origin, and 85 for those of mid-Eastern origin. The corresponding figures for the kibbutz-reared children were 115 in each case. Not only did the kibbutz children score higher on IQ tests in general, their rearing appears capable of closing a gap between the two ethnic groups which was even greater than that between American negroes and caucasians in Jensen's (1969) study.

The second study to be considered was carried out by Barbara Tizard (1974) in London residential nurseries which contain children from a wide variety of ethnic origins. Tizard and her team examined three groups of children aged from 2 to nearly 5 years who had been in the institution for at least 6 months. One group was white, one black (African or West Indian parents) and one group was of mixed race. There were no significant differences amongst the three groups, all of whom performed at average level. At a later date, Tizard tested children from each of the three racial groups who had been admitted to the nurseries by the age of 4 months and who had remained there until at least age 2 years. Some of these children were still institutionalized, but some had been adopted by white parents and some had been restored to their mothers (generally one parent families). The results were striking. In general, children who had been adopted were performing at a level far above those restored to their mothers, whilst the institutionalized children were somewhere between. The pattern of results was similar in all three racial groups. We may thus infer that racial origin is not an important variable in the development of the children's IQ; of far more importance is the pattern of early care to which they are exposed.

Conclusions

What can be learnt from all this?
1   Perhaps, at least temporarily, the Race–IQ debate is dead. It is a debate that has generated more heat than light. As Bodmer and Cavalli-Sforza (1970) warned us, apart from its social nuisance value, the debate was never likely to throw much light on the genetic control of IQ because any race differences would furnish such 'a small fraction of the total variation in IQ'. And then, whilst noting the undesirability, in principle, of control of scientific enquiry, they state:

> since for the present, at least, no good case can be made for such studies on either scientific or practical grounds, we do not see any point in particularly encouraging the use of public funds for their support. There are many more useful biological problems for the scientist to attack (p.29).

2   We must look critically at the 'classic' studies in behaviour genetics: at their methods of measurement, their methodologies, their calculations and their inferences. Psychologists are as fallible as anyone else: they can be the victims of fraud, error, miscalculation, bias, and sheer bad luck.
3   Developmental psychologists are no longer claiming 80 per cent inheritance of mental characteristics such as IQ. The argument that any genotype can produce as many phenotypes as there are numbers of nurturing environments is now more acceptable than it was when the race–IQ debate was at its height.
4   New methods of studying behaviour genetics are urgently needed. Studies

of half-siblings–that is, children whose mother or father marries another partner and thus creates two separate households (Rose and others, 1979) look particularly promising–especially where measures of the phenotypic similarities/differences in (say) IQ are accompanied by reliable measures of genetic similarity, such as fingerprint ridge counts. As well as new methods of study, new statistical techniques for handling the data have been developed–often of mind-blowing complexity (e.g. Royce and Mos, 1979).

5   It is important to remind ourselves that *behaviour* cannot be inherited. What genes do is to specify the large molecules (polypeptides) that constitute proteins. Differences between individuals in these proteins could however result in differences in behaviour and perhaps in intelligence. One way in which this might occur is through differences in the efficiency with which internal communication in the brain takes place, since this communication involves 'transmission proteins' (Reed, 1984). Whether a gene is switched on or not will depend upon the environment, as Jacob and Monod described (see above).

6   Behaviour genetics is an intellectual minefield. It is very, very difficult to design a study, even less devise a theory, which is not instantly vulnerable to attack by other workers in the field.

Further reading

EYSENCK, H. J. versus KAMIN, K. (1981) *Intelligence: The Battle for the Mind.* London: Pan Books.
   Not so much a debate as a prize fight between two heavy weights, espousing respectively views of a strongly genetic and a strongly environmental determination of IQ.
WELLS, B.W.P. (1980) *Personality and Heredity.* London: Longman.
   A balanced, largely non-technical account of research in 'psychogenetics covering IQ, personality and mental illness.

Discussion topics

● What is meant by the term 'heritability'? What particular problems should you look out for in its use?
● How have twin studies been used in the study of the inheritance of psychological characteristics? What are some of the difficulties of such studies?

CHAPTER TWENTY

Early brain development and experience
Mark Trueman and S. J. Hutt

Early human brain development

The human brain is the biological computer that controls both our bodily and mental processes. An appreciation of its structural and functional maturation may provide valuable clues towards an understanding of mental development in early life. In purely physical terms, the development of the brain during the first two decades of life is extremely interesting. An early, but informative, picture (Figure 20.1) was provided by Tanner (1960) comparing the growth of the human brain at different ages with general body growth and the development of the sexual organs, as a percentage of their adult levels. As might be expected, the development of the sexual organs occurs relatively late; the growth of the internal organs, such as liver and spleen, increases more or

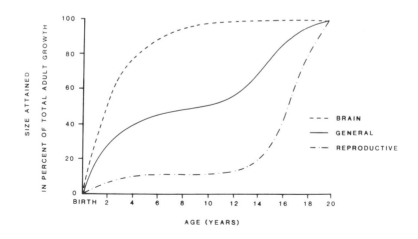

20.1   Growth curves for different parts of the body.

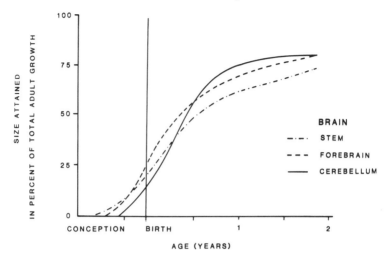

20.2   Growth rates for total number of cells in three areas of the human brain.

less linearly. In contrast, the brain achieves almost all of its mass in the first few years of life; indeed, in a more recent summary, Tanner (1978) shows that some 25 per cent of adult brain weight is reached at birth, nearly 50 per cent at 6 months, 75 per cent at 2 years, 90 per cent at 5 years and 95 per cent by the age of 10 years.

A more recent picture (Figure 20.2) of brain growth was based upon a study of 139 human brains, ranging in area from 10 weeks gestation to 7 years after birth (Dobbing and Sands, 1973). It modifies the earlier one in a number of ways. First, what the authors term the 'brain growth spurt' begins prenatally, notably in the last third of pregnancy. Secondly, there are marked differences in brain growth between different areas. Thirdly, the area of the brain with the fastest rate of growth, the cerebellum, achieves its growth plateau even earlier than would have been predicted from Tanner's (1960) exploratory study.

There are broadly two types of cell in the brain: *neurons,* or nerve cells; and *glia,* the connective tissue of the nervous system. While the neurons are the transmitters of impulses and messages, they are very dependent upon glial cells for their health and efficiency. One of the functions of glial cells is to form an insulating sheath of myelin (a fatty substance) around part of the neuron. This increases the speed and efficiency whereby messages are sent from one nueron to another. Dobbing's work has documented two overlapping phases in the brain growth spurt: the first, in which new neurons are produced; and the second, in which glial cells are produced. The neurons mainly develop prenatally while the glial cells largely develop in the first two years of postnatal life. The development of neurons and glial cells, together with the increasingly complex interconnections between neurons, are the main features of the growing brain that are affected by environmental influences.

'Critical', 'sensitive' and 'vulnerable' periods in development

Since at least the time of Plato, it has been taken for granted that the early years of life are of particular importance in the development of man. The importance of early experiences are stressed in many of the major psychological theories of human development (e.g. Freud and Rogers, mentioned in Chapter 13). The most recent formulations of this idea have used the terms 'critical', 'sensitive' and 'vulnerable' to denote a period when some aspect of an animal's development can be greatly influenced by the environment. These three terms (critical, sensitive and vulnerable) have somewhat different meanings and will be explored in more detail below.

The notion of a 'critical period' in development came from the research of Lorenz on imprinting, which is summarized in Chapter 18. It is argued that there may be critical periods in early life during which the nervous system is optimally tuned to learn certain responses, which it cannot learn earlier or later. For instance, Bloom (1964) calculated that 80 per cent of adult levels of IQ developed by the age of four years. Such evidence, together with the fear of wasting these precious years, prompted the Plowden Committee's (1967) demand for a physical and psychological environment that would ensure the child's optimal development in nursery and primary schools.

These early notions about the nature of critical periods were subject to criticism from several sources. More recent work on imprinting showed that the beginning and end of critical periods were not as clear-cut as had originally been argued. The classic studies of critical periods in humans (e.g. Bloom, 1964) were convincingly criticized by Clarke and Clarke (1976) who also provided considerable evidence that the experiences of early life might not have the importance that had once been thought. The Clarkes assembled an impressive series of articles showing how children who had suffered extreme social and/or perceptual deprivation in early life had developed apparently normally in social, emotional and cognitive terms, provided that they had been placed in a stimulating and caring environment for a number of years subsequent to the original trauma. (We shall return to this idea of the beneficial effects of a stimulating environment following trauma.) The criticisms of the notion of a critical period led to the development of the idea of the 'sensitive period'. This term implies that during a period of neuronal development, usually early in life, learning some patterns of behaviour (for example, learning to speak a language, learning to swim or cycle) may be especially easy; while this behaviour may be learnable earlier or later, it would not be with the same facility.

A good example of a period of special sensitivity to early experiences is provided by work on 'enrichment' in animals. As we saw in the previous chapter, rats that have been reared from weaning to sexual maturity in environments providing greater than normal opportunities to explore objects and to engage in social interaction are better at maze learning than animals raised under usual laboratory conditions. The effect upon later performance was greatest if the enriched environment was experienced immediately after weaning. In animals for whom the enrichment experience was delayed, the effect upon performance was weaker, though it was still present. Similar findings have been reported for cats, squirrels and monkeys (Rosenzweig, 1984).

While the terms 'critical' and 'sensitive' periods have often been used to denote times during which particular behaviours might develop, the term 'vulnerable period' had always been reserved for discussions of abnormal environmental effects on brain development. A biological system is most sensitive to 'good' or 'bad' environmental influences during periods of rapid growth (Walter, 1958). The brain growth spurt marks a time of especial vulnerability of the brain to damage or insult (Dobbing and Smart, 1974). The range of early life-experiences that are claimed to place significant constraints upon the human nervous system's ability to adapt to future environmental challenges is very wide. Among such factors, prenatally, are the hormones to which the foetus is exposed; the drugs ingested by the mother, including alcohol and nicotine: and the mother's emotional state. Postnatally, the number of factors that may affect development is even greater and includes: the circumstances surrounding the child's birth; the child's nutritional state; the child's exposure to disease or pollutents; and the quantity and quality of stimulation received.

We do not have space to consider all these influences upon brain development and some are covered in more detail in Chapter 16. We will consider just two that are of current interest: some effects of malnutrition and some effects of febrile convulsions. The widespread occurrence of malnutrition in pre-industrial countries is a matter of present-day political and humanitarian concern. The study of the behavioural, as well as the health effects of malnutrition is thus of great current interest. Febrile convulsions are of interest because they are the most common neurological insult suffered by pre-school children in industrialized societies. It may be of interest, therefore, to examine briefly some results emerging from a current study by the authors. Both malnutrition and febrile convulsions appear to have their major impact during the 'brain growth spurt'.

Intelligence and early malnutrition

Malnutrition is a deficiency disease caused by inadequate intake of proteins and/or calories. It has been estimated that over 100 million children under the age of five years currently suffer from moderate or severe malnutrition. As will be seen below, the effects of malnutrition on brain and behavioural development vary considerably according to the severity and duration of the episode, and the age and social circumstances of the child.

There is some evidence that relatively brief periods of malnutrition appear to have few adverse or long-term effects upon development. The Nazi embargo on food to occupied areas of the Netherlands resulted in the Dutch famine of 1944–45. Children who were born during and just after that famine have been studied as young adults (Stein and others, 1972) and no evidence of reduction in stature or intellectual ability was found among those born in areas affected by the famine compared with those from unaffected areas. One notable finding of this study was that the birth weights of children during the famine were not lowered, a fact that augured well for their subsequent development. Nevertheless, mortality increased, and the authors of this study argue for an all-or-none effect of prenatal undernutrition: the survivors were able to withstand the effects of the famine because the mothers absorbed the deleterious effects of the famine until their own nutrient stores were depleted; after such depletion, death would be inevitable.

It is estimated that some 10 million children under the age of five years suffer from one of the three major varieties of *severe* malnutrition: kwashiorkor, marasmus and undifferentiated kwashiorkor-marasmus. Kwashiorkor results from a diet that is adequate in calories but not in proteins. This condition is usually caused by the early weaning of one infant when the mother finds out that she is expecting another child. (Indeed, the name kwashiorkor means 'displaced child'.) Marasmus is the product of an inadequate amount of proteins and calories. The child with undifferentiated kwashiorkor-marasmus is suffering the effects of both conditions, or might be in a state of transition from one to the other. As much of the development of the human brain occurs after birth, dietary conditions early in life are as important as those prevailing prenatally. If the child suffers a period of severe malnourishment during the brain growth spurt then it is unlikely that the child will fulfill its full genotypic potential (see Chapter 19). If, however, the episode occurs after the brain growth spurt then the prognosis is far more optimistic. Restitution of a proper diet will enable the child to catch up considerably in terms of both general somatic and cognitive development.

Undernourished children are shorter and weigh less than well-fed ones. However, the effects of severe malnutrition upon the growth and development of the immature brain are far more serious than the effect upon physical growth. There is a reduction in the number of cells, principally the glia, but the number of cortical neurons may also be reduced. Malnutrition reduces the amount of lipid or fatty substance in the brain which is essential for myelination of the axons as well as development of interconnecting cells (Winick and Rosso, 1969; Marcondes and others, 1973). Finally, the effects on the cerebellum, the part of the brain with the greatest rate of postnatal growth, are likely to lead to clumsiness, deficient motor control and coordination, and impairment of attention (Dobbing and Smart, 1974; Tizard, J. 1974).

Detailed studies of the behaviour and performance of malnourished children have revealed, however, that malnutrition is seldom a factor acting in isolation. For instance, a large-scale study of 300 children in Mexico (Cravioto and Arrieta, 1983) showed that many of the homes of children who came to be clinically diagnosed as malnourished were impoverished in many other respects as well-lack of play material, reduced adult contact and stimulation, poor housing, a restricted range of experience and so on. Thus, as Tizard, J. (1974) points out, 'malnutrition and sociocultural factors are likely to act synergistically to depress both growth and development'.

Studies carried out in Jamaica support this interpretation (Richardson, 1976). In these studies, the researchers sought to answer two questions: (i) how do children malnourished in the first two years of life compare with their better-fed siblings and classmates in intellectual competence at later ages; and (ii) is the brain differentially sensitive to malnutrition during different periods of the first two years? The average IQ of previously malnourished boys when they were between the ages of 5–10 years was 57.7, while the IQ obtained by their nearest male siblings was 61.8, and that of their classmate peers was 65.9. (The meaning of these IQs can be better understood by recalling the material in Chapters 16 and 19.) Thus the children who suffered malnutrition in infancy and early childhood fared worse, both on intelligence tests and in school performance than their sibs or their classmates. The fact that the sibs of the malnourished children performed more poorly than the classmates suggests that unfavourable sociocultural conditions played a significant role in depressing performance, though the possibility that the sibs also suffered from some degree of undernutrition cannot be ruled out. When the period during which the children became ill was examined, there was no association between the degrees of intellectual impairment and the time of malnutrition. It appears that the brain was vulnerable to the adverse effects of malnutrition throughout the whole of the first two years of life. However, this latter conclusion needs to be considered critically. The Jamaican study involved children with undifferentiated kwashiorkor-marasmus; if we review studies that have examined children with either marasmus or kwashiorkor we find that there are specific patterns of effects that are age-dependent.

Cases of only marasmus or kwashiorkor are uncommon, but in general the former is a feature of early life while the latter results from a change in diet later in life. Thomson and Pollitt (1977) show that the mean age of hospitalization for the marasmic child is lower than the mean age of hospitalization for the child with kwashiorkor (10.6 and 15 months respectively). The important point is that the marasmic child suffers a lack of protein during the most rapid phase of the brain growth spurt, while the child with kwashiorkor has passed the period of greatest vulnerability to neural 'insult'. Studies of marasmus indicate definite loss of neurons and abnormal neural development (Winick and Rosso, 1969), low levels of cognitive performance and poor social development. Studies of children with kwashiorkor show that the levels of neurological, cognitive and behavioural deficit are milder than those found in children with marasmus. Furthermore, there is evidence that some of the effects of kwashiorkor are reversible if the child is given adequate diet, whereas the effects of marasmus are largely irreversible (Thomson and Pollitt, 1977).

In general, malnutrition is seldom a unitary cause of poor development.

Children who receive an inadequate diet have little energy to move about, investigate and explore; they are quiet, apathetic and undemanding and thus demand little attention from adults and receive little stimulation. They are also more susceptible to infection and their illness further debilitates them. A poorly fed child is a child who is manifestly more vulnerable to the vicissitudes of life.

Intelligence and febrile convulsions in infancy

Some of the complexities involved in trying to investigate the developing brain can be seen in some recent research we have carried out. We have looked at the effects of febrile convulsions on the development of young children. Febrile convulsions are epileptic fits that are preceded by an illness with a high temperature (100°F. or higher) in children under five years of age. As such convulsions affect between 2–5 per cent of the population they represent the most common neurological disorder found among pre-school children. In the present context they are important because the peak time of onset for febrile convulsions is during the brain growth spurt. This provides us with an opportunity to investigate the effects of the same type of neurological 'insult' during and after the spurt.

Although the brain growth spurt continues into the second year of life, the fastest rate of development of glial cells has occurred by just after the first year. Thus, the first year would seem to mark a period of great vulnerability to the effects of neural insult. Our results also support this suggestion. Febrile convulsive children who had suffered their first convulsion during the first 13 months of life had a lower IQ (mean = 98) than either children whose convulsion occurred after 13 months of age (mean = 110), or non-convulsive, control children (mean = 108). These results suggest that febrile convulsions produce important intellectual deficits if they occur during the period of the brain growth spurt, but few such effects if they occur later.

However, age at onset was not the only variable that affected the behavioural expression of febrile convulsions in our study. We found that early convulsing girls suffered greater intellectual deficits than early convulsing boys when compared with their controls. There was a 7 IQ point difference between early convulsing males and their controls, while this increases to a 15 IQ point difference between early convulsing females and their controls. Interestingly, the later convulsing children had slightly higher IQ scores than the controls with the males scoring an average of 107 and the females an average of 113. This pattern of results suggest that, not only is the end of the first year of life a time of significant change in the developing brain, but also that this development is rather different for the two sexes.

Why should this be? One possible explanation is provided by the 'differential cerebral maturation' hypothesis of Taylor and Ounsted (1971). This hypothesis is of particular importance because it links neural damage caused by febrile convulsions with sex differences in the brain. They found that as children get older they are less likely to have a convulsion while suffering a febrile illness. Indeed, only 5 per cent of febrile convulsions occur in children over five years of age. More significantly, Taylor and Ounsted found that girls seemed to 'grow out' of febrile convulsions rather earlier than boys. They argued that this was because the female brain develops faster than the male brain. If we take it that early convulsing females are suffering an insult at a time of more rapid neural development than early convulsing males, then we might expect a more serious effect on IQ for the more vulnerable females. As shown above, this is what we found. Thus the differential cerebral maturation hypothesis provides us with an explanation of both our age at onset results and our sex difference results.

Stimulation and compensation for cerebral insult

The idea that the negative effects of an insult to the brain might be ameliorated by stimulation or an 'enriched environment' has been mentioned above. Much of the early work on this topic developed from animal studies such as those of Rosenzweig (1971) who showed that animals exposed to enriched environments immediately after weaning had more advanced brain growth relative to animals brought up in bare cages. Building on some of the ideas generated by this animal work, a number of researchers have investigated the uses of stimulation or 'enrichment' for humans who have suffered insult (Walsh and Greenough, 1976). Indeed, there have been some interesting studies that have looked at the ameliorative effects of stimulation for malnourished children. For example, in the Jamaican study (Tizard, 1974) mentioned above, the authors found that the children who performed worst intellectually were those who suffered from malnutrition and had also experienced a poor home environment. When children were separated according to whether they had been malnourished or not, and as to whether their home provided good intellectual stimulation or not, the IQ scores of the four groups were as follows:

	Good stimulation	Poor stimulation
Malnourished cases	62.7	52.9
Comparison group	71.4	60.5

The brightest group turned out to be the one in which both nutritional conditions and the home environment were favourable, and conversely, the dullest group was that in which both nutrition and environmental experiences were deficient. The similarity in the performance of the two other groups indicates that good environmental stimulation can do much to compensate for the detrimental consequences of malnutrition, and is a finding of some import for the developing nations.

This finding was confirmed in a rather more direct investigation of the effects of stimulation on improving the prognosis of severely malnourished children carried out by Winick and others (1975). Winick and his colleagues examined data on three groups of Korean girls who had been severely malnourished, moderately malnourished or well-nourished in the first two years of life and had been adopted by American families before their third birthday. These workers found that both the severely and moderately malnourished groups had exceeded the Korean norms for height, weight and IQ after six years of living in America. They further found that even the severely malnourished children had attained an average IQ of 102 by this time.

This research has been used to good effect in subsequent work on malnutrition by Grantham-McGregor and others (1980). The authors compared three groups: children aged 6–24 months, being treated in a West Indian hospital for severe malnutrition; a similar age group of well-nourished children admitted to the hospital for other clinical conditions; and a malnourished group who were treated in hospital in the same way as the first group, but who were also exposed to a special regime of 'psychosocial stimulation'. The last group had one hour a day of structured play while in hospital with a 'community health aid' who continued with the play sessions after discharge for one hour a week for six months in the child's home. At the end of six months the developmental quotient (in effect, an infant IQ scale) of the undernourished group receiving psychosocial stimulation was markedly higher than that of the unstimulated malnourished group and was only slightly lower than that of the adequately nourished group.

Conclusions

What then may we say about the relationship between early brain development and experience? First, between the last three months of pregnancy and age two, there occurs a 'brain growth spurt'. Secondly, during the brain growth spurt changes within the body, such as malnourishment or convulsions, have effects both upon measures of central nervous system maturity and behaviour. Thirdly, that environmental changes, such as the amount of stimulation, have effects although these are less easily detected in research. While the evidence of 'critical periods' for the effects of stimulation is not strong, there is support for the notion that there are times when the brain is particularly 'sensitive' to environmental effects. However, to maximize the potential for ameliorating the effects of environmental insult, enrichment programmes would need to commence before the end of the brain growth spurt.

Further reading

BRIERLEY, J. (1976) *The Growing Brain*. Windsor, Berks.: NFER.

An excellent basic level text that goes into more detail on many of the points raised in this chapter.

CRAVIOTO, J. and DeLICARDIE, E.R. (1979) Nutrition, Mental Development, and Learning. In: FAULKNER, F. and TANNER, J.M. (Eds) *Human Growth*. Volume 3. London: Plenum Press.
An advanced level review of the cognitive effects of malnutrition.

Discussion topics

- What are some of the ways in which the development of the brain can go wrong?
- What evidence is there that the brain is particularly susceptible to damage at certain times?

CHAPTER TWENTY-ONE

The different abilities of the two halves of the brain
Mark Trueman

Introduction

An obvious feature of the brain of man is that the cerebal cortex (the upper and most recently evolved part) is divided into two halves, the right and left hemispheres. Each hemisphere controls the movements and sensations of the opposite side of the body so that, for instance, the right hand is controlled by the left hemisphere. In addition it has become apparent over the last 120 years that each hemisphere fulfils subtly different functions. For most people the left hemisphere controls language, while the right hemisphere seems to be specialized to control visual-spatial functions. (These are described in Chapter 22). This pattern, which has been labelled cerebral asymmetry of

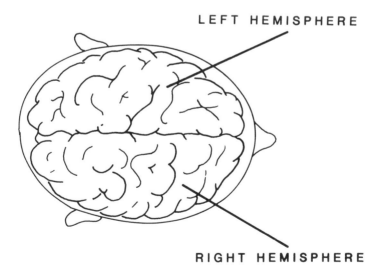

LEFT HEMISPHERE

RIGHT HEMISPHERE

21.1   Illustration of human brain seen from above.

function, holds for some 95 per cent of right-handed and even for 70 per cent of left-hand people.

In this chapter we shall examine some of the evidence for cerebral asymmetry, discuss some of the psychological functions that are asymmetrically represented in the two hemispheres, and then ask if cerebral asymmetry develops as the individual matures.

Studies of patients with damage to one side of the brain

The first hints that the two sides of the brain might be involved in controlling different functions came from work carried out by Dax and Broca in mid-nineteenth century France. They independently found that damage to the left side of the brain resulted in disturbance in the ability to speak or understand language. This kind of disability later became called aphasia. As Broca was unable to find cases where aphasia was associated with right hemisphere damage he concluded that language abilities seemed to be chiefly located in the left hemisphere and relatively absent in the right hemisphere.

More specifically, Broca's research established that damage limited to the rear part of the left frontal lobe of the brain (Broca's Area) caused the patient to have great difficulty in producing speech (see Figure 21.2). Broca's Aphasia, as this condition became called, is characterized by the patient having enormous difficulty in articulating what he is trying to say. Furthermore, conversation from the patient tends to consist of a series of key words while conjunctions,

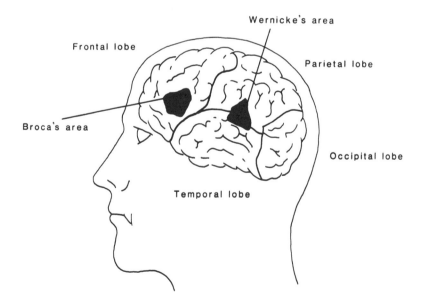

21.2 Diagram of the left cerebral hemisphere showing Broca's and Wernicke's areas.

adjectives, adverbs and articles are omitted. This gives the conversation of a Broca's Aphasic the style of a telegram.

A few years later, the German neurologist Wernicke discovered that damage to the rear part of the left temporal lobe (later called Wernicke's area) resulted in problems of understanding speech or producing understandable speech. Although patients with Wernicke's Aphasia are fluent in their production of speech, what they say can be quite meaningless. They have difficulty in finding appropriate words and resort to using inappropriate or even non-existent words. Geschwind (1970) provides an example of the speech of a Wernicke's Aphasic patient: 'I was over in the other one, and then after they had been in the department, I was in this one'. As Geschwind points out, although there is grammatical structure in the sentence there is a lack of words with specific meaning.

The work of Broca and Wernicke thus established that damage to Broca's and Wernicke's areas in the left hemisphere caused disruption of language functions, while damage to the same areas on the opposite side of the brain caused no such dysfunction. Indeed, it was not for quite some time that it was realized that damage to areas of the right hemisphere caused any abnormal behaviour.

The British neurologist, Hughlings Jackson, was one of the earliest investigators of the specialized functions of the right hemisphere. He noted that a patient with a tumour in the right hemisphere had great difficulty in recognizing objects, persons and places. However, it took until the end of the First World War before clinicians began to discover the nature of the functions controlled by the right hemisphere. One of the most startling findings was that patients with large-scale damage to the parietal lobe of the right hemisphere neglected and ignored the left half of their body. The patient would not dress that side of his body, not protect it from harm and would even go so far as to declare that it did not belong to him.

More recently psychologists have examined the effects of damage on each side of the brain to the four cortical lobes: frontal, temporal, parietal and occipital. Of particular interest are findings concerning damage to the frontal and temporal lobes.

Damage to the right frontal lobe can result in the patient having difficulty in tasks that require constructing shapes out of blocks or tasks that require the copying of designs. A particularly interesting asymmetry found in some patients shows that damage to part of the left frontal lobe is associated with impairment in 'verbal fluency'. That is, the ability to name as many words as possible beginning with a particular letter in five minutes. Damage to the same part of the right frontal lobe reveals difficulty in a task of 'design fleuncy'. In this latter task the patient is asked to draw as many shapes as he can in five minutes using just four lines. Normal controls produced an average of 35 shapes, left frontal lobe patients drew about 24 shapes and right frontal lobe patients produced an average of 15 drawings.

It is important to realize that the symptoms of brain damage are complex.

Not all frontal lobe patients show all, or indeed any, of the symptoms so far described. This is not just because the frontal lobes can be broken down into many smaller and more specific areas; rather it is because several parts of the brain are involved in producing particular pieces of behaviour. For instance, we have already seen that both Broca's and Wernicke's areas are involved in controlling language functions.

The main focus of recent interest in the study of unilateral damage in the temporal lobes has been on its effects on memory. Left sided damage is associated with deficits in verbal memory while right sided damage might be associated with deficits in nonverbal memory.

Although considerable advances had been made in establishing the functions of the two hemispheres in the hundred years following Broca's initial findings, there is one particular limitation with this methodology. Most of the patients were admitted to hospital because of the effects of tumour, strokes, accidents and head wounds received in wartime. The nature of these forms of damage to the brain (lesions) ensures that there is usually at least some functional cortex in both hemispheres. Therefore, any findings from unilateral lesion studies can only hint at the isolated functions of each hemisphere. This is primarily because there are extensive interconnecting bundles of fibres that share information between the two cortical hemispheres. However, an unusual operation has been performed on a small number of patients, which involves cutting through these interconnecting fibres in an effort to prevent severe epileptic seizures spreading from one side of the brain to the other. This is known as the split-brain operation.

Studies with 'split-brain' patients

The 'split-brain' operation involves cutting the neural connections between the left and right hemispheres, including the corpus callosum and the anterior commissure (see Figure 21.3). It is important to realize that there are still extensive intact connections between the cortex and mid-brain structures, and that each hemisphere can receive sensory information from both sides and can control the muscles of the body. However, the two hemispheres cannot communicate directly with each other.

This lack of inter-hemispheric communication was shown in the following early experiment carried out by Gazzaniga (1967). A split-brain patient sat in front of a board with a row of lights on it. The patient was asked to stare at a central point on this board while to the right of this point the lights were briefly flashed. The flash of light lasted a mere tenth of a second, which ensured that the patient did not have time to move his eyes from the central point. The patient reported that he had seen the lights flash on and off. However, when the patient again fixated at the central point and the lights to the left were flashed the patient said that nothing had happened. Even more extraordinary was that while the patient reported *seeing* nothing when the

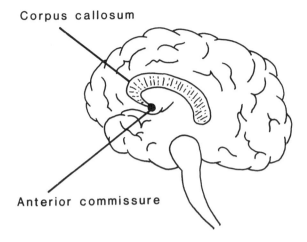

21.3   Section through the brain showing the commissures.

left-hand lights were illuminated, he was able to *point* accurately to the lights that had been flashed. How might one explain these rather strange findings?

First we need to know a little about how visual information is processed by the normal brain. Visual data are largely processed by part of the cortex on the opposite side of the brain to where the visual data orginated in space. As shown in Figure 21.4, the right-hand side of the eye sends its visual information to be processed in the right hemisphere; while visual information appearing in the left-hand side of the eye is processed by the left hemisphere. Thus objects lying to the *left* of centre are perceived by the *right* hemisphere. The information that the lights to the left of the central point (in the left visual field) were flashed was sent to the right hemisphere. Similarly, the information that the lights to the right of the central point (in the right visual field) were not flashed was sent to the left hemisphere. Because of the short duration of the illumination the experimenter could be sure that data from each visual field were sent only to the opposite hemisphere. In the normal intact brain the information held by the two hemispheres is shared via the corpus callosum and the other cerebral commissures. Once the brain has collected all the information about which lights were flashed and which were not it can then report its conclusions. In the normal brain this reporting is done verbally under the control of the left hemisphere.

If this is what happens in the normal brain then what is going on in the brain of a split-brain patient? First, the information from the left visual field of both eyes that the lights were flashed was sent to the right hemisphere. Similarly, the information that the lights in the right visual field of both eyes were not flashed was sent to the left hemisphere. However, these two pieces of information cannot be shared because of the severed inter-hemispheric connections. When asked 'What did you see?' only the left hemisphere is linguistically capable of giving a spoken reply. However, the accuracy of its

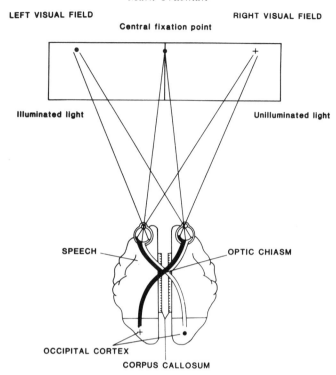

LEFT VISUAL FIELD   **RIGHT VISUAL FIELD**
                    Central fixation point

Illuminated light   **Unilluminated light**

SPEECH   **OPTIC CHIASM**

OCCIPITAL CORTEX
              CORPUS CALLOSUM

21.4   Diagram showing how information presented to one visual half-field is processed by cortex on the opposite side.

reply is limited to the information contained in the left hemisphere. Therefore we are told that 'Nothing happened'. However, when the patient is told to respond by pointing at the lights that have flashed, the patient's right hand (which is mainly controlled by the left hemisphere) does nothing, while his left hand (which is mainly controlled by the right hemisphere) correctly pointed to the the lights in the left visual field. In this study, Gazzaniga has demonstrated that the hemispheres in split-brain patients do not share information and because of this they must make independent decisions. Furthermore, Gazzaniga has provided more evidence for the notion of cerebral asymmetry because the primary mode of response for the left hemisphere was verbal while the primary mode of response for the right hemisphere was non-verbal.

Further research has indicated that the left hemisphere not only responds verbally but that it is also superior in carrying out tasks with verbal materials. It has been suggested that the left hemisphere processes information by breaking it down into smaller meaningful features and sequences and then attaches verbal labels to these features. Meanwhile, research into the abilities of the right hemisphere showed that it was superior in drawing (but not writing) tasks, constructing shapes out of blocks and in handling material which was relatively meaningless (e.g. nonsense syllables) and incapable of being described with a verbal label. It has been suggested that there may be differences in processing strategies between the two hemispheres: the left hemisphere is good at dealing with sequences, while the right hemisphere is good at dealing with wholes. That is, while the left hemisphere will tend to analyse a stimulus as a sequence of elements, the right hemisphere deals simultaneously with its overall configuration.

In spite of the impressive differences between the two hemispheres it is necessary to sound a note of caution. These patients represent a very small group of subjects with very abnormal brains. Years of epilepsy will probably have brought about many changes in the functional organization of the brain (see the section on Plasticity of function, below). Consequently, it would be unwise to apply research findings gained from split-brain patients directly to a normal population. Before this can be done we need research with neurologically normal subjects, which might lend independent support for the notion of cerebral asymmetry.

Studies of cerebral asymmetry with normal populations

The tachistoscope is an electrical device which presents visual information for very short periods of time. The tachistoscope provides a more controlled way of displaying visual material to the half visual fields of each eye than the methodology used in the experiment of Gazzaniga (1967) described above. Experimenters project information to one or other visual field and then examine the accuracy or speed of response of each hemisphere. Obviously with normal subjects information projected to the left visual field will first be sent to the right hemisphere and then will be shared with the left hemisphere via the corpus callosem. The point is that the right hemisphere will have both quicker and more direct access to the stimuli than the left hemisphere. Following this logic it might be expected that, if there were no differences between the hemispheres, then whichever hemisphere received the information first would be the one to initiate the faster or more accurate response. Often this has not been found with normal subjects and in fact each hemisphere appears capable of superior processing performance with particular stimuli, irrespective of which hemisphere had initial access to those stimuli. These findings are clearly in line with the notion of cerebral asymmetry of function.

As might be expected from the findings with brain damaged and split-brain patients, much of the early work with normal subjects showed a left hemisphere superiority for processing verbal stimuli and a right hemisphere superiority for processing non-verbal stimuli. For instance, the left hemisphere was found to be better at both recall accuracy and manual reaction time with words, strings of letters, single letters and digits. The right hemisphere was shown to be superior in the recognition of unfamiliar faces and the matching of meaningless shapes. However, it was soon found that task performance could not be predicted from just a knowledge of the verbal or non-verbal nature of the stimulus material. For example, the two stimuli 'A' and 'A' are more quickly recognized as being the same letter when presented to the right hemisphere than when presented to the left hemisphere. However, when the stimuli 'A' and 'a' are presented it is the left hemisphere which shows the superior performance. It is clear that the two hemispheres are dealing with this 'verbal' material in very different ways. The right hemisphere seems to be matching on the basis of appearance while the left hemisphere is matching on the name of the letter.

Although early research (Kimura, 1968) had suggested that music is processed in the right hemisphere, Simpson (1979) points out that music is not a single entity but embraces three distinct components: melody, harmony and rhythm. While there is good evidence for right hemisphere superiority in recognizing both melody and harmony, Simpson shows that there is a left hemisphere advantage for rhythm. These findings provide more support for considering the information processing strategies of the two hemispheres, rather than the type of stimuli, as being important. The right hemisphere's holistic processing strategy will assist in the recognition of melody and harmony (the notes being related in some overall structure), while the left hemisphere's sequential processing assists in the recognition of rhythm, which is clearly organized temporally.

The main conclusion to be drawn from the above studies of cerebral asymmetry is the remarkable similarity of the results in spite of the employment of very diverse methods with different groups of subjects. The superficial linking of left hemisphere with the processing of verbal stimuli and the right hemisphere with the processing of non-verbal, visual-spatial stimuli has been replaced by descriptions in terms of the overall information processing strategies used by each hemisphere.

Does cerebral asymmetry develop?

The physical structures of the brain develop and change as children grow. The human brain increases about two and a half times in length from birth to adulthood. Within the first two years of life the brain develops most of its adult number of brain cells. During childhood and adolescence these cells establish increasingly complex interconnections with other cells. Throughout the life span the process of myelination occurs. This involves the laying down of a fatty sheath around each nerve fibre, which results in an improvement in the efficiency and speed of transmission of messages throughout the brain. It is interesting to note that the corpus callosum, which is so important in the sharing of information between the hemispheres, greatly increases its size between birth and adulthood. Furthermore, the corpus callosum is not completely myelinated until well into adolescence. Given all of these structural changes within the brain it is interesting to consider whether cerebral asymmetry also develops.

Unfortunately, the answer is not a simple one, and it is instructive to examine some of the evidence, since it shows how difficult it is to establish with certainty facts about the brain.

Until the last ten years or so the evidence seemed to favour the view that the left side of the child's brain only slowly becomes specialized for language so that there was progressive lateralization. A particularly influential review by Lenneberg (1967) compared the occurrence of speech disorders following one-sided brain damage in children who had suffered their insult before the age of ten years and subjects whose insult occurred in adulthood.

As can be seen from the results summarized in Table 21.1 a much larger proportion of children (47 per cent) showed language loss following right-sided brain damage than did adults, and a rather smaller proportion showed language loss after left-sided damage, than did adults. This pattern of results suggested to Lenneberg that language functions only slowly become specialized in the left hemisphere.

		Damage on right side	Damage on left side
Age when damage occurred	Under 10 years	47 per cent	87 per cent
	Adult	3 per cent	97 per cent

Table 21.1   Disturbances of speech following one-sided brain damage occurring during childhood or adulthood.

However, more recent studies have failed to support Lenneberg's conclusion. Carter *et al.* (1982), for example, reviewed 171 cases of children in whom language loss followed brain damage, and found that the children showed the same pattern of results as did adults. That is, disruption of language following left hemisphere damage was common among children and among adults.

It is hard to see why these studies have come up with different findings, but it is possible that the children reviewed by Lenneberg had in fact suffered some damage to both hemispheres, but that this did not show up with the techniques available at the time.

The suggestion that even young children show left-sided representation of language is consistent with two other types of evidence. First, Geschwind and Levitsky (1968) showed that there are actually anatomical differences between the left and right hemispheres, such that a part of Wernicke's area (called the *'planum temporale'*) is actually larger in the left hemisphere than the right. As was mentioned earlier, damage to Wernicke's area in the left hemisphere produces difficulty in understanding speech, so this anatomical difference could well be an important one. Geschwind's work involved adults, but Witelson and Pallie (1973) have shown that the same anatomical difference occurs in newborn children.

Secondly, studies such as those described earlier, in which material is presented in the right visual field or left visual field have been employed with children, and so have studies involving presenting auditory material to either right ear or left ear. By and large, these studies do not show an increasing asymmetry with age and so have failed to support the notion of progressive lateralization (see Bryden, 1982).

Overall then, there do not seem to be profound changes in hemispheric specialization as the brain matures–rather, the left hemisphere seems to be organized to assume control of language function from birth.

Plasticity of function

An interesting insight into the nature of brain function has come from studies of recovery from brain damage. Under some circumstances, it appears that one part of the brain can take over functions normally covered by the injured part. This is known as 'plasticity of function'.

One type of evidence for plasticity of function comes from studies of patients who have suffered some form of one-sided brain damage, which (sometimes years later) led to the complete removal of the damaged half of the brain. This operation, known as a 'hemispherectomy' is occasionally performed to prevent the spread of malignant tumours from one side of the brain to the other, or to control intractable epilepsy. Examination of patients who have had such a hemispherectomy shows that in some cases the remaining hemisphere has taken over the control of functions normally associated with the damaged hemisphere.

Quite how long this period of plasticity lasts has been a matter of some dispute, as has been the extent of plasticity. Lenneberg (1967) described a number of cases in which damage to the left hemisphere had occurred prior to 13 years of age, and in which subsequent removal of this hemisphere produced little loss of language. If the damage had occurred after 13 years however, the same operation produced considerable loss of language. However, this interpretation has been challenged by subsequent research with patients who had early damage in the left half of the brain. Subsequent removal of the left hemisphere revealed that the intact right hemisphere never attains the same level of linguistic sophistication of an undamaged left hemisphere (Dennis and Whitaker, 1977).

In the debate over how long the brain retains its ability to reorganize the functions of the hemispheres, McFie (1961) and Annett (1973) have argued that the likelihood of recovery of function is most promising in cases of insult occurring during the first year of life, Krashen (1973) and Lenneberg (1967) argued that this period of plasticity lasted for five and thirteen years respectively, while Teuber (1975) found better recovery of language functions in wounded soldiers who were under the age of 22 when they were injured compared with soldiers who were 23 years and older. In general, it would appear that the damaged younger brain does achieve more complete recovery of function than the damaged older brain. However, we are as yet in no position to fix developmental limits for this process (Parker, 1982).

We might note an apparent contradiction. As was shown in the previous chapter, the brain is most susceptible to damage in the first year of life. However, there is also a greater chance in the first year of life of the effects of damage being reduced through plasticity, in that disrupted functions are taken over by another (undamaged) part of the brain.

There are two ways of understanding this contradiction. Rutter (1983) suggests that if damage is limited to one hemisphere, the functions normally carried out in that hemisphere can be taken over by the other, undamaged, hemisphere. An alternative view is that there is a great deal of spare capacity in the brain, so that under some circumstances, even quite extensive damage may have little obvious effect (Lorber, 1981; 1983). However, the issue of the relationship between 'vulnerability' and 'plasticity' in the first year of life remains debatable.

Conclusion

We have seen that there is asymmetrical organization of psychological function in the human brain. The left hemisphere seems to be preferentially involved with information that requires sequential, analytic processing as epitomized in the case of language. Furthermore, the right hemisphere seems organized to deal preferentially with simultaneously presented data that require processing as a whole, as is the case with complex visual-spatial information. The evidence that this cerebral asymmetry increases during the course of development is weak. The brain seems predisposed from birth to develop linguistic functions in the left hemisphere and spatial functions in the right. If, however, damage occurs sufficiently early in life, the other hemisphere can take over these functions, though they may never develop to the same level of sophistication as in the normal brain.

Further reading

BEAUMONT, J.G. (1983) *Introduction to neuropsychology.* Oxford: Blackwell.
    A thorough and critical account of present-day neuropsychology, which I
    would recommend to the advanced student.
SPRINGER, S.P. and DEUTSCH, G. (1981) *Left brain right brain.* Oxford: Freeman.
    An excellent starting place for the student who wants more details of the
    studies mentioned in this chapter.
WITTROCK, M.C. (Ed.) (1977) *The human brain.* New Jersey: Prentice Hall.

Chapters 4, 5 and 6 provide a readable and informative account of the abilities of the left and right hemispheres.

Discussion topics

- In what ways are the two halves of the brain different?
- What happens to the brain in the first year of life?

CHAPTER TWENTY-TWO

Sex differences in the development of cognitive ability: evidence, explanations and implications
Hope M. Macdonald

Introduction

Try this test of cognitive ability. The subject is presented with a series of drawings like those in Figure 22.1, depicting orderly piles of cubes. In each pile, some of the cubes are either partially or totally obscured. The subject's task is to count, in a limited time period, the number of cubes in each drawing.

How well a particular group of children perform on this task, known as 'Cube Counting', depends on several factors such as age, education, social-class background. But unlike many other mental tests, the outcome also depends on whether males or females are being tested. Males tend to be far more accurate than females. For instance, in 1932, the Cube Counting test was completed by all the 11-year-olds in Halifax, Yorkshire–a total of 1278 boys

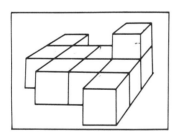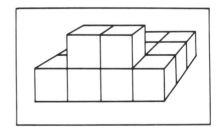

22.1   Items from a Cube Counting test.

and girls. The results showed that 60 per cent of the boys were able to answer at least half of the test items correctly, but only 35 per cent of the girls achieved similar scores (SCRE, 1933). This male superiority, which is evident as early as six years of age, has emerged in several other studies of the Cube Counting test.

What is it about this task that makes it easier to solve for boys than for girls? Considering that the Halifax boys and girls did not differ on a test of verbal ability, it seems unlikely that boys are simply more intelligent than girls. Perhaps boys are better at counting. The many studies of enumerating in school-age children provide little support for this idea (see Maccoby and Jacklin, 1974). An alternative explanation is that the Cube Counting task measures a special cognitive skill–'spatial ability'–on which males excel.

Claims regarding the special abilities of each sex have frequently appeared in the psychological literature but most have not withstood objective appraisal (Maccoby and Jacklin, 1974). Spatial ability is one of the few exceptions to this rule. Most researchers agree that the available evidence supports the notion that when group scores are compared, males are superior to females. Another difference which is thought to be well established, is that females tend to excel, especially during childhood, on tests of verbal ability. While these findings are not generally disputed there is continuing controversy about another question: what causes these sex differences? In this chapter we will focus on spatial ability and review some of the possible answers to this question. As we will see, the study of the sex difference in spatial ability offers some promising opportunities to explore how biological and environmental factors operate in the development of cognitive differences. But before proceeding with these causal issues, let us take a closer look at the nature of the sex difference in spatial ability.

Sex differences in spatial ability

Spatial ability, in the most general sense, involves the effective perception and organization of information about objects and their spatial relationships. It may be manifest in abilities such as aiming at a target, arranging objects into a given pattern, imagining how an object will look if rotated, or having a good sense of direction. The precise nature and limits of the hypothesized ability are not entirely understood. Indeed, there are probably several distinguishable spatial abilities. What is clear, is that scores on the various tests used to measure spatial abilities are all highly related. In contrast, scores on the same spatial tests have only a very weak relationship to scores on verbal tests. Moreover, spatial tests have proven especially useful in predicting success in certain fields: mathematics, architecture, drafting, engineering. So, in addition to being of academic interest, spatial ability is of practical importance.

The critical component in several spatial tests is 'mental rotation'. Shepard and Metzler (1971) developed a set of drawings showing combinations of ten blocks assembled in different ways. They asked subjects whether or not two such drawings–like the pairs shown in Figure 22.2–showed the same set of blocks but in differing spatial orientations. Both the performance of the subjects and their subjective reports suggested that they rotated one of the forms in their 'mind's eye' before making the judgement. On the paper-and-pencil version of this test, known as the Mental Rotation Test (MRT), males consistently surpass females in mean score (Vandenberg and Kuse, 1979). I have recently completed testing 117 British college students. Of the male students, 50 per cent achieved scores higher than 11.5 but only 7 per cent of the female students surpassed this median male score. As sex differences go, the male superiority is a large one. Nonetheless, the distributions of male and female scores overlap: some females do better than the average male and some males do worse than the average female. So the statistical relationship that holds between groups of males and females (males scoring higher) will not necessarily hold for individuals.

Because the Mental Rotation Test and many other standard tests of spatial ability are not appropriate for use with young children, there is a lack of information concerning the age at which male superiority emerges. Some researchers have argued that the sex difference is not apparent until adolescence. However, there is reason to believe that males excel, at least in certain tests, at a much earlier age. For example, several studies of children aged between four and ten have shown that boys outscore girls on the Corsi Block Tapping Test. In this test, which involves an array of wooden blocks, the subject observes the experimenter tapping a series of blocks and is then required to imitate this sequence of block tapping (e.g. Orsini, Schiappa and

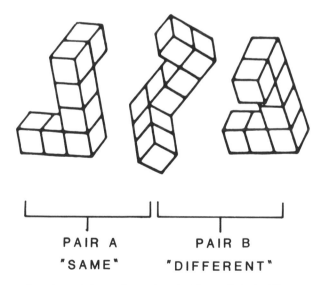

PAIR A   PAIR B

"SAME"   "DIFFERENT"

22.2 Perspective view of three-dimensional objects. Pair A differ only in rotation, whereas pair B differ in shape as well as in rotation.

Grossi, 1981). In both pre-school and school children, boys have also been found to be more accurate than girls at constructing three-dimensional scale models of their classrooms and towns (e.g. Siegel and Schadler, 1977).

One of the earliest and simplest spatial tests was devised by Porteus in 1913. It requires the subject to trace the correct path through a printed labyrinth or maze. Porteus (1965) has summarized the results of fifty years of Porteus Maze research involving a wide range of cultural groups (e.g. Japanese, Chinese, Americans, Indians, Australasians) and age groups. Of 105 sex comparisons, 99 showed a higher mean score in males. More recent investigations using other maze tests have repeatedly shown that from as early as four years of age, boys outperform girls (e.g. Fairweather and Butterworth, 1977).

Another test on which males excel is the Embedded Figures Test (EFT). In the EFT the subject views a simple geometric form and then attempts to find or 'disembed' this form in a more complex geometric design, like the examples in Figure 22.3. Studies using the pre-school version of the EFT (suitable for three to six-year-olds) typically do not find a difference in favour of boys, but through the remaining years of childhood and adolescence, a male superiority appears with increasing frequency (Maccoby and Jacklin, 1974).

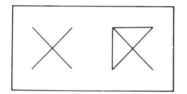 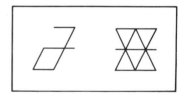

22.3   Items from an Embedded Figures Test.

The superior spatial ability of males might enhance their understanding of the physical world, e.g. they may be better at appreciating the principle that still water remains gravitationally horizontal regardless of the tilt of its container. Piaget and Inhelder (1956) hypothesized that mastery of this principle depends on the capacity to conceptualize space in an integrated grid of horizontals and verticals. Using the 'water-level test', in which children were asked to anticipate (by drawing a line) the water level in a tilted container, Piaget observed that children passed through several stages in their understanding of horizontality. At one early stage, children represent the liquid with a line parallel to the container's base, regardless of the tilt of the container. In the final stage, which occurred at about 12 years, children recognized the liquid's invariant horizontality. In the case of boys, Piaget's analysis is by and large accurate. However, girls–at all ages–lag behind boys in performance on the water-level test.

On the basis of their studies, Thomas, Jamison and Hummel (1973) estimate that at least 50 per cent of college women fail to produce horizontal water-levels. In contrast, it is apparently unusual to find college men who do not know the principle. Individuals who perform poorly on the water-level test also tend to perform poorly on other spatial tests such as the Mental Rotation Test-a finding that provides some support for Piaget's suggestion that subjects who do badly on this task lack a spatial context into which observations may be fit.

In summary then, males generally do better on spatial tests than do females. Though this male superiority appears most consistently in adulthood, early sex differences do emerge on a variety of spatial tests.

Explanation of the male spatial superiority

Individuals differ widely from one another in spatial ability. As we have seen, some of this variation-indeed sometimes quite a substantial amount-is due to the sex of the subject. This sex difference provides a 'clue' that something which differentiates boys from girls, men from women, is involved in the development of spatial ability. This 'something' might have biological origins. But biological raw materials cannot operate in isolation from environmental factors, or vice versa. All behaviour, including thinking, is the result of the interplay of biological factors and environmental factors (as described in Chapter 19). In order to go beyond this general statement, however, and to specify how biology and environment interact to produce an observable phenomenon, it is often necessary first of all to identify the important factors. For this reason, researchers tend to focus (as we will do in the following sections) on specific biological or environmental influences, none of which are in fact working in isolation.

Genetics

Studies of twins can be used to investigate whether genetics influence the development of particular abilities, as discussed in Chapter 19. A number of studies have revealed that the spatial-test scores of identical twins are significantly more similar than the spatial scores of ordinary (fraternal) twins. Identical twins, of course, have an identical genetic make-up since they grow from a single fertilized ovum. Fraternal twins result from the fertilization of two ova at about the same time and are no more closely related genetically than ordinary brothers and sisters. The finding that, the closer the genetic relationship the more similar are spatial scores, is usually interpreted to mean that spatial ability has an important heritable or genetic component.

Could genetic differences between the sexes account for the observed difference in spatial ability? In 1943 O'Connor suggested that his data on spatial abilities were consistent with 'recessive sex-linked determination', meaning a recessive gene carried on the X chromosome. O'Connor had observed that only approximately 25 per cent of the females in his sample scored above the male median on a test of spatial ability. The potential significance of this observation will be clarified if we review some of the basic features of the genetic determination of sex.

Every human cell contains 46 chromosomes arranged in 23 pairs. One of each pair is contributed by the mother of the individual, and one by the father. The twenty-third pair, which differ in males and females, are called the sex chromosomes. If the individual is female the sex chromosomes have a structure designated as XX; if male, the pair have the XY structure. Since the mother can endow her child only with an X chromosome, it is the father–whose fertilizing sperm carries either an X or a Y chromosome–who determines the sex of the offspring. Genes carried on the sex chromosomes are described as sex-linked genes and all but one of those currently identified are carried on the X chromosome. An X-linked recessive trait, therefore, can be expressed in females only if it is present on both the X contributed by the mother and the X contributed by the father. If only one X carries the recessive gene, its effects will be masked by the dominant counterpart on the other X chromosome. On the other hand, in males who inherit this one X-linked recessive gene, the trait will be expressed. This is because males, whose sex chromosome structure is XY, have no other X chromosome which could carry a dominant, masking gene.

Unlike most recessive traits, which are detrimental or pathological in effect (as described in Chapter 16), the X-linked gene hypothesized by O'Connor (1943) would *enhance* spatial ability. According to this model, a female will show a high degree of spatial ability only if she inherits two of the recessive genes for this trait. But a male will exhibit enhanced spatial ability if his one X chromosome is tagged for this trait. Therefore, the sexes will differ in the proportion expressing the trait, with about 50 per cent of males and 25 per cent of females, having enhanced spatial ability. Indeed, O'Connor's (1943) study and several others have reported distributions similar to these (see Vandenberg and Kuse, 1979).

The sex-linked gene hypothesis also makes specific and testable predictions about the similarity between the spatial abilities of parents and their offspring. The reasoning goes like this. A father carrying the X-linked recessive gene cannot transmit it to his son because he contributes only a Y chromosome to his son. Therefore, we would not expect a boy to resemble his father in spatial ability. But he should resemble his mother from whom he inherited one X chromosome. In the case of girls, they will resemble their fathers more than their mothers because though their mothers may carry the gene on one X chromosome without it being expressed, their fathers will show spatial enhancement so long as their one X carries the recessive gene. A father with poor spatial ability will endow his daughter with an untagged X, so the daughter (regardless of the nature of the X inherited from her mother) will also have relatively poor spatial ability. Girls who are high in spatial ability will have inherited one of their two X-linked genes from a father with good spatial ability.

If we were to examine the correlations of spatial scores among family members, we would expect the highest associations to occur for mother–son and father–daughter, the next highest for mother–daughter and the lowest for father–son. Several of the original investigations of this sort, support the predictions of the X-linkage model (see Vandenberg and Kuse, 1979). Corah (1965) for example, who examined scores on the Embedded Figures Test, found that the highest and only significant correlations were between the spatial scores of mother–son and father–daughter.

These early studies aroused considerable interest and led to many more tests of the X-linkage model. However, these more recent studies, which have tended to use larger samples and more spatial tests, failed to uncover the unique pattern of correlation predicted by the X-linkage model. Detailed assessments of both sets of studies have failed to uncover any systematic differences which could account for the discrepancy in findings (Vandenberg and Kuse, 1979).

The fact that recent studies do not support the X-linkage model of transmission of enhanced spatial ability does not necessarily mean that genetic differences between the sexes play no role in the development of the sex difference in spatial ability. That the model has been disputed, and in the eyes of some refuted, has led to new hypotheses of genetic transmission. Now hypotheses mean more research and, hopefully more answers.

Hormones

Evidence which might provide some clue to the biological sources of male spatial superiority, comes from the study of individuals with Turner's syndrome—a condition characterized by short stature, rudimentary or missing ovaries and other physical abnormalities. The majority of Turner's syndrome females have a single X chromosome, which is designated XO, rather than the usual XX structure.

According to the X-linked recessive model, we would expect these individuals to resemble males in spatial ability because, like males, they have only one X chromosome. In fact though, this is not the case. Although Turner's syndrome females have verbal IQs in the above-average range, their scores on spatial tests (e.g. Mental Rotation Test, Embedded Figures Test, Block Design) are particularly *low*. Clearly, this impairment of spatial ability in Turner's syndrome is difficult to reconcile with a genetic model implicating the X chromosome. On the other hand, it is possible that the impairment seen in these XO individuals is caused by another abnormality associated with the syndrome. Individuals with Turner's syndrome, although feminine in appearance, suffer from gonadal agenesis; that is, their ovaries deteriorate and fail to function normally. The result is that unless they are treated with sex hormones, these females remain sexually infantile and sterile.

In normal females, functional ovaries secrete sex hormones. Hence, some researchers have suggested that the expression of the spatial trait may depend on a normal environment of sex hormones.

Hormones are powerful and highly specialized chemical substances that interact with cells that have differentiated in such a way as to be able to receive the hormonal 'message' and to act upon it. Sex hormones, which are produced primarily by the gonads (ovaries and testes) and the adrenal gland, play a crucial role in the development and maintenance of primary (reproductive tract) and secondary (e.g. facial and pubic hair) sex characteristics. Males and females each have small amounts of the opposite sex hormone in their bodies, but there is an important difference between the sexes in the relative proportion of male (androgens) and female (estrogens and progesterones) hormones. A normal, mature female produces more estrogens than androgens, whereas in the normal mature male, the converse is true. An individual's sexual characteristics can be affected by the proportions of male and female hormones in the body both prenatally and postnatally. For instance, inordinately high levels of androgens in girls can result in body masculinization at puberty.

Is there any evidence to suggest that differences in spatial ability are linked to sex-hormone levels? Bearing in mind that research in this emergent field is limited in quantity and suffers from methodological difficulties associated with measuring hormone status, the answer is a tentative 'yes'.

Reasoning that gonadal hormones are responsible for the development of secondary sex characteristics (e.g. body shape, body hair, genital development), a few investigators have used these physical manifestations to infer hormonal status. Petersen (1976) obtained physical measures of hormonal influence at ages 13, 16 and 18, and then examined the relationship between these physical traits and certain cognitive traits. She measured both spatial ability (using the Wechsler Block Design subtest and the Space subtest of the Primary Mental Abilities test) and verbal fluency.

If more male hormones produce proficiency at a 'male' skill such as spatial ability, then we would expect high-spatial females to manifest physically the influence of male hormones, i.e. they should appear more masculine than other girls. This is just what Petersen (1976) found. Spatial scores were lower in more feminine-looking girls and higher in the girls who looked more masculine. In the case of boys though, the pattern of results was just the opposite. Spatial scores were higher in boys who looked less masculine and lower in boys who looked more masculine. In other words, for both sexes an extreme imbalance between the levels of androgens and estrogens is associated with lower spatial scores.

The links between hormones and behaviour are never direct. If, as these and other findings suggest (see Wittig and Petersen, 1979) there is an optimal balance of male–female hormones that facilitates spatial ability, we must ask through what mechanism the influence occurs. One idea which has generated much controversy is that during some critical stage of foetal development, the sex hormones 'prime' or organize the brain for later sex-related behaviour.

Brain organization

Most of the studies demonstrating a link between sex hormones and sex differences in both behaviour and the brain, have been conducted using animals as subjects. Although all behaviours seen in male animals are apparent in female animals, and vice versa, there are some behaviours that are seen more frequently in males or females. It is known that these 'sex-typical' behaviours are strongly influenced by the presence or absence of sex hormones during early foetal development. For instance, the addition of the masculinizing hormone androgen during early development of the female leads to increased levels of male-like behaviour (e.g. mounting other animals, aggression) in adulthood.

Another well-documented finding, is that the same hormones that affect sex-typical behaviour, also play a primary role in producing the sexual differentiation of the brain that occurs prenatally. For example, it has been clearly shown that in animals the hypothalamus (a portion of the brain that is intimately involved in sexual behaviour) is organized into a male type by exposure to androgen during early development. The absence of sufficient amounts of androgen results in a female type of hypothalamus. In a recent study, Arendash and Gorski (1982) demonstrated that 'sex of the brain' can be manipulated through brain transplants. They transplanted brain tissue from neonate (newly-born) male rats into the brains of neonate female rats. The result was that during adulthood, the females with male-brain transplants showed substantially more male-like behaviour than a group of control females.

Hutt (1972) has commented that humans would be curious anomalies if, in contrast to other animals, the sexual differentiation of the brain was not accompanied by some behavioural and psychological difference. But what in regard to humans is meant by sexual differentiation of the brain? While there is certainly no consensus in regard to this question, there is a sizeable body of research which suggests that there is a fundamental difference between the sexes in how the cerebral hemispheres of the brain are functionally organized.

As discussed in Chapter 21, the two halves (hemispheres) of the brain are not mirror images of each other. Some tasks are done predominantly by one side, some by the other. The brain is also structurally asymmetrical. The upper surface of the temporal lobe is on average, larger on the left than on the right, a difference that is established during foetal development. The temporal lobes play the major role in dealing with the analysis of sounds, and indeed it is the left hemisphere (which has the larger temporal lobe) that predominates in the receiving, processing and production of language. The right hemisphere is chiefly concerned in the processing of spatial information, either visual or tactile.

So, the distinction between verbal and spatial skills appears both in brain organization (verbal in the left, spatial in the right hemisphere) and in sex differences (females superior in verbal, males in spatial). And according to some researchers like Levy (1974), there may be a causal link between the two sets of findings. Levy has hypothesized that in order for spatial functioning to be at its best, the right hemisphere must be fully and appropriately organized for spatial processing. If, in the course of neural development, language encroaches upon the right hemisphere and it becomes partially organized for verbal functions, rather than spatial functions, the individual will consequently manifest perceptual–spatial difficulties. This theory was initially based on Levy's finding that left-handers show worse spatial skills than right-handers. Left-handers are known to be 'bilateralized', that is, compared to right-handers, their verbal and spatial functions are less strictly separated or lateralized in the left and right hemispheres. Levy went on to propose that the poorer spatial ability of females is likewise a result of their greater bilateralization of function.

There have been other explanations of male spatial superiority that implicate cerebral lateralization, but the picture we now have of sex differences in brain organization fits more closely with Levy's theory than with any other competing hypothesis. McGlone (1980), who has recently reviewed the evidence regarding sex differences in hemispheric lateralization, has concluded that the research does support the idea that females are less lateralized (or more bilateralized) than males in their cerebral representation of both spatial and verbal functions. Clinical studies indicate that the impact of brain injury on abilities varies with sex of the patient. Females generally suffer less impairment following brain injury to one hemisphere than do males, suggesting that one part of the brain can 'take over' for another more easily in females than males. Adult males and females also tend to differ in the degree of laterality shown on behavioural tests of cerebral specialization (see Chapter 21 for an explanation of these tests). On tachistoscopic tests, males show a stronger right-field superiority for verbal stimuli and a stronger, more consistent, left-field superiority for spatial material. In dichotic tests, where different messages are played through earphones to each ear, the usual advantage of the right ear for processing verbal material tends to be stronger for men than for women.

If sex differences in cerebral lateralization are real, could they be the cause of the sex difference in spatial ability? One way of supporting Levy's theory that high spatial ability is the consequence of a high degree of hemispheric lateralization, would be to show that this association holds for each sex. Of the studies of this sort, some have produced positive results. For example, among both males and females, subjects who show a high degree of lateralization (as measured by dichotic listening and tachistoscopic tests) tend to score higher on the Embedded Figures Test than subjects who are bilateralized (e.g. Oltman, Ehrlichman and Cox, 1977).

If further research does demonstrate that variations in spatial ability are associated with differing degrees of cerebral lateralization, the nature of this association will need to be clarified. One frequently mentioned possibility, is that the bilateralization of language functions in females' brains predisposes them to use language strategies when solving spatial problems. If language strategies are a less efficient way to solve spatial problems, then their scores will be lower than those of males who rely almost exclusively on spatial strategies. Females are more likely to describe their approach to spatial tasks as 'verbal' as opposed to 'visual'. However, as yet there is no direct support for the speculation that the sexes differ in the cognitive mechanisms used to solve spatial problems.

Socialization

At birth almost all individuals can be classified as male or female on the basis of biological criteria. However, one's status as male or female in society is not simply or solely biological. Each male or female is born into a social environment that exists prior to the individual and is the context in which the individual develops. It is through interaction with this social environment– where sex is a highly salient and important characteristic of an individual–that the biological organism becomes extensively modified (as discussed in Chapter 14). Therefore, the possibility that sex differences in spatial abilities are a consequence of the process of socialization as males versus females must be examined.

A large body of cross-cultural research suggests that experiential factors are related to performance on spatial tests. Berry (1966), for instance, found that Canadian Eskimos scored higher on tests of spatial ability than people from the Temne tribe of Africa. The Temne are farmers who rarely leave their village. In contrast, the Eskimos, who must hunt to survive, travel extensively on land and sea surveying their environment. Perhaps, as Berry has argued, the activities of the Eskimos foster directional sense and spatial skills. In the area of sex differences, Berry reports some other intriguing findings. Although the usual male superiority was found in the Temne tribe, the Eskimo males and females achieved similar spatial scores. If the sex difference in spatial ability is influenced by the nature of the social roles assigned to the two sexes, we would expect to find some cultural differences in sex-roles. In fact, Berry did observe that the roles of males and females tended to overlap more in the Eskimo culture. For instance, male and female Eskimos shared equally in the hunting and travelling experiences thought to facilitate and require spatial ability.

Although Berry's failure to find a male spatial superiority amongst Eskimos is the exception rather than the rule in studies on contrasting cultures, this finding does point to the possibility that the usual sex difference is one outcome of the roles and activities which society prescribes for each sex. Sherman (1967) has argued that a number of activities which seem likely to foster spatial abilities (e.g. building with blocks, model building, tinkering with cars) are 'masculine' ones, that is, males are more likely to engage in these activities. Thus, from an early age, males may be practising their spatial skills more than females.

A few studies (e.g. Serbin and Connor, 1979) have found that children who prefer masculine activities (e.g. playing with puzzles and building toys) scored higher on spatial tests such as the Embedded Figures Test than children who prefer feminine activities (e.g. doll play, playing in a toy kitchen). Of course, these associations do not prove that engaging in certain activities fosters spatial ability. It might be that children with high spatial ability select these activities in order to engage their strength. Long-term studies of the development of both spatial activities and abilities in children might reveal the causal nature of the association.

One implication of Sherman's (1967) hypothesis, is that the gap in the spatial performance of males and females can be reduced or closed if the relevant remedial practice in spatial thinking is provided. Sherman has stated that the disappearance of the sex difference after practice would be evidence that males were closer to realizing their potential spatial ability than females. The evidence relating to this issue is conflicting.

The most positive results have occurred with the Embedded Figures Test (EFT). Amongst both children and adults, females benefit more from EFT training than males (e.g. Connor, Schackman and Serbin, 1978). Conversely, performance on the Piagetian water-level test seems quite resistant to the effects of training. Thomas and others (1973) studied 63 females who had performed inaccurately on this horizontality task. These females were subsequently trained to adjust the pretend water line on a mock container so that it matched the water level on a real container of water. This training program had little success: only 12 of the 63 females showed an improvement in performance. Other attempts to teach the concept of horizontality to girls and women have also had limited success.

Performance on many other spatial tests does improve with training. Macdonald (1984) examined the effects of training and practice on the Mental Rotation Test (MRT) scores of 12-year-old boys and girls. The two one-hour training sessions comprised several tasks, including block building and manipulation of plastic replicas of the MRT figures. MRT scores were obtained immediately before and after the training, and again ten weeks later. The scores of the training group were compared to a control group (matched for age, sex and initial MRT scores) who did not receive training. The result was that the mean score of the trained children increased significantly more than that of the control children. However, the male superiority that was evident at the initial testing, persisted. So, although spatial training did lead to a substantial improvement in the scores of both boys and girls, the greater improvement in females, which Sherman's hypothesis predicts, did not occur.

The few training experiments which have successfully eliminated the sex difference in spatial scores have sometimes been taken to mean that environmental factors are the whole cause, or nearly the whole cause, of male superiority. This interpretation often rests on the erroneous belief that any behaviour that is biologically rooted cannot be modified. Biological predispositions *can* be accentuated, attenuated or even negated by the manipulation of the social environment.

Implications of the male spatial superiority

We have reviewed four of the major explanations of the sex difference in spatial ability. These theories are all tentative ones which might, on the basis of future research, turn out to be simply wrong. This would not be unusual: one of the ways in which scientific theories and understanding advance is through discarding explanations that prove not to be useful. However conclusions about sex differences in abilities, even the most tentative ones, can have ramifications which extend beyond the domain of science into our everyday life. These effects are less likely to be detrimental ones if we bear in mind two points–both of which have already been mentioned.

The first point is that a difference that is rooted in a biological predisposition can be magnified or reduced by environmental influences. Hence, although we are not sure what the long-term benefits of spatial training are, it is possible that compensatory training might remedy the spatial deficiencies observed in some children.

The second point to remember is that we have been discussing differences between groups of males and females. Within each group there is a wide range of individual differences in spatial skill. Consequently, a person's membership in a group provides little or no information about his or her spatial ability. Thus the sex difference in spatial ability does not provide justification for the segregation of certain occupations according to sex. Differences in ability, rather than differences in sex, should be considered when choosing the best person for a job. Nor does the male spatial superiority explain the predominance of males in those jobs thought to require high spatial ability (e.g. architecture, engineering). If spatial ability was the determining factor we would expect (on the basis of spatial-test scores) at least one-third of these positions to be filled by women. In fact though, about one per cent of architects and engineers are female. This gap is too wide to be explained by spatial ability alone.

Further reading

HUTT, C. (1972) *Males and Females.* Harmondsworth: Penguin.
   A readable, wide ranging introductory book that emphasizes the biological bases of sex differences in intelligence, ability and personality.
McGEE, M.G. (1979) *Human Spatial Abilities: Sources of Sex Differences.* Praeger.
   A good source of further information concerning different types of spatial ability, and the social relevance and importance of these skills.
WITTIG, M.A. and PETERSEN, A.C. (1979) (Eds) *Sex-Related Differences in Cognitive Functioning.* New York: Academic Press.
   A collection of scholarly papers that review research and theories about sex differences in various cognitive abilities. Topics include the influence of sex-role socialization (Chapter 12), hormones (Chapter 8), genes (Chapters 2 and 3) and cerebral organization (Chapter 5).

Discussion topics

- Why are males superior at spatial tasks and females superior at verbal tasks?
- Why should research focus on the development of sex differences in cognitive performance?

References

ACHENBACH, T.M. (1973) 'Surprise and memory as indices of concrete operational development'. *Psychological Reports*, 33, 47-57.

ADAMS, B., GHODSIAN, M. and RICHARDSON, K. (1976) 'Evidence for a low upper limit of heritability.' *Nature*, 263, 314-16.

ADAMS, C. and LAURIKIETIS, R. (1976) *The Gender Trap. Book 1. Education and Work.* London: Virago.

ANGLIN, J.M. (1977) *Word, object, and conceptual development.* New York: Norton.

ANNETT, M. (1973) 'Laterality of childhood hemiplegia and the growth of speech and intelligence'. *Cortex*, 9, 1-33.

ARENDASH, G.W. and GORSKI, R.A. (1982) 'Enhancement of sexual behavior in female rats by neonatal transplantation of brain tissue from males.' *Science*, 217, 1276-8.

ARONSON, E. (1984) *The social animal.* San Francisco: Freeman.

BAKER, L. (1979) 'Comprehension monitoring: identifying and coping with text confusions.' *Journal of Reading Behavior*, 11, 363-74.

BATESON, P.P.G. (1973) 'Internal influences on early learning in birds.' In HINDE, R.A. and STEVENSON-HINDE J. (Eds) *Constraints on Learning: Limitations and Predispositions.* London: Academic Press.

BATESON, P.P.G. and CHANTREY, D.F. (1972) 'Retardation of discrimination learning in monkeys and chicks previously exposed to both stimuli.' *Nature*, 237, 173-4.

BEATTIE, G. (1979) 'That's no way to treat a lady'. *Bulletin of British Psychological Society*, 32, 97-9.

BEATTIE, G. (1980) 'Separating the men from the boys'. *Bulletin of the British Psychological Society*, 33, 51-3.

BEM, S.L. (1972) 'Psychology looks at sex roles: where have all the androgynous people gone?' Paper presented at the UCLA Symposium on Women, May 1972. Reported in KAPLAN, A.G. and SEDNEY, M.A. (1980) *Psychology and Sex Roles-an adnrogynous perspective.* Boston: Little Brown.

BEM, S.L. (1975) 'Sex role adaptability: one consequence of psychological androgyny'. *Journal of Personality and Social Psychology*, 31, 634-43.

BENDER, L. (1947) 'Psychopathic behaviour disorders in children'. Reported in Bowlby, J. (1951) *Maternal Care and Mental Health.* World Health Organisation, Geneva.

BERGER, P.L. and LUCKMANN, T. (1966) *The social construction of reality: A treatise in the sociology of knowledge.* Garden City, N.Y.: Doubleday.

BERNSTEIN, B. (1962) 'Social class, linguistic codes and grammatical elements'. *Language and Speech*, 5, 221–40.

BERRY, J.W. (1966) 'Temne and Eskimo perceptual skills'. *International Journal of Psychology*, 1, 207–29.

BIRCH, H.G. (1945) 'The relation of previous experience to insightful problem solving'. *Journal of Comparative Psychology*, 38, 267–83.

BLAKEMORE, C. (1973) 'Environmental constraints on development in the visual system'. In HINDE R.A. and STEVENSON-HINDE J. (Eds) *Constraints on Learning.* London: Academic Press.

BLOOM, B.S. (1964) *Stability and Change in Human Characteristics.* New York: Wiley.

BLOOM, B.S. (1969) 'To the Editors'. *Harvard Educational Review*, 39, 419–21.

BLOOM, L. (1970) *Language development: form and function in emerging grammars.* Cambridge, Mass.: MIT Press.

BLOOM, L. (1971) *The Social Psychology of Race Relations.* London: Allen and Unwin.

BLURTON-JONES, N. (1972) *Ethological Studies of Child Behaviour.* Cambridge: Cambridge University Press.

BODMER, W.F. (1972) 'Race and IQ: The Genetic Background'. In RICHARDSON, K. and SPEARS, D. (Eds) *Race, Culture and Intelligence.* Harmondsworth: Penguin.

BODMER, W.F. and CAVALLI-SFORZA, L.L. (1970) Intelligence and Race. *Scientific American*, 223, 19–29.

BODMER, W.F.and CAVALLI-SFORZA, L.L. (1975) *Genetics, Evolution and Man.* San Francisco: Freeman.

BOWER, T.G.R. (1966) 'The visual world of infants'. *Scientific American*, 215, 80–92.

BOWER, T.G.R. (1977) *A primer of infant development.* San Francisco: Freeman.

BOWERMAN, M. (1976) 'Semantic factors in the acquisition of rules for word use and sentence construction'. In MOREHEAD, D.M. and MOREHEAD, A.E. (Eds) *Normal and deficient child language.* Baltimore: University Park Press.

BOWLBY, J. (1946) *Forty-four Juvenile Thieves: their Characters and Home Life.* London: Bailliere, Tindall and Cox.

BOWLBY, J. (1951) *Maternal Care and Mental Health.* World Health Organisation, Geneva.

BOWLBY, J. (1969) *Attachment and Loss. Volume 1: Attachment.* London: Hogarth.

BRANSFORD, J.D. (1979) *Human Cognition.* Belmont: Wadsworth.

BROADHURST, P.B. (1960) 'Applications of biometrical genetics to the inheritance of behaviour'. In EYSENCK, H.J. (Ed.) *Experiments in Personality. Volume I: Psychogenetics and Psychopharmacology.* London: Routledge.

BROWN, A.L. and CAMPIONE, J.C. (1978) 'The effects of knowledge and experience on the formation of retrieval plans for studying from texts'. In GRUNEBERG, M.M., MORRIS, P.E. and SYKES, R.N. (Eds) *Practical Aspects of Memory.* London: Academic Press.

BROWN, A.L., CAMPIONE, J.C. and DAY, J.D. (1981) 'Learning to learn: on training students to learn from texts'. *Educational Researcher*, 10, 14–21.

BROWN, C. (1984) *Black and white in Britain.* London: Heinemann.

BROWN, R. (1965) *Social Psychology.* New York: Macmillan.

BROWN, R. (1973) *A first language: the early stages.* London: Allen and Unwin.

BRUNER, J.S. (1978) 'Learning how to do things with words'. In BRUNER, J.S. and GARTON, A. (Eds) *Human Growth and Development.* Oxford: Clarendon Press.

BRUNER, J.S., JOLLY, A. and SYLVA, K. (1976) *Play: its role in development and evolution.*

Harmondsworth: Penguin.

BRUNER, J.S., OLVER, R.R. and GREENFIELD, P.M. (1966) *Studies in Cognitive Growth.* New York: John Wiley.

BRYANT, P.E. (1982) 'The role of conflict and agreement between intellectual strategies in children's ideas about measurement'. *British Journal of Psychology*, 73, 243–51.

BRYANT, P.E. and TRABASSO, T. (1971) Transitive inferences and memory in young children. *Nature*, 232, 456–8.

BRYDEN, M.P. (1982) *Laterality: functional asymmetry in the intact brain.* London: Academic Press.

BURT, C. (1966) 'The genetic determination of differences in intelligence: a study of monozygotic twins reared together and apart'. *British Journal of Psychology*, 57, 137–53.

BUSBY, L.J. (1975) 'Sex-role research on the mass media'. *Journal of Communication*, 25, 107–31.

BUTLER, N.R. and GOLDSTEIN, H. (1973) 'Smoking in pregnancy and subsequent child development'. *British Medical Journal*, 4, 573–5.

CAREY, S. (1982) 'Semantic development: The state of the art'. In WANNER, E. and GLEITMAN, L.R. (Eds) *Language acquisition: The state of the art.* London: Cambridge University Press.

CARPENTER, G. (1975) 'Mother's face and the newborn'. In LEWIN, R. (Ed.) *Child Alive.* London: Temple Smith.

CARTER, R.L., HOHENEGGER, M.K. and SATZ, P. (1982) 'Aphasia and speech organisation in children'. *Science*, 218, 797–9.

CASLER, L. (1968) 'Perceptual deprivation in institutional settings'. In NEWTON, G. and LEVINE S. (Eds) *Early Experience and Behaviour.* Springfield, Illinois: C.C. Thomas.

CHANTREY, D.F. (1972) 'Enhancement and retardation of discrimination learning in chicks after exposure to the discriminanda'. *Journal of Comparative and Physiological Psychology*, 82, 256–61.

CHASE, W.G. and CHI, M.T.H. (1980) 'Cognitive skill: implications for spatial skill in large-scale environments'. In HARVEY, J. (Ed.) *Cognition, Social Behaviour, and the Environment.* Potomac: Erlbaum.

CICCHETTI, D. and SROUFE, L.A. (1976) 'The relationship between affective and cognitive development in Down's Syndrome infants'. *Child Development.* 47, 920–29.

CLARK, E.V. (1973) 'What's in a word? On the child's acquisition of semantics in his first language'. In MOORE, T.E. (Ed.) *Cognitive development and the acqusition of language.* New York: Academic Press.

CLARK, E.V. (1978) From gesture to word: on the natural history of deixis in language acquisition. In BRUNER, J.S. and GARTON, A. (Eds) *Human Growth and Development.* Oxford: Clarendon Press.

CLARK, E.V. (1979) 'Building a vocabulary: words for objects, actions and relations'. In FLETCHER, P. and GARMAN, M. (Eds) *Language Acquisition.* London: Cambridge University Press.

CLARK, E.V. (1982) 'The young word-maker: a case study of innovation in the child's lexicon'. In WANNER, E. and GLEITMAN, L.R. (Eds) *Language Acquisition: The state of the art.* London: Cambridge University Press.

CLARK, H.H. and CLARK, E.V. (1977) *Psychology and Language.* New York: Harcourt Brace, Jovanovich.

CLARK, K.B. and CLARK, M.P. (1947) 'Racial identification and preference in Negro children'. In NEWCOMBE, J.M. and HARTLEY, E.L. (Eds) *Readings in Social*

Psychology. New York: Holt.

CLARKE, A.M. and CLARKE, A.D.B. (1976) *Early Experience: Myth and Evidence*. London: Open Books.

COLE, M. and SCRIBNER, S. (1974) *Culture and Thought*. New York: Wiley.

COLE, M. and SCRIBNER, S. (1977) 'Cross-cultural studies of memory and cognition'. In KAIL, R.V. and HAGEN, J.W. (Eds), *Perspectives on the Development of Memory and Cognition*. Hillsdale, N.J.: Lawrence Erlbaum.

COLE, M., GAY, J., GLICK, J.A. and SHARP, D.W. (1971) *The Cultural Context of Learning and Thinking*. London: Methuen.

COLLIAS, N.E. (1956) 'The analysis of socialisation of sheep and goats'. *Ecology*, 37, 228–9.

CONDON, W. (1975) 'Speech makes babies move'. In LEWIN, R. (Ed.) *Child Alive*. London: Temple Smith.

CONDON, W. (1979) 'Neonatal entrainment and enculturation'. In BULLOWA, M. (Ed.) *Before Speech*. Cambridge: Cambridge University Press.

CONNOR, J.M., SCHACKMAN, M. and SERBIN, L.A. (1978) 'Sex-related differences in response to practice on a visual-spatial test and generalization to a related test'. *Child Development*, 49, 24–9.

COOPER, R.M. and ZUBEK, J.P. (1958) 'Effects of enriched and restricted early environments on the learning ability of bright and dull rats'. *Canadian Journal of Psychology*, 12, 159–64.

CORAH, N.L. (1965) 'Differentiation in children and their parents. *Journal of Personality*, 33, 300–308.

COWIE, V. (1981) 'Unprotected from the outside world'. *Nursing Mirror*, 77, 46–8.

CRAVIOTO, J. and ARRIETA, R. (1983) 'Malnutrition in childhood'. In RUTTER, M. (Ed.) *Developmental Neuropsychiatry*. London: Guilford Press.

DAVEY, A.G. and MULLIN, P.M. (1980) 'Ethnic identification and preference of British primary school children'. *Journal of Child Psychology and Psychiatry*, 21, 241–51.

DAVIE, C.E., HUTT, S.J., VINCENT, E. and MASON, M. (1984) *The Young Child at Home*. Windsor: NFER–Nelson.

DAWKINS, R. (1976) *The Selfish Gene*. London: Oxford University Press.

DEARDEN, R.F. (1967) 'The concept of play'. In PETERS, R.S. (Ed.) *The Concept of Education*. London: Routledge Kegan Paul.

DeFLEUR, M.L. (1964) 'Occupational roles as portrayed on television'. *Public Opinion Quarterly*, 28, 57–74.

DENNIS, M. and WHITAKER, H.M. (1977) 'Hemispheric equipotentiality and language acquisition'. In SEGALOWITZ S.J. and GRUBER, F.A. (Eds.) *Language development and neurological theory*. New York: Academic Press.

DEUTSCH, F. (1975) 'Effects of sex of subject and story characters on pre-schooler's perceptions of affective responses and intrapersonal behaviour in story sequences'. *Developmental Psychology*, 114, 112–5.

DiBERADINA, M.A., HOFFNER, N.J. and ELKIN, L.D. (1984) 'Activation of dormant genes in specialised cells'. *Science*, 224, 946–51.

DOBBING, J. and SANDS, J. (1973) 'Quantitive growth and development of human brain'. *Archives of the Disabled Child*, 48, 757–67.

DOBBING, J. and SMART, J.L. (1974) 'Vulnerability of developing brain and behaviour'. *British Medical Bulletin*, 30, 164–8.

DOHRMANN (1975) 'A gender profile of children's educational TV' *Journal of Communication*, 24, 4.

DONALDSON, M. (1978) *Children's Minds*. Glasgow: William Collins.

DONALDSON, M. (1982) 'Conservation: What is the question?' *British Journal of Psychology*, 73, 199–207.

DOUGLAS, J.W.B., ROSS, J.H. and SIMPSON, H.R. (1968) *All our Future: a Longitudinal Study of Secondary Education*. London: Peter Davies.

DOWDELL, P.M. (1981) Alcohol and Pregnancy. *Nursing Times*, 77, 43, 1825–31.

DUBE, E.F. (1982) 'Literacy, cultural familiarity, and "intelligence" as determinants of story recall'. In NEISSER, U. (Ed.) *Memory Observed*. San Francisco: Freeman.

ERLENMEYER-KIMLING, L. and JARVIK, L.F. (1963) 'Genetics and Intelligence: a review'. *Science*, 142, 1477–9.

EWING, A.E. (1963) 'Attempts to select for spontaneous activity in *Drosophila melanogaster*'. *Animal Behaviour*, 11, 369–78.

FAIRWEATHER, H. and BUTTERWORTH, G. (1977) The WPSI at 4 years: A sex difference in Verbal Performance discrepancies. *British Journal of Educational Psychology*, 47, 85–90.

FANTZ, R.L. (1961) 'The origin of form perception'. *Scientific American*, 204, 66–72.

FELDMAN, H., GOLDIN-MEADOW, S. and GLEITMAN, L. (1978) 'Beyond Herodotus: The creation of language by linguistically deprived deaf children'. In LOCK, A. (Ed.) *Action, gesture and symbol: The emergence of language*. London: Academic Press.

FOULDS, G.A. (1976) *The Hierarchical Nature of Personal Illness*. London: Academic Press.

FREEMAN, N. (1980) *Strategies of representation in young children*. London: Academic Press.

GALLUP, G.G. (1979) 'Self-recognition in chimpanzees and man'. In LEWIS, M. and ROSENBLUM, L. (Eds) *The child and its family: The genesis of behavior* (Volume 2). New York: Plenum.

GARDNER, H. (1980) *Artful Scribbles*. London: Jill Norman.

GARDNER, H. and WOLF, D. (1983) 'Waves and streams of symbolization: notes on the development of symbolic capacities in young children'. In ROGERS, D. and SLOBODA, J.A. (Eds) *The Acquisition of Symbolic Skills*. New York: Plenum Press.

GAZZANIGA, M.S. (1967) 'The split brain in man'. *Scientific American*, 217, 24–9.

GELMAN, R. (1979) Preschool thought. *American Psychologist*, 34, 900–905.

GELMAN, R., SPELKE, E.S. and MECK, E. (1983) 'What preschoolers know about animate and inanimate objects'. In ROGERS, D. and SLOBODA, J.A. (Eds) *The Acquisition of Symbolic Skills*. London: Plenum.

GESCHWIND, N. and LEVITSKY, W. (1968) 'Human brain: left-right asymmetries in temporal speech region'. *Science*, 161, 186–7.

GESCHWIND, N. (1970) 'The organisation of language and the brain'. *Science*, 170, 940–4.

GIBSON, E. (1969) *Principles of Perceptual Learning and Development*. New York: Appleton Century Crofts.

GINSBURG, H. and OPPER, S. (1979) *Piaget's theory of intellectual development: An Introduction*. Englewood Cliffs, N.J.: Prentice Hall.

GOLINKOFF, R.M. (1983) 'The preverbal negotiation of failed messages: Insights into the transition period'. In GOLINKOFF, R.M. (Ed.) *The transition from prelinguistic to linguistic communication*. Hillsdale, N.J.: Erlbaum.

GOODNOW, J.J. (1977) *Children's Drawing*. London: Fontana.

GOODNOW, J.J. and LEVINE, R.A. (1973) 'The grammar of action: sequence and syntax in children's copying of simple shapes'. *Cognitive Psychology*, 4, 82–98.

GRAHAM, D. (1972) *Moral Learning and Development*. London: Batsford.

GRANTHAM-McGREGOR, S., STEWART, M.E. and SCHOFIELD, W.N. (1980) 'Effect of long-term psychosocial stimulation on mental development of severely malnourished children.' *The Lancet*, 785-9.

GREEN, R. (1974) *Sexual Identity Conflict in Children and Adults*. New York: Basic Books.

GREENWALD, H.J. and OPPENHEIM. D.B. (1968) 'Reported magnitude of self-misidentification among Negro children: Artifact?' *Journal of Personality and Social Psychology*, 8, 49-52.

HANCOCK, C.R. (1963) 'Lady and woman'. *American Speech*, 38, 234-5.

HARDING, C.G. (1983) 'Setting the stage for language acquisition: Communication development in the first year'. In GOLINKOFF, R.M. (Ed.) *The transition from prelinguistic to linguistic communication*. Hillsdale, N.J.: Erlbaum.

HARLOW, H.F. (1961) 'The development of affectional patterns in infant monkeys'. In FOSS, B.M. (Ed.) *Determinants of Infant Behaviour*. Volume 2. London: Methuen.

HARLOW, H.F. and HARLOW, M.K. (1969) 'Effects of various mother-infant relationships on rhesus monkey behaviours'. In FOSS, B.M. (Ed.) *Determinants of Infant Behaviour*. Volume 4. London: Methuen.

HARRIS, P.L. (1979) Perception and Cognition in infancy. In CONNOLLY, K. (Ed.) *Psychology Survey No. 2*. London: Allen and Unwin.

HARTLEY, E.L., SCHWARTZ, S. and ROSENBAUM, M. (1948) 'Children's use of ethnic frames of reference'. *Journal of Psychology*, 26, 367-86.

HEARNSHAW, L.S. (1979) *Cyril Burt, psychologist*. Ithaca, N.Y.: Cornell University Press.

HEELEY, J. (1983) 'Boys' comics: Violence Rules'. *Sunday Times Newspapers*, February 27th.

HENDERSON, N.D. (1975) 'Gene-environment interaction in human behavioral development'. In SCHAIE, K.W. ANDERSON, V.E. McCLEARN G.E. and MONEY, J. (Eds) *Developmental Human Behavior Genetics*. Lexington, Mass.: Lexington Books.

HERSHER, L., RICHMOND, J.B. and MOORE, A.U. (1963) 'Modifiability of the critical period for the development of maternal behaviour in sheep and goats'. *Behaviour*, 20, 311-20.

HINDE, R.A. (1970) *Animal Behaviour: a synthesis of ethology and comparative psychology*. New York: McGraw Hill.

HINDE, R.A. (1974) *Biological Bases of Human Social Behaviour*. New York: McGraw-Hill.

HINDE, R.A. (1979) *Towards Understanding Relationships*. London: Academic Press.

HINDE, R.A. and DAVIES, L. (1972) 'Removing infant rhesus from mother for 13 days compared with removing mother from infant'. *Journal of Child Psychology and Psychiatry*, 13, 227-37.

HIRSCH, J. (1967) *Behavior-Genetic Analysis*. New York: McGraw-Hill.

HOFFMAN, M.L. (1979) 'Development of moral thought, feeling and behaviour'. *American Psychologist*, 34, 958-66.

HONZIK, M.P. (1957) 'Developmental studies of parent-child resemblance in intelligence'. *Child Development*, 28, 215-28.

HOWE, C. (1976) 'The meanings of two-word utterances in the speech of young children'. *Journal of Child Language*, 3, 29-47.

HUBEL, D.H., and WIESEL, T.N. (1962) 'Receptive fields and functional architecture in the cat's visual cortex'. *Journal of Physiology (London)*, 160, 106-54.

HUNTER, I.M.L. (1976) 'Memory: theory and application'. In VARMA, V.F. and WILLIAMS, P. (Eds) *Piaget, Psychology and Education*. London: Hodder and Stoughton (109-19).

HUNTER, I.M.L. (1979) 'Memory in everyday life'. In GRUNNEBERG, M.M. and MORRIS, P.E. (Eds)

Applied Problems in Memory. New York: Academic Press (1-24).

HUNTER, I.M.L. (1984) 'Lengthy verbatim recall (LVR) and the mythical gift of tape-recorder memory'. In LAGERSPETZ, K. and NIEMI, P. (Eds) *Psychology in the 1990s.* Amsterdam: North-Holland (425-40).

HUTT, C (1966) 'Exploration and play in children'. *Symposia of the Zoological Society in London.* In BRUNER, J.S., JOLLY, A. and SYLVA, K. (1976) *Play.* Harmondsworth: Penguin.

HUTT, C. (1972) *Males and Females.* Harmondsworth: Penguin.

HUTT, C. (1979a) 'Play in the under-fives: form, development and function'. In HOWELLS, J.G. (Ed.) *Modern perspectives in the Psychiatry of Infancy.* New York: Brunner/Mazel.

HUTT, C. (1979b) 'Exploration and play'. In SUTTON-SMITH, B. (Ed.) *Play and Learning.* New York: Gardner Press.

JACOB, F. and MONOD, J. (1961) 'On the regulation of gene activity'. *Cold Spring Harbor Symposium on Quantitative Biology*, 26, 193-209.

JAHODA, G. (1963) 'The development of children's ideas about country and nationality'. *British Journal of Educational Psychology*, 33, 47-60.

JAHODA, G., THOMPSON, S.S., and BHATT, S. (1972) 'Ethnic identity and preferences among Asian immigrant children in Glasgow: a replicated study'. *European Journal of Social Psychology*, 2, 19-32.

JAMES, W. (1890) *Principles of Psychology.* New York: Holt.

JENNINGS, S.A. (1975) 'Effects of sex typing in children's stories on preference and recall'. *Child Development*, 46, 220-3.

JENSEN, A.R. (1969) 'How much can we boost IQ and scholastic achievement?' *Harvard Educational Review*, 39, 1-123.

JOBLING, M. (1975) Highlight No. 18. *Drugs and Disease in Pregnancy.* National Children's Bureau Information Service.

JUEL-NIELSEN, N. (1965) 'Individual and environment: A psychiatric–psychological investigation of monozygous twins reared apart'. *Acta Psychiatrica et Neurologica Scandinavica*, Supplement 183.

KAIL, R. (1979) *The Development of Memory in Children.* San Francisco: Freeman.

KAIL, R.D. and HAGEN, J.W. (Eds.) (1977) *Perspectives on the Development of Memory and Cognition.* Hillsdale, N.J.: Lawrence Erlbaum.

KAMIN, L.J. (1977) *The Science and Politics of IQ.* Harmondsworth: Penguin.

KELLER, H. (1958) *The Story of My Life.* London: Hodder and Stoughton.

KELLOGG, R. (1969) *Analyzing Children's Art.* Palo Alto: Mayfield.

KELLOGG, R. (1979) *Children's Drawings/Children's Minds.* Palo Alto: Mayfield.

KEMPE, R.S. and KEMPE, H. (1978) *Child Abuse.* London: Fontana.

KIMURA, D. (1968) 'Left-right differences in the perception of melodies'. *Quarterly Journal of Experimental Psychology*, 16, 355-8.

KING'S FUND CENTRE (1976) *Collaboration between parents and professionals.* Mental Handicap Papers 9. London: King's Fund Centre.

KING, J.C. (1971) *The Biology of Race.* New York: Harcourt Brace Jovanovich.

KLAUS, M.H., JERAULD, R., KREGER, N., McALPINE, W., STEFFA, M. and KENNELL, J.H. (1972) 'Maternal attachment–importance of the first post-partum days'. *New England Journal of Medicine.* 286, 460-3.

KLIMA, E.S. and BELLUGI, U. (1966) 'Syntactic Regularities in the speech of children'. Reprinted in FERGUSON, C.A. and SLOBIN, D.I. (Eds) (1973) *Studies of Child Language Development.* New York: Holt, Rinehart and Winston.

KOBASIGAWA, A. (1974) 'Utilization of retrieval cues by children in recall'. *Child Development*, 45, 127-34.

KOHLER, W. (1957) *The mentality of apes*. Harmondsworth: Penguin.

KOLERS, P.A. (1972) 'Experiments in reading'. *Scientific American*, 227, 84-91.

KRASHEN, S. (1973) 'Lateralization, language learning and the critical period: some new evidence'. *Language Learning*, 23, 63-74.

KUHN, M.H. (1960) 'Self attitudes by age, sex and professional training'. *Sociology Quarterly*, 1, 39-55.

KUO, Z.Y. (1932) 'Ontogeny of embryonic behavior in Aves'. *Journal of Comparative Psychology*, 14, 109-22.

LABOV, W. (1972) 'The logic of non-standard English'. In GIGLIOLI, P. (Ed.) *Language and Social Context*. Harmondsworth: Penguin.

LAKOFF, R. (1975) *Language and Woman's Place*. New York: Harper Colophon Books.

LAYZER, D. (1972) 'Science or superstition? (A physical scientist looks at the IQ controversy)'. *Cognition*, 1, 265-300.

LEACH, P. (1983) *Babyhood*. Harmondsworth: Penguin.

LEBOYER, F. (1977) *Birth Without Violence*. London: Fontana.

LENNEBERG, E.H. (1967) *Biological foundations of language*. London: Wiley.

LESHAN, L. (1977) *You can fight for your life: Emotional factors in the causation of cancer*. New York: Evans.

LEVY, J. (1974) 'Psychobiological implications of bilateral asymmetry'. In DIMOND, S.J. and BEAUMONT, J.G. (Eds.) *Hemisphere Function in the Human Brain*. New York: John Wiley.

LEWIN, R. (1975) *Child Alive*. London: Temple Smith.

LEWIS, M. (1972) 'Parents and Children: Sex role development'. *The School Review*, 80, 229-40.

LEWIS, M. (1982) 'Play as whimsy'. *Behavioral and Brain Sciences*, 5, 166.

LEWIS, M., and GOLDBERG, S. (1969). 'The acquisition and violation of expectancy: an experimental paradigm'. *Journal of Experimental Child Psychology*, 7, 70-80.

LOEHLIN, J.C. and NICOLS, R.C. (1976) *Heredity, Environment and Personality* Austin: University of Texas Press.

LONEY, J. (1980) 'Hyperkinesis comes of age'. *American Journal of Orthopsychiatry*, 50, 28-42.

LORBER, J. (1981) 'The disposable cortex'. *Psychology Today*, 15, 126.

LORBER, J. (1983) 'Is your brain really necessary?' In VOTH, D.. GUTJAHR, P. and GLEES, P. (Eds) *Hydrocephalus in Fruhen Kindesalter* Stuttgart: F.E. Verlag.

MACCOBY, E.E. and JACKLIN, C.N. (1974) *The Psychology of Sex Differences*. Stanford: Stanford University Press.

MACDONALD, H.M. (1984) *Sex differences and hemispheric organization in cognitive functioning*. Unpublished Ph.D. thesis, Keele University.

MACFARLANE, A. (1975) 'The first hours, and the smile'. In LEWIN, R. (Ed.) *Child Alive*. London: Temple Smith.

MARCONDES, E., LEFEVRE, A., MACHADO, D., GARCIA DE BARROS, N., CAVALLO, A., GAZAL, S., QUARENTEI, G., SETIAN, N., VALENTE, M., and BARBIERI, D. (1973) 'Neuropsychomotor development and pneumoencephalographic changes in children with severe malnutrition'. *Environmental Child Health*, 19, 135-39.

MARGOLIES, P.J. (1977) 'Behavioural approaches to the treatment of early infantile autism'. *Psychological Bulletin*, 84, 249-64.

MARKMAN, E.M. (1977) 'Realizing that you don't understand: a preliminary investigation'. *Child Development*, 48, 986-92.

MARKMAN, E.M. and GORIN, L. (1981) 'Children's ability to adjust their standards for evaluating comprehension'. *Journal of Educational Psychology*, 73, 3, 320-5.

MASH, E. and DALBY, T. (1978) 'Behavioural interventions for hyperactivity'. In TRITES, R. (Ed.) *Hyperactivity in Children: Etiology, measurement and treatment*. Baltimore: University Park Press.

MAYNARD SMITH, J. (1977) 'Parental investment: a prospective analysis'. *Animal Behaviour*, 25, 1-9.

McASKIE, M. and CLARKE, A.M. (1976) 'Parent-offspring resemblance in intelligence: theories and evidence'. *British Journal of Psychology*, 67, 243-73.

McCLEARN, G.E. and DeFRIES, J.C. (1973) *Introduction to Behavioral Genetics*. San Francisco: Freeman.

McFIE, J. (1961) 'The effects of hemispherectomy on intellectual functioning in cases of infantile hemiplegia'. *Journal of Neurological and Neurosurgical Psychiatry*, 24, 240-49.

McGAUGH, J.L., JENNINGS, R.D. and THOMSON, C.W. (1962) 'Effect of distribution of practice on the maze learning of descendants of the Tryon maze bright and maze dull strains'. *Psychological Reports*, 10, 147-150.

McGLONE, J. (1980) 'Sex differences in human brain asymmetry'. *Behavioral and Brain Sciences*, 3, 215-64.

McNEILL, D. (1966) 'Developmental Psycholinguistics'. In SMITH, F. and MILLER, G. (Eds) *The Genesis of Language: A Psycholinguistic Approach*. Cambridge, Mass: MIT Press.

McSHANE, J. and WHITTAKER, S. (1983) 'The role of symbolic thought in language development'. In ROGERS, D.R. and SLOBODA, J.A. (Eds) *The Acquisition of Symbolic Skills*. London: Plenum Press.

MEAD, G.H. (1934) *Mind, Self and Society*. Chicago: Chicago University Press.

MEDAWAR, P.B. (1957) *The Uniqueness of the Individual*. London: Methuen.

MEICHENBAUM, D. (1977) *Cognitive Behaviour Modification: An Integrative Approach*. New York: Plenum.

MILNER, D. (1975) *Children and Race*. Harmondsworth: Penguin.

MILNER, D. (1983) *Children and Race: ten years on*. London: Ward Lock Educational.

MITTLER, P. (1971) *The Study of Twins*. Harmondsworth: Penguin.

MONEY, J. (1974) 'Prenatal hormones and post-natal socialisation in gender identity differentiation'. In COLE, J.K. and DIENSTBIER, R. (Eds) *Nebraska Symposium on Motivation*. Lincoln: University of Nebraska Press.

MONEY, J. and EHRHARDT, A. (1972) *Man, Woman, Boy and Girl*. Baltimore: Johns Hopkins University Press.

MONEY, J., HAMPSON, J.G. and HAMPSON, J.L. (1957) 'Imprinting and the establishment of gender role'. *Archives of Neurology and Psychiatry*, 77, 333-6.

MONEY, J. and TUCKER, P. (1977) *Sexual Signatures: on being a man or a woman*. Sphere Books Ltd.

MORGAN, J., O'NEILL, C. and HARRE, R. (1979) *Nicknames*. London: Routledge and Kegan Paul.

MOSKOWITZ, B.A. (1978) 'The acquisition of language'. *Scientific American*, 239, 82-96.

MUNSINGER, H. (1975) 'The adopted child's IQ: a critical review'. *Psychological Bulletin*, 82, 623-59.

MUSSEN, P.H., CONGER, J.J. and KAGAN, J. (1965) *Child Development and Personality*. New York: Harper and Row.

NEISSER, U. (1982) *Memory Observed*. San Francisco: Freeman.

NEWMAN, H.H., FREEMAN, F.M. and HOLZINGER, K.J. (1937) *Twins: a study of heredity and environment*. Chicago: University of Chicago Press.

NEWSON, E. and HIPGRAVE, T. (1982) *Getting through to your Handicapped Child*. Cambridge: Cambridge University Press.

NEWSON, J. and NEWSON, E. (1979) 'Intersubjectivity and the transmission of culture'. Reprinted in: Oates, J. (Ed.) *Early cognitive development* London: Croom Helm.

O'CONNOR, J. (1943) *Structural Visualization*. Boston: Human Engineering Laboratory.

OLMSTEAD, D.L. (1971) *Out of the Mouth of Babes*. The Hague: Mouton.

OLTMAN, P.K., EHRLICHMAN, H. and COX, P.W. (1977) 'Field independence and laterality in the perception of faces'. *Perceptual and Motor Skills*, 45, 255–60.

ORSINI, A., SCHIAPPA, O. and GROSSI, D. (1981) 'Sex and cultural differences in children's spatial and verbal memory span'. *Perceptual and Motor Skills*, 53, 39–42.

OSGOOD, C.E., MAY, W.H. and MIRON, M.S. (1975) *Cross-cultural Universals of Affective Meaning*. Illinois: University of Illinois Press.

PARKE, R.D. (1981) *Fathering*. London: Fontana.

PARKER, D.M. (1982) 'Determinant and plastic principles in neuropsychological development'. In DICKERSON, J.W.T. and McGURK, H. (Eds) *Brain and behavioural development*. London: Surrey University Press.

PATTON, R.G. and GARDNER, L.I. (1963) *Growth Failure in Maternal Deprivation*. Springfield, Illinois: C.C. Thomas.

PETERSEN, A.C. (1976) 'Physical androgyny and cognitive functioning in adolescence'. *Developmental Psychology*, 12, 533–42.

PIAGET, J. (1926) *The Language and Thought of the Child*. London: Routledge Kegan Paul.

PIAGET, J. (1930) *The Child's Conception of Physical Causality*. London: Kegan Paul.

PIAGET, J. (1932) *The Moral Judgement of the Child*. London: Routledge Kegan Paul.

PIAGET, J. (1952) *The Origins of Intelligence in Children*. New York: International Universities Press.

PIAGET, J. and INHELDER, B. (1956) *The Child's Conception of Space*. New York: Norton.

PICK, A.D. (1965) 'Improvement of visual and tactual form discrimination'. *Journal of Experimental Psychology*, 69, 331–339.

PLOMIN, R., DeFRIES, J.C. and McCLEARN, G.E. (1980) *Behavioural Genetics: a primer*. San Francisco: Freeman.

PLOWDEN COMMITTEE (1967) *Children and their Primary Schools*. London: HMSO.

PORTEUS, S.D. (1965) *Porteus Maze Test: Fifty Years' Application*. Palo Alto: Pacific Books.

PROSSER, G.V. (1974) 'Questions asked and social class'. In ROBINSON, W.P. (Ed.) *Education, Curiosity and Questioning*. Southampton: University of Southampton.

PROSSER, G.V., HUTT, C., HUTT, S.J., MAHINDADASA, K.J. and GOONETILLEKE, M.D.J. (1984) *Children's Play in Sri Lanka: a cross-cultural study*. (In preparation).

REED, T.E. (1984) 'Mechanism for hereditability of intelligence'. *Nature*, 311, 417.

RHEINGOLD, H.L. and COOK, K.V. (1975) 'The contents of boys' and girls' rooms as an index of parents' behaviour'. *Child Development*, 46, 459–63.

RICHARDSON, S.A. (1976) 'The influence of severe malnutrition in infancy on the intelligence of children at school age: an ecological perspective'. In WALSH, R.N. and GREENOUGH, W.T. (Eds) *Environments as therapy for brain dysfunction*. New York: Plenum.

RICHARDSON, S.A., BIRCH, H.G. and HERTZIG, M.E. (1973) 'School performance of children who were severely malnourished in infancy'. *American Journal of Mental Deficiency*, 77, 623—32.

ROBERTSON, J. and ROBERTSON, J. (1967) *Young Children in Brief Separation*. London: Tavistock Child Development Research Unit.

ROSCH, E. (1977) 'Classification of real-world objects: origins and representations in cognition'. Reprinted in JOHNSON-LAIRD, P.N. and WASON, P.C. *Thinking: Readings in Cognitive Science*. London: Cambridge University Press.

ROSE, R.J., HARRIS, E.L., CHRISTIAN, J.C. and NANCE, W.E. (1979) 'Genetic variance in non-verbal intelligence: data from the kinships of identical twins'. *Science*, 205, 1153-5.

ROSENZWEIG, M.R. (1971) 'Effects of environment on development of brain and behaviour'. In TOBACH, E., ARONSON, E.L. and SHAW, E. (Eds) *The Biopsychology of Development*. New York: Academic Press.

ROSENWEIG, M.R. (1984) 'Experience, memory and the brain'. *American Psychologist*, 39, 365-76.

ROYCE, J.R. and MOS, L.P. (Eds) (1979) *Theoretical Advances in Behavioural Genetics*. Amsterdam: Sijhoff and Noordhoff.

RUBIN, Z. (1980) *Children's friendships*. London: Fontana.

RUFFY, M. (1981) 'Influence of social factors in the development of the young child's moral judgment'. *European Journal of Social Psychology*, 11, 61-76.

RUTTER, M. (1981) *Maternal Deprivation Reassessed*. Harmondsworth: Penguin.

RUTTER, M. (1983) 'Issues and prospects in developmental neuropsychiatry'. In RUTTER, M. (Ed.) *Developmental Neuropsychiatry*. London: Guilford Press.

SCARR, S. (1968) 'Environmental bias in twin studies'. *Eugenics Quarterly*, 15, 34-40.

SCARR-SALAPATEK, S. (1971) 'Race, social class and IQ'. *Science*, 174, 1285-95.

SCHAFFER, R. (1977) *Mothering*. London: Fontana.

SCHIEFFELIN, B.B. and OCHS, E. (1983) 'A cultural perspective on the transition from prelinguistic to linguistic communication'. In GOLINKOFF, R.M. (Ed.) *The transition from prelinguistic to linguistic communication*. Hillsdale, N.J.: Erlbaum.

SCHWARTZMAN, H.B. (1982) 'Play as a mode'. *Behavioural and Brain Sciences*, 5, 168-69.

SCOTTISH COUNCIL FOR RESEARCH IN EDUCATION (1933) *The Intelligence of Scottish Children: A National Survey of an Age-Group*. London: University of London Press.

SCRIBNER, S. and COLE, M. (1981) *The Psychology of Literacy*. Cambridge, Mass.: Harvard University Press.

SERBIN, L.A. and CONNOR, J.M. (1979) 'Sex-typing of children's play preferences and patterns of cognitive performance'. *Journal of Genetic Psychology*, 134, 315-16.

SHEPARD, R.N. and METZLER, J. (1971) 'Mental rotation of three-dimensional objects'. *Science*, 171, 701-703.

SHERMAN, J.A. (1967) 'Problem of sex differences in space perception and aspects of intellectual functioning'. *Psychological Review*, 74, 290-99.

SHIELDS, J. (1962) *Monozygotic twins brought up apart and brought up together*. London: Oxford University Press.

SIEGEL, A.W. and SCHADLER, M. (1977) 'The development of young children's spatial representations of their classroom'. *Child Development*, 48, 388-94.

SIMPSON, A.J. (1979) 'Hemispheric differences in cognitive processes: evidence from experimental psychology'. In CONNOLY, K. (Ed.) *Psychology Survey No. 2*. London: George Allen and Unwin.

SKODAK, M. and SKEELS, H.M. (1949) 'A final follow-up of one hundred adopted children'. *Journal of Genetic Psychology*, 75, 85-125.

SLOBIN, D.I. and WELSH, C.A. (1973) 'Elicited imitation as a research tool in developmental psycholinguistics'. In FERGUSON, C.A. and SLOBIN, D.I. (Eds) *Studies of Child Language Development*. New York: Holt Rinehart and Winston.

SLUCKIN, W., HERBERT, M. and SLUCKIN, A. (1983) *Maternal Bonding*. Oxford: Blackwell.

SMITH, P.K. (1975) 'Ethological methods'. In FOSS, B. (Ed.) *New Perspectives in Child Development*. Harmondsworth: Penguin.

SMITH, P.K. (1982) 'Does play matter? Functional and evolutionary aspects of animal and human play'. *Behavioural and Brain Sciences*, 5, 139-84.

SMITH, R.T. (1965) 'A comparison of socioenvironmental factors in monozygotic and dizygotic twins, testing an assumption'. In VANDENBERG, S.G. (Ed.) *Methods and Goals in Human Behaviour Genetics*. New York: Academic Press.

SNOW, C.E. (1972) 'Mothers' speech to children learning language'. *Child Development*, 43, 549-65.

SNOW, C.E. (1977) 'The development of conversation between mothers and babies'. *Journal of Child Language*, 4, 1, 1-22.

SNOW, C.E. and FERGUSON, C.A. (1977) *Talking to children: language input and acquisition*. London: Cambridge University Press.

SPITZ, R.A. (1945) 'Hospitalism: an inquiry into the genesis of psychiatric conditions in early childhood'. *Psychoanalytic Study of the Child*, 1, 53-74.

SPITZ, R.A. (1946a) 'Anaclitic depression'. *Psychoanalytic Study of the Child*. 2, 313-42.

SPITZ, R.A. (1946b) 'Hospitalism: a follow-up report'. *Psychoanalytic Study of the Child*, 2, 113-18.

STEIN, Z., SUSSER, M., SAENGER, G. and MAROLLA, F. (1972) 'Nutrition and Mental Performance', *Science*, 178, 708-13.

STOPPARD, T. (1978) *Professional Foul*. London: Faber and Faber.

STUART, R.B. (1967) 'Decentration in the development of children's concepts of moral and causal judgment'. *Journal of Genetic Psychology*, 3, 59-68.

SYLVA, K., BRUNER, J.S. and GENOVA, P. (1976) 'The role of play in the problem-solving of children 3-5 years old'. In BRUNER, J.S., JOLLY, A., and SYLVA, K. (1976) *Play*. Harmondsworth: Penguin.

TAJFEL, H. and JAHODA, G. (1966) 'Development in children of concepts and attitudes about their own and other countries'. *Proceedings XVIII International Congress of Psychology, Moscow* Symposium 36, 17-33.

TAJFEL, H., JAHODA, G., NEMETH, C., RIM, Y. and JOHNSON, N.B. (1972) 'The devaluation by children of their own national and ethnic group: two case studies'. *British Journal of Social and Clinical Psychology*, 11, 235-43.

TANNER, J.M. (1960) *Education and Physical Growth*. London: University of London Press.

TANNER, J.M. (1978) *Foetus into Man*. London: Open Books.

TAYLOR, D.C. and OUNSTED, C. (1971) 'Biological mechanisms influencing the outcome of seizures in response to fever'. *Epilepsia*, 12, 33-45.

TEUBER, H.L. (1975) 'Recovery of function after brain injury in man'. In CIBA Symposium 34 (new series) *Outcome of severe damage to the CNS* Amsterdam: Elsevier.

THOMAS, A., CHESS, S. and BIRCH, H.G. (1970) 'The Origin of Personality'. In ATKINSON, R. (Ed.) *Contemporary Psychology: Readings from Scientific American*. San Francisco: Freeman.

THOMAS, H., JAMISON, W. and HUMMEL, D.D. (1973) 'Observation is insufficient for discovering that the surface of still water is invariantly horizontal'. *Science*, 81,

173-4.

THOMSON, C.A. and POLLITT, E. (1977) 'Effects of severe protein-calorie malnutrition on behaviour in human populations'. In GREENE, L.S. (Ed.) *Malnutrition, Behaviour, and Social Organisation*. London: Academic Press.

TIZARD, B. (1974) 'IQ and race'. *Nature*, 247, 316.

TIZARD, J. (1974) 'Early malnutrition, growth and mental development in man'. *British Medical Bulletin* 30, 169-174.

TREVARTHEN, C. (1975) 'Early attempts at speech'. In LEWIN, R. (Ed.) *Child Alive*. London: Temple Smith.

UNGER, R.K. (1980) *Female and Male: Psychological Perspectives*. New York: Harper and Row.

VANDENBERG, S.G. and KUSE, A.R. (1979) 'Spatial ability: A critical review of the sex-linked major gene hypothesis'. In WITTIG, M.A. and PETERSEN, A.C. (Eds) *Sex-Related Differences in Cognitive Functioning*. New York: Academic Press.

VAUGHAN, G. (1978) 'Social categorisation and intergroup behaviour in children'. In TAJFEL, H. (Ed.) *Differentiation between Social Groups*. London: Academic Press.

VETTA, A. (1977) 'Estimation of heritability from IQ data on twins'. *Nature*, **266**, 279.

VYGOTSKY, L.S. (1962) *Thought and Language*. New York: Wiley.

WALK, R.D. and GIBSON, E.J. (1961) 'A comparative and analytical study of visual depth perception'. *Psychological Monographs*, **75**, 1.

WALSH, R.N. and GREENOUGH, W.T. (Eds) (1976) *Environments as Therapy for brain dysfunction*. London: Plenum.

WALTER, W.G. (1958) In TANNER, J.M. and INHELDER, B., (Eds.) *Discussions in Child Development*. Volume 3. London: Tavistock.

WATTS, J. (1983) 'Dr Michel Odent: a Labour of Love'. *Observer Magazine*. 6th November. Observer Newspapers.

WEBER, S.J., JESIEN, G.S., SHEARER, D.E., BLUMA, S.M., HILLIARD, J.M., SHEARER, M.S., SCHORTINGUIS, N.E. and BOYD, R.D. (1975) *The Portage Guide to Home Teaching*. C.E.S.A. 12, Portage, Wisconsin.

WEISKRANTZ, L. (1972) 'Behavioural analysis of the monkey's visual nervous system'. *Proceedings of the Royal Society B*, 182, 427-55.

WERTHEIMER, M. (1961) 'Psychomotor coordination of audio-visual space at birth'. *Science*, 134, 1692.

WILSON, E.O. (1975) *Sociobiology: the new synthesis*. Cambridge, Mass.: Harvard University Press.

WINICK, M. and ROSSO, P. (1969) 'Head circumference and cellular growth of the brain in normal and marasmic children'. *Journal of Pediatrics*, 74, 774-8.

WINICK, M., MEYER, K.K. and HARRIS, R.C. (1975) 'Malnutrition and environmental enrichment by early adoption'. *Science*, 190, 1173-5.

WINNER, E. (1979) 'New names for old things: The emergence of metaphoric language'. *Journal of Child Language*, 6, 469-92.

WITELSON, S.F. and PALLIE, W. (1973) 'Left hemisphere specialisation for language in the newborn: neuroanatomical evidence of asymmetry'. *Brain*, 96, 641-6.

WITTIG, M.A. and PETERSEN, A.C. (1979) (Eds.) *Sex-related Differences in Cognitive Functioning*. New York: Academic Press.

WOLFF, P.H. (1959) 'States in newborn infants'. *Psychosomatic Medicine*, 21, 110-18.

WOLFF, P.H. (1963) 'Observations on the early development of smiling'. In FOSS, B.M. (Ed.) *Determinants of Infant Behaviour*. Volume 2. London: Wiley.

WOLFF, P.H. (1969) 'The natural history of crying and other vocalisations in early infancy'. In foss, b.m. (Ed.) *Determinants of Infant Behaviour.* Volume IV. London: Methuen.

wright, d. (1971) *The Psychology of Moral Behaviour.* Harmondsworth: Penguin.

Subject Index

Author Index